The Gifted Kids' Survival Guide

A Teen Handbook

Revised, Expanded, and Updated Edition

JUDY GALBRAITH, M.A., AND JIM DELISLE, PH.D.

Edited by Pamela Espeland

free spirit
PUBLiSHiNG®

Works
for kids®

Library of Congress Cataloging-in-Publication Data

Galbraith, Judy.
    The gifted kids' survival guide : a teen handbook / Judy Galbraith and Jim Delisle : edited by Pamela Espeland.
        p.   cm.
    Includes bibliographical references and index.
    Summary: Examines issues that are of concern for young people who have been labeled "gifted," discussing what the label means, intelligence testing, educational options, and relationships with parents and friends. Includes first-person essays on being gifted.
    ISBN 1-57542-003-1
    1. Gifted teenagers—Juvenile literature. [1. Gifted children.] I. Delisle, James R., 1953–   . II. Espeland, Pamela. III. Title.
BF724.3.G53G35   1996
305.9'0829—dc20   96-29430
                                                                                                        CIP
                                                                                                        AC

Interior design by Rick Korab, Punch Design
Cover design by MacLean & Tuminelly
Interior illustrations by Harry Pulver, Jr.
Index compiled by Eileen Quam and Theresa Wolner

10 9 8 7 6 5 4

Printed in Canada

Free Spirit Publishing Inc.
400 First Avenue North, Suite 616
Minneapolis, MN 55401-1724
(612) 338-2068
help4kids@freespirit.com
www.freespirit.com

Dedication

To gifted young people everywhere, whose great minds, enthusiasm, sensitivity, and free spirited natures are a constant source of inspiration for me. And to my lifelong friend and editor, Pamela Espeland, whose steadfast caring and encouragement mean more to me than words can ever express.

J.G.

Sometimes children teach us as much as—or more than—we teach them. With this in mind, I dedicate this book to Matt, Chuck, Dan, and Rob, all intelligent and sensitive young men who have taught me a great deal. Also, and of equal importance, this book is dedicated to Chris, Jon, and Leah. May they all see themselves somewhere on these pages, for they are here. Finally, this book is for Matt F., whose questions about life permeate these pages. Hang in there, Matt, and call whenever you'd like!

J.D.

Contents

Taking Charge of Your Education

Relationships

Introduction

Many schools today have strong, effective, exciting gifted programs in place. Countless teachers are dedicated to ensuring that *all* students, including gifted students, are given the chance to learn, grow, and succeed. In many communities, giftedness is encouraged, respected, and rewarded. If you are part of such a program, favored with such teachers, and nurtured by such a community, then you may not need this book, and the information in it may seem irrelevant to you. But if you have ever felt confused, conflicted, frustrated, excluded, or unhappy with your school, your environment, your life, and/or yourself, and if you suspect that it has something to do with being gifted, read on.

How and Why We Wrote This Book

This is not a book *about* gifted young people. It's a book *for* gifted young people. And it takes sides—yours. We wrote it with help from hundreds of gifted teenagers from New Jersey to California, Ontario to Slovenia who responded to a survey asking them to identify their questions and concerns about growing up gifted*—and from hundreds more we've interviewed, spoken with, listened to, and heard from over the years. We drew on the expertise of forward-thinking teachers, parents, and other experts on giftedness, and on current research and findings. And we thought deeply about our own experience as educators of and advocates for gifted children and teenagers.

Although this will probably sound strange coming from the authors, we wish this book wasn't necessary. If every school fully met the needs of its brightest students, if our culture genuinely valued giftedness and every individual was encouraged to reach his or her potential, then it wouldn't be necessary to write a book like this one. Schools would teach all students in the ways they learn best, and gifted students wouldn't have the kinds of problems they sometimes do—boredom at school, feelings of isolation and loneliness and differentness, difficulties that arise from being labeled, self-destructive perfectionistic tendencies, and more.** But that's not the way things are, and it's not the way they will be in the near future, if ever.

In fact, this book may be even *more* necessary now than when the first edition was published in 1983. (*The Gifted Kids Survival Guide II* followed four years later, in 1987.) It's true that many gifted teens today are better educated, more street-smart, more confident and "with it" than the gifted teens of 15 or even 10 years ago. Because of the growing emphasis on self-awareness, self-esteem, and self-help, and because at least some of the stigma associated with giftedness has dissipated, gifted students today are probably better off in some ways than their predecessors. So you might say that things have never been brighter for gifted teens than they are at the present time.

---

* Our heartfelt thanks go out to everyone who participated in our survey. If you weren't part of the original survey group, we invite you to contribute your thoughts and ideas for the next edition of this book. You'll find the survey on pages 280–83.
** Not all gifted students have all of these problems, but many gifted students have told us that they have one or more. We're not being negative, we're just telling it like it is.

Or you might say that things have seldom been worse. In fact, giftedness and gifted education are both under fire. Many school districts, faced with shrinking budgets and cutbacks, have dropped their gifted programs altogether. (Not that the common once-a-week pull-out class constituted a "program," but at least it was something.) Tighter budgets mean fewer teachers and heavier workloads, and that in turn means fewer opportunities to give gifted kids the individualized education they thrive on.

The rise of the "inclusive classroom" has also taken its toll. Inclusiveness—bringing all students into the regular classroom, including those with special education needs and severe learning difficulties—was never meant to take attention away from high-ability kids, but that's what sometimes happens. Students who do well in school and don't have to struggle to learn may not be getting the attention they need and deserve. Gifted students may be left to fend for themselves, or they may be expected to teach other kids in cooperative learning groups. For some of these students, school is one dull day after another, a time when they seldom learn anything new and instead slog (or sleep) through repetitive information.

Because more parents hold full-time jobs, greater demands are placed on teachers. Things parents used to teach have become the responsibility of schools. Subjects like anti-drug education, health care, human sexuality, social skills, and life skills take up class time that used to be devoted to academics. With more areas to cover, teachers have less time to spend with you—less time to spend with every student.

Then there's the fact that giftedness is given lip service as a "good thing" in our culture but isn't really valued day-to-day. Brainy, successful people are esteemed—and resented. Top students earn the high grades, but athletes get the awards, kudos, letter jackets, and full scholarships. Smart kids may be labeled "geeks," "nerds," "dorks," "teacher's pets," or whatever the current (usually worse) word happens to be. They may be picked on and attacked, sometimes violently.

In 1993, the U.S. Department of Education released a report titled *National Excellence: A Case for Developing America's Talent*, which calls on educators to address the "quiet crisis" that exists in the way we educate (or fail to educate) our top students. The report highlights the conflicts in our culture's perception of giftedness:

"Today, exceptional talent is viewed as both a valuable human resource and a troublesome expression of eccentricity. As a culture, we admire and reward the brilliant, creative mind after it has invented something practical or produced tangible results. Yet we are not inclined to support those who want to pursue an artistic or intellectual life, and we find ways of discouraging those who wish to do so. . . . The nation's high-ability students receive mixed messages. Our society urges these young people to do well in school; but it also encourages them not to flaunt their intelligence and, in some cases, to avoid high grades and excellent academic achievement altogether. . . . Negative stereotypes of high-achieving students have created an atmosphere in which students do not want to be identified as very smart."

In the words of Gregory Anrig, president of the Educational Testing Service, "As a culture, we seem to value beauty and brawn far more than brains."

About This Book

The Gifted Kids' Survival Guide: A Teen Handbook presents facts, findings, ideas, insights, strategies, tips, how-tos, and more about giftedness, intelligence, testing, school survival, goal setting, college preparation, expectations, time management, relationships, stress, and other topics of interest and importance to gifted students today. To get an overview, skim the Contents, scan the Index, or flip through the pages and stop when you see something you want to know more about.

We've also included thought-provoking and inspiring quotations, boxes, cartoons, questions to think about and talk about, and lists of resources to consult when you want to learn more about a particular topic or issue. An Additional Resources section (pages 284–86) points you toward other organizations, publications, and Web sites you may want to pursue.

Over the years, gifted students have told us that problems with school and teachers are their #1 concern, so we've included a hefty chapter about taking charge of your education through proper planning and action. Gifted young people have identified confusion about giftedness and relationships with peers as other pressing concerns, so we've devoted considerable space to these topics. We offer solid advice on how to handle the elevated expectations parents often have of their gifted children—and we explain what it's like to be the parent of a gifted kid, because it always helps to see complex issues from another perspective. We've included many observations and questions from gifted young people who took part in our survey, and several "Speak Out" essays contributed by gifted teenagers and adults, because it's reassuring to know that you're not alone and there are other people out there who think and feel as you do. Throughout, we try to give you the tools you need to take control of your life, make good choices, and get what you want and need.

You should know up front that this book doesn't contain any quick fixes or easy solutions. In order to make the changes in your life, family, social group, and school that you feel are most important, you need to be willing to work, experiment, question authority, examine your own thinking, assess your goals and objectives, and persist in spite of setbacks, mistakes, and failures. We have made every effort to avoid preaching, moralizing, shoulds, got tos, and ought tos, although sometimes we can't help ourselves (after all, we're teachers and one of us is a parent). If you want to try some of our suggestions, that's great; we hope you will find them useful. If you don't, that's okay, too. Sometimes the things we say may appear self-evident to you, even boringly obvious. But before you dismiss a suggestion, *try it.* No matter how plain, ordinary, or simplistic it might seem.

We wrote this book for gifted students ages 11–18, but we hope that some people under 11 will read it—and a lot of people over 18, including teachers and parents of gifted kids. We believe that it can give teachers and parents a clearer understanding of the gifted young people in their classrooms and families. We've both noticed that when a problem exists between teachers and/or parents and kids, it's often rooted in a lack of mutual respect. Parents or teachers may think, "You don't know anything because you're just a kid." Students may think, "My teachers don't care about me because I'm one in 100," or "My parents think that just because I'm gifted, I should be able to do everything on my own." Each side is guilty of assuming that the other has little or nothing to offer.

On the other hand, we've noticed that problems between teachers and/or parents and kids seem to diminish as respect grows. We hope that this book will help teachers and parents become more respectful of the knowledge and abilities that young people (especially bright young people) have. We want adults to start asking, "What can I learn from you?" We also hope that this book will help students become more respectful of the wisdom and experience their teachers and parents have to offer. It all gets easier when the two sides stop arguing and working against each other. To that end, we have included several suggestions young people can use to get their needs met constructively, working *with* their parents and teachers whenever possible.

We don't claim to have the last word on giftedness and what gifted teens want and need. We're smart enough (and so are you) to know that if you don't find what you're looking for in this book, you'll keep looking until you do.

It's been said that life is a journey. We hope that your journey—with or without this book—will be more than an exercise in survival. We hope that it will be challenging, happy, and fulfilling. We hope that you will learn to accept your giftedness as an asset, if you haven't already, and use it to make the most of who you are.

Best wishes,

Judy Galbraith and Jim Delisle
Free Spirit Publishing Inc.
400 First Avenue North, Suite 616
Minneapolis, MN 55401-1724
help4kids@freespirit.com
www.freespirit.com

On Being "Gifted"

Let's assume that if you're reading this book, you've probably been identified as "gifted" somewhere along the way.* Maybe you were tested as a toddler or a preschooler because your parents suspected that you were smarter, more creative, or more precocious than other kids your age. Maybe one of your teachers noticed that you had special talents or abilities. Maybe high grades and/or test scores qualified you for a spot in the "gifted program" in elementary or middle school. For whatever reason, like it or not, you've been labeled, and you may not even have a clear idea of what "gifted" means.

"WHY IS THERE SUCH A THING AS BEING 'GIFTED'?"
JOSH, 12

---

* Or maybe you haven't been identified as "gifted" but you believe you *are* gifted. Either way, keep reading! Not every gifted person is recognized as such, for reasons we'll explain later.

Dueling Definitions

If anyone has told you what "gifted" means, chances are the definition was vague or confusing, because nobody can *agree* on a single definition. There are government definitions, school definitions, teacher definitions, administrative definitions, researchers' definitions, authors' definitions, and dictionary definitions. And they all differ in some ways. Examples:

● *From* Merriam Webster's Collegiate® Dictionary, *Tenth Edition (1993):*

> **gifted 1:** having great natural ability:
> TALENTED (~ children)
> **2:** revealing a special gift (~ voices).

● *From the U.S. Department of Education:*

> " 'Gifted and talented children' means children and, whenever applicable, youth, who are identified at the preschool, elementary, or secondary level as possessing demonstrated or potential abilities that give evidence of high performance capability in areas such as intellectual, creative, specific academic, or leadership ability, or in the performing and visual arts, and who by reason thereof require services or activities not ordinarily provided by the school."

● *From the National Association for Gifted Children's mission statement (1996):*

> " . . . children and youth with demonstrated gifts and talents as well as those who may be able to develop their talent potential with appropriate educational experiences."

● *From three respected experts on giftedness:*

> **Lewis Terman** (1925): "The top one percent level in general intelligence ability as measured by the Stanford-Binet Intelligence Scale or a comparable instrument."

> **Paul Witty** (1940): "There are children whose outstanding potentialities in art, in writing, or in social leadership can be recognized largely by their performance. Hence, we have recommended that the definition of giftedness be expanded and that we consider any child gifted whose performance in a potentially valuable line of human activity is consistently remarkable."

Dr. Joseph Renzulli (1978): "Giftedness consists of an interaction among three basic clusters of human traits—these clusters being above average general abilities, high levels of task commitment, and high levels of creativity."

What can we conclude from the above? That existing definitions of giftedness have problems because:

1. they're too general AND
2. they're too restrictive. (Curious, isn't it?)

It can also be argued that the main problem with any definition isn't *what it says* but *how it's used.* Adults use definitions of giftedness to develop criteria for identifying students who then receive special opportunities and more challenging educational programs. That's fine, except that sometimes definitions include people who really shouldn't be included—or they exclude people who really shouldn't be excluded.

We recently discovered another definition of giftedness that seems like a step in the right direction:*

"Giftedness can be defined as *the ability to solve complex problems in effective, efficient, elegant, and economical ways.* Using this definition, a gifted individual is one who can use existing knowledge when necessary and can apply known methods when appropriate, therefore reaching solutions based on the best available knowledge and methods. However, a gifted individual can also abandon existing knowledge and concepts, redefine problems, devise new methods, and reach entirely different solutions."

Of all these definitions, which one(s) do you prefer, and why?

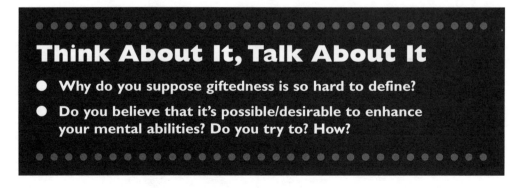

Think About It, Talk About It

● **Why do you suppose giftedness is so hard to define?**

● **Do you believe that it's possible/desirable to enhance your mental abilities? Do you try to? How?**

---

* Reported by C. June Maker in "Identification of Gifted Minority Students: A National Problem, Needed Changes and a Promising Solution," *Gifted Child Quarterly,* Volume 40, No. 1 (Winter 1996), p. 44. Based on work by Howard Gardner, C.J. Maker, A.B. Nielson, J.A. Rogers, and P. Bauerie.

Who Gets Left Out?

No matter how diligently teachers and administrators work to identify gifted students fairly and accurately (so the "right" students can receive more challenging educational programs), some gifted kids get left out. They aren't identified because they don't satisfy certain criteria. If you don't fit the description, you miss out on opportunities that might enable you to demonstrate and enhance your giftedness.

Those who are most often passed over when the gifted program Selection Day comes along include:

Gifted Girls

They may be excluded not because they aren't as smart or talented as boys, but because they may have learned to cover up or deny

> **"WE ARE EXPECTED TO BE PRETTY AND POPULAR, AND IT IS SO HARD TO BE INTELLIGENT AND LET IT SHOW IN SCHOOL." GIRL, 14**

their abilities in order to be popular or feel "normal." (This is especially true in middle school/junior high.) Or, if they are identified as gifted, they may choose not to participate in the gifted program due to social pressures.

People with Disabilities

They may be left out if their physical, emotional, or learning disabilities hinder their capacity to demonstrate their giftedness in the most recognizable and acceptable ways. The traditional methods used to identify gifted kids would have failed to notice Helen Keller.

Gifted people with disabilities have been called an "unseen minority." As researcher Nick Colangelo has observed, when teacher and parent groups are asked to imagine a "gifted child," they rarely conjure up the image of a gifted child with disabilities.

Troublemakers

They often aren't considered because some teachers associate "good" behavior with being gifted and "bad" behavior with being unwilling or unable to learn. Thomas Edison was considered a little hellion in school (and, in fact, he never graduated from grade school).

People from Minority or Other Non-Mainstream Groups

Their gifts may not be measured by standard IQ and achievement tests, which are often biased to majority (white middle- to upper-class) students. Also, their gifts may lie in areas that are not celebrated or valued by the mainstream society.

People Who Perform Poorly on Tests

Some gifted students simply aren't good at taking tests. They may know the material, but the test situation is too stressful for them, and they perform poorly as a result. They may be penalized with low test scores due to a poorly trained test administrator, or they may have personal problems that prevent them from concentrating and performing up to their true capabilities. Since test scores are one of the principle methods used to identify gifted individuals, this clearly puts them at a disadvantage.

Borderline Cases

Regardless of the system used to identify and select gifted students, there are always some "marginal" cases who fall between the cracks. (See page 12 for a list of notable achievers whose gifts may not have been recognized early on.)

How the Gifted Are Identified

Generally speaking, teachers and school administrators rely on the following three measures for identifying students as gifted and selecting them for participation in the gifted program (if one exists):

1. IQ tests (those who score in the top 3–5 percent on the Stanford-Binet IQ test or another similar test)

2. achievement tests (those who score at the 95th percentile or above on achievement tests)

3. teacher evaluations.

15 People Who Probably Wouldn't Have Made the Cut

1. John F. Kennedy received constant reports of "poor achievement" and was a lousy speller.

2. Beethoven's music teacher once said of him, "As a composer, he is hopeless."

3. Winston Churchill failed sixth grade and finished last in his class at Harrow, England.

4. Walt Disney was fired by a newspaper editor because he had "no good ideas" and he "doodled too much."

5. Sally Jesse Raphael was fired at least 19 times before becoming the host of her own TV and radio shows.

6. Paul Orfalea, founder of the successful Kinko's Copy Centers chain, was placed in a class for retarded students after he failed second grade due to dyslexia.

7. Isaac Newton—who discovered calculus, authored the theory of universal gravitation, originated the three laws of motion, and formulated the binomial theorem—did poorly in grade school.

8. Singer-dancer-choreographer Debbie Allen was turned down by a dance school.

9. Dr. Robert Jarvick was rejected by 15 American medical schools. He later invented an artificial heart.

10. Madeleine L'Engle's book, *A Wrinkle in Time,* was rejected by almost every major publisher before Farrar, Straus, and Giroux agreed to do it—after warning that the book would probably not sell. It went on to win the Newbery Medal.

11. Babe Ruth struck out 2,000 times on his way to becoming one of baseball's all-time greatest home-run hitters.

12. Tina Brown—former editor of *Vanity Fair,* current editor of the *New Yorker*—was expelled from school.

13. So was swimming champion Diana Nyad.

14. So was Roger Daltrey—composer, musician, and lead singer of the rock group The Who.

15. Albert Einstein flunked math.

You'll learn more about tests and testing on pages 47–64. You'll find an example of a teacher screening form on page 14. (As you'll see, evaluations tend to be open to individual interpretation.) In addition to teacher evaluations, some schools ask for recommendations from parents. And in a few instances, students might be allowed to nominate themselves by completing a questionnaire.

Take a few moments to read through the teacher screening form. How many of these characteristics do you have?

Obviously, no one will exhibit *all* of the characteristics listed in any evaluation; for example, a gifted mathematician will probably show different abilities than a gifted dancer. Evaluations attempt to identify those students who demonstrate excellence or strong potential to achieve in one or more of the following five areas. Which descriptions fit you?

Academic
- *High rate of success in subjects of interest*
- *Pursues certain areas with vigor*
- *Good memory*
- *Comprehends well*
- *Acquires knowledge quickly*
- *Widely read in special areas*

Leadership
- *Likes structure*
- *Self-confident*
- *Well-accepted by peers*
- *Shows good judgment, common sense*
- *Responsible*
- *Articulate, verbally fluent*
- *Foresees the consequences of things*

Creativity
- *Independent thinker*
- *Expressive (orally or in writing)*
- *Keen sense of humor*
- *Is resourceful*
- *Doesn't mind being different*
- *Is original, unconventional, imaginative*

Intellectual
- *Observant*
- *Gets excited about new ideas*
- *Inquisitive*
- *Learns rapidly, easily*
- *Independent learner*
- *Has a large vocabulary compared to others of same age*
- *Thinks abstractly*
- *Enjoys hypothesizing*
- *Intense*

Visual/Performing Arts
- *Ability to express feelings, thoughts, and moods through art, dance, drama, or music*
- *Good coordination*
- *Exhibits creativity, imagination*
- *Observant*
- *Likes to produce original products*
- *Flexible*

TEACHER SCREENING FORM FOR GIFTED EDUCATION

Please take a few minutes to list the names of the students who come into your mind *first* as you read through the descriptions below. This should be done as "free association," very rapidly. You don't need to fill in every space. It's likely that you will be able to name more than one student per description.

1. Learns easily, quickly

2. Original, imaginative, creative, unconventional

3. Widely informed, informed in unusual areas

4. Thinks of unusual ways to solve problems

5. Persistent, resourceful, self-directed (does things without being told)

6. Persuasive, able to influence others

7. Shows common sense, may not tolerate foolishness

8. Inquisitive, skeptical, curious about knowing the how and why

9. Adapts to a variety of situations, new surroundings

10. Clever at making things out of ordinary materials

11. Abilities in the arts (music, dancing, drawing, etc.)

12. Understands the importance of nature (weather, moon, sun, stars, soil, etc.)

13. Outstanding vocabulary, verbally fluent

14. Easily learns new languages

15. Independent worker, shows initiative

16. Good judgment, logical

17. Flexible, open

18. Versatile, many interests, interests go beyond chronological age

19. Shows unusual insights

20. Shows high level of sensitivity, empathy toward others

21. Has excellent sense of humor

22. Resists routine and drill

23. Expresses ideas and reactions, sometimes in an argumentative way

24. Sensitive to truth and honor

Quick Answers to Two Common Questions

Where does giftedness come from?

Nature—and nurture. In part, your giftedness is inherited from your parent(s) or grandparent(s). It has also been affected by your environment. Everything around you—your experiences with friends, family members, and at school; books you've read, games you've played—has enhanced your abilities.

While no one knows exactly which of these factors is most important, we do know that there are specific things you can do to maximize (or minimize) your giftedness. For example: If you're active, read a lot, meet new people, travel, are inquisitive, and take advantage of life's opportunities, you'll stretch your mind, grow as a person, and become more knowledgeable and creative. On the other hand, if you're sedentary, watch a lot of TV, eschew books, and do your best to keep people, ideas, and experiences at a distance, you'll limit your natural ability to learn. Studies have shown that IQ can vary as much as 20 points over a person's lifetime.

How many people are gifted?

It's estimated that there are between 2–3 million gifted kids in the United States alone. Worldwide, perhaps 5 percent of the population would be identified as gifted, using various definitions and selection practices.

Not everyone agrees with these numbers. A few educators suggest that broadening our definitions would result in up to 60 percent of the population being defined as gifted. Some even believe that *everyone* is gifted in some way.

The Gifted Kids' Survival Guide

"In our society to admit inferiority is to be a fool, and to admit superiority is to be an outcast. Those who are in reality superior in intelligence can be accepted by their fellows only if they pretend they are not."
Marya Mannes

The "Gifted" Label: Burden or Blessing?

In an ideal world, we wouldn't need labels of any kind. In our less-than-ideal world, labels help us to communicate, understand, make decisions—and allocate funding. The "gifted" label exists in schools today because the needs of bright, talented, creative students often aren't met by the regular curriculum. Identifying these students as gifted gives schools a way to justify special programs that come closer to meeting the students' needs, and also to select kids for inclusion in gifted programs.

The problem with the "gifted" label isn't the label itself but rather how people perceive it and use it. When it's attached to certain nouns (athlete, musician, writer, actor, etc.), it's usually acceptable and considered a compliment. But when it's used in reference to academic or scholarly pursuits, it's not necessarily an asset. In fact, many students experience the label in conjunction with such negative nicknames as "geek," "nerd," "dweeb," "junior genius," "dork," or worse, none of which promote feelings of acceptance or popularity. And this in turn leads some gifted students to downplay or deny their giftedness.

Every gifted person we've ever taught, interviewed, talked with, worked with, or lived with admits to enjoying the benefits of being intelligent. Knowing how to think deeply, think creatively, feel intensely, understand complex concepts, explore a variety of interests, make connections that others don't see, solve problems, come up with unique ideas, and so on makes life interesting and exciting. So why does the "gifted" label—when linked with intellectual pursuits—end up as more of a burden than a blessing?

At least part of the answer lies in the way our culture values (or devalues) academic effort and achievement. Consider these facts:*

- *Americans spend less time in school than the people of most other industrialized countries.*
- *We devote less than half as much time as other nations to core subjects.*
- *Less than half of a typical American school day is devoted to academic activities.*
- *The three main television stations in one major metropolitan area give up to 30 times more coverage to student athletes than to student scholars.*

---

* From the dissertation titled "Brains, Beauty, or Brawn: A Context Analysis of Adolescent Response to Three Superlatives" by Stephen Schroeder-Davis, Ed.D.; copyright ©1995. For permission to reprint this excerpt, please contact: Stephen Schroeder-Davis, Ed.D., Vandenberg Jr. High, 948 Proctor Ave., Elk River, MN 55330.

- *Two-thirds of our students state that student athletes are more respected than student scholars.*
- *The "pure scholar" (the non-athletic academic achiever) is the least popular student in a typical school.*
- *Over two-thirds of our brightest students report deliberate under-achievement to avoid being labeled a "nerd" by classmates.*
- *Less than a third of our students (30 percent) report a "positive school climate."*
- *Students report spending more time per week on virtually anything other than schoolwork, including socializing, sports, extracurricular activities, TV, work, and listening to the radio.*

The Board of Education in one Nevada county has come up with a revealing series of euphemisms to describe students' academic performance. Those who earn D's or F's are "emerging." Those who earn B's and C's are "developing." And those who earn A's are merely "extending." (As opposed to "succeeding," "achieving," or "excelling," all of which might imply that the A students are doing better than the others.)

> **"BEING GIFTED ISN'T NECESSARILY A GOOD THING IN AMERICAN SOCIETY. AVERAGE INTELLIGENCE IS VALUED MORE. WHO WOULDN'T WANT TO COVER IT UP?"**
> IVORY, 12

No wonder so many gifted students struggle with insensitive and uninformed comments from teach-

> **"HOW DOES A PERSON AVOID BEING RIDICULED FOR HAVING AN ADVANCED VOCABULARY OR WHATEVER? I MEAN, SAYING 'I CAN'T HELP IT, I'M GIFTED' ISN'T EXACTLY A GOOD COMEBACK, IS IT?"**
> PETER, 12

ers, peers, and/or parents. For some kids, the best response is simply to ignore the ridicule. They refuse to allow others to damage or destroy their self-esteem.

Staying centered and strong takes determination and practice. One thing that helps is making a list of the pluses in your life—the benefits that come from being smart, creative, and talented. It also helps to consider the minuses—the drawbacks of the label—so you can decide which ones you'll try to change and which ones you'll just have to live with.

Some Possible Advantages of Being Gifted

- *You may have access to challenging programs, classes, and other educational opportunities that match your ability level and interests.*
- *Being gifted may open the door to scholarships, awards, and competitions.*
- *Adults may assume that you're more responsible, which can lead to increased freedom.*

- *You are able to tackle and surmount many types of problems and challenges, often with greater speed and finesse than people of average or low ability.*
- *Some teachers appreciate (some even prefer) the opportunity to work with smart students. In fact, you make their day!*
- *Having a good mind can mean a more interesting life (depending on the choices you make).*

"**AT THE SCHOOL I GO TO, PEOPLE STRIVE TO PUT THEIR TALENTS AND INTELLIGENCE TO GREAT CHALLENGES. WE AREN'T LABELED FREAKS, AND IT'S ACTUALLY 'COOL' TO BE GIFTED." JAY, 15**

- What other advantages can you think of? Come up with your own list, then consult (and update) it frequently—or whenever the "gifted" label seems more of a burden than a blessing.*

Some Possible Disadvantages of Being Gifted

- *People who don't understand what being gifted means (and doesn't mean) may equate giftedness with perfection. As a result, some people may have unreasonable expectations of you, from your grades to your behavior.*
- *Labels are easy excuses for put-downs and insults. Being "gifted" may make you a potential target.*
- *When someone asks you what "gifted" means, there really is no "right" answer, which makes it awkward to explain.*
- *Your classes and schoolwork are often too easy—and dull. Much of your schoolwork may seem irrelevant.*
- *Friends who really understand and accept you may be few and far between.*
- *You sometimes feel overwhelmed by the number of things you can do. How can you make good choices? How can you decide which direction(s) and interest(s) to pursue in life?*
- *You may feel "different" from other kids your age—and if you view being different as a deficit, you may try to suppress your true self.*
- *Because you are knowledgeable, sensitive, and smart, you may be more aware of and concerned about world problems than some of your peers. On the other hand, you may feel helpless to do anything about them, and that can be frustrating and frightening.*

"In this world people have to pay an extortionate price for any exceptional gift whatever."
Willa Cather

Make your own list of disadvantages. Throughout this book, we'll offer suggestions for dealing with some of the most common "minuses" of being gifted.

---

* TIP: If you enjoy journaling, you may want to keep a journal as you read this book. Use it to record your lists, thoughts, questions, reactions, and ideas.

Maddening Myths

There are many misconceptions about what it means to be gifted. Here are ten of the most common myths we've encountered over the years:

Myth #1: Gifted kids have it made and will succeed in life no matter what. They don't need any special help in school or anywhere else.
Fact: Everyone needs encouragement—and help—to make the most of their abilities and succeed in life.

Myth #2: Gifted kids should love school, get high grades, and greet each new schoolday with enthusiasm.
Fact: Most schools are geared for average learners, not gifted learners, which makes it hard for gifted students to get excited about going. Some of the most talented students in the United States actually choose to drop out of school altogether.

Myth #3: Gifted students come from white middle- and upper-class families.
Fact: They come from all cultural, ethnic, and socioeconomic groups.

Myth #4: Gifted kids are good at everything they do.
Fact: Some gifted students are good at many things; others are exceptionally able at only a few things. Some gifted students are also learning disabled,* which means that they might not be very good at schoolwork. For more about giftedness and LD, see pages 22–24.

Myth #5: Teachers love to have gifted students in their classes.
Fact: Some do, some don't. Certain teachers feel uncomfortable with gifted students and get defensive when they suspect that their students know more than they do.

Myth #6: If gifted students are grouped together, they will become snobbish and elitist.
Fact: Some will, some won't. What's especially pernicious about this myth is that some adults use it to rationalize decisions about *not* allowing gifted students to work or study together or *not* providing them with opportunities that meet their learning needs.

Myth #7: All gifted kids have trouble adjusting to school and forming friendships.
Fact: Some do, some don't—just like other kids.

Myth #8: Gifted students don't know that they're "different" unless someone tells them.
Fact: Most gifted kids don't need to be identified or labeled before they know that they're not quite like their age peers.

Myth #9: Gifted students must constantly be challenged and kept busy or they'll get lazy.
Fact: They might get bored, but they won't necessarily get lazy.

Myth #10: Gifted kids are equally mature in all areas—academic, physical, social, and emotional.
Fact: That would be convenient, but it's not a reasonable expectation. On the other hand, it's not fair to assume that just because someone is advanced intellectually, he or she will lag behind in other developmental areas.

"Arguments of elitism are foolish. This nation fosters a sense of elitism when it comes to sports or the entertainment industry. Certainly there needs to be no apology for those who wish to nurture the minds of the best young students."
James Gray

---

*We prefer the term "learning different" because we believe that it more accurately reflects individual characteristics.

What This Means to You

Not everyone who is gifted has been identified as such. You may have friends, brothers, and/or sisters who are gifted but haven't been spotted by the school's selection system. (If your test scores drop, *you* may be labeled "gifted" one year and not the next. Which doesn't make a lot of sense, but that's the way it is.) Some schools don't check for giftedness at all, so students in those schools are never identified. And some schools that formerly identified gifted kids don't anymore because their gifted programs have been eliminated, so why bother?

What you need to remember, in the midst of all the confusion, inconsistencies, and inequities, is this: *The system isn't perfect.* People make mistakes. Right or wrong, most teachers aren't required to take training in gifted education. Therefore, many teachers know very little about giftedness and are not adequately equipped to identify gifted students.

What matters most is what *you* think of yourself and your abilities. Whether someone else believes that you're gifted is incidental and even irrelevant. It's up to you to decide how and whether you will use your gifts; it's up to you to determine the direction your present and future will take. *Never let anyone else decide for you how smart you are.*

Being gifted won't guarantee you a particular GPA or success in school. It won't automatically lead to a satisfying and meaningful career (or series of careers). It won't reward you with fame, friendships, and happiness. It won't make you kinder, more compassionate, and more caring than other people. Like everyone else, you're going to have to work at who you want to be and what you want from life.

But, let's face it, being gifted *will* give you an edge. You just have to know when and how to use it.

> "Our highest responsibility, finally, unavoidably, is the stewardship of our potential—being all we can be."
> **Marilyn Ferguson**

GIFTED PEOPLE SPEAK OUT
Vamir, 15

I was classified as "gifted" in second grade. This was really driven home when I skipped two grades, going from fifth grade to seventh over winter break. Though the social adjustment was rough initially, since then I have been fine both socially and academically. My major problem now is relationships with girls—I don't know too many my own age, and college girls are rather reluctant to have a relationship with someone so young.

Throughout the years, I have found myself and my gifted classmates to be motivated, curious, creative, and strong-willed (well . . . stubborn). In high school, especially, I noticed the independence of gifted students.

I don't know about you, but I've never liked the word "gifted." I don't think "capable" or "special" are specific enough, and "intelligent" isn't at all subtle. "Talented" seems to be okay, but if you've got a better word, I'm all ears.

A little bit about myself: My parents are both highly educated professionals, and I think that I am gifted entirely because of them (but my accomplishments are my own). My mother is a physician and my father is an engineer. Both of them apply science to their jobs. At the University, I am majoring in physics and math, possibly with another major and at least a substantial minor in economics. After college, there'll be more study, but I'm not sure what—either graduate physics or business (or possibly both, in time).

I am interested in science (especially physics), mathematics (algebra), philosophy (logic) and finance (futures trading). I like to read about these topics and some science fiction and espionage, as well as the "classics" that I started reading in my Humanities and Social Science classes. I also participate in College Bowl and Model United Nations, too.

Here are some of my concerns as a "gifted student." I hate it when adults are condescending to me simply because of my age (if it's because I've done something stupid, it's my fault). Most people don't give kids enough credit, so I try to treat younger children like they are my age, and those that can talk are usually mature enough to act that way. I also hate it when my parents (usually my dad) shows me off to friends and acquaintances. I talked to him about it and he does it less and less, but he still does it.

I hate it when I have so many thoughts that I lose one (which has happened to me at least a dozen times while writing this). I also hate it when I cannot think of anything, and when I have a really neat thought that I can't investigate more deeply because I just don't have the educational background.

I worry too much. I worry about "losing my talents." I worry about becoming average. I worry about my "lost childhood" and the opportunities I've missed because of my advancement. I worry I will burn out or overspecialize. I worry about how successful I will be in my career and whether my colleagues will accept me (and whether they do now).

Competition, standards, and records I am striving for confuse me. Do I really want to do this? I cannot decide. Should

I keep speeding up? The answer must be no, right? These questions make me doubt myself, my abilities, my sanity. It hurts.

About deciding on a career: Just like a little philosophy makes one an atheist while a lot makes you religious, a little knowledge makes you certain about your career, while more makes you uncertain once again. I have so many ideas for what to do and who to be.

I wish you luck as you grow up gifted. Always examine how you feel about school, learning, friends, and yourself.

Vamir is a freshman at a major midwestern university.

"Twice Exceptional": Gifted and LD

Some gifted students have needs in two areas that seem to contradict each other: They are gifted *and* learning disabled (LD). In recent years, gifted students with LD have been labeled "twice exceptional." Like all labels, this one has its shortcomings, but at least it calls attention to students whose giftedness might otherwise be overlooked.

For example, a student who is easily distracted and has difficulty completing assignments or concentrating on tests may be passed over when teachers are identifying students for enrichment opportunities. Since school success is often evaluated on the basis of graded assignments and test scores, a student who doesn't perform well on these tasks may not be seen as "smart," even though he or she is, in fact, intellectually, creatively, or otherwise gifted.

Another example is the student who has trouble with traditional written assignments (organizing content, handwriting, etc.). Unless alternatives are available—oral reports, artistic projects, access to computers—his or her giftedness may not be recognized.

Gifted students with LD may have uneven academic skills and may appear unmotivated. They may have "processing problems" with the way they see and hear, causing them to seem "slow." They may have motor skills problems that affect their handwriting. And because they are often frustrated with school, they may act out and have low self-esteem.

On the other hand, many gifted students with LD score in the gifted range on ability, achievement, and creativity tests. They may have a wide range of knowledge about a variety of topics and a fertile imagination. They may have a superior vocabulary and sophisticated ideas.

"Twice exceptional" students benefit when educators and parents focus on strengths, not perceived deficiencies. These students also need opportunities to learn and to show what they know in ways that are more natural and effective for them.

GIFTED PEOPLE SPEAK OUT

Aaron Samouelian

My struggles aren't over. They began early in my education. I always found it so difficult to understand what was being said in class! For example, when the teacher told us to follow multiple directions ("Fold your paper like a hot dog and then turn it 90 degrees"), I would not have a visual picture of what the final result should look like. Therefore, I would immediately rely on my neighbor's product for clues. I felt like crying knowing I couldn't rely on my own abilities. They were there, but I didn't know how to apply them.

This led to feelings of stupidity. Stupidity is not a motivating feeling to have at any time. But for me, it was a constant and exhausting struggle just to complete assignments and turn them in. I was insecure of their quality and value. Furthermore, when class discussion was going on, I would know the answers but not take a chance in answering for fear of looking stupid if I was wrong. This was a big factor in my life: feeling afraid to fail.

Struggling in high school can be very lonely and depressing. The schools I went to did not have a supportive environment in which I could learn, especially the high schools I attended. High school consists of peers and fitting in, so when you combine peers, rigid high school teaching styles, feelings of insecurity, and stupidity, you have a person who really knows what the word "struggle" means.

It got so bad for me that lying became automatic. Through lying I fooled my family, friends, and teachers—and probably myself. For example, I would change a report card grade or show my parents old homework when they asked to see current assignments. It became easier to fool everyone than to do the work. At the end of my sophomore year, I ran away from home because I was finally caught at failing. This turned out to be the first time that failure was good for me. In desperation, my parents had me tested, and we all discovered that I had a very high IQ, being deficient only in language retrieval. This enabled me to get admitted to a school for the gifted and talented. It was there that my successes began.

"Evidence suggests that the conventional educational system may be focusing on the wrong kinds of skills and . . . weeding out many of those who might have the most to give. . . . Different kinds of problems and different kinds of tools may require different talents and favor different kinds of brains."
Thomas G. West

There were many factors that contributed to my success. One was that the students and faculty at my new school made me feel a part of their community. This began on the first day of school, when I was greeted with open arms and a smile. I hadn't been used to these! I now belonged to a learning institution filled with a kind, caring faculty. They were there for me and my fellow students and not just for the paycheck. This attitude was evident through their understanding and acceptance of my special needs. They showed an interest in my learning styles and, even though my opinions and ideas were different from others, for the first time in my academic career, different was accepted.

Secondly, I started learning about myself and the styles in which I learned best. I no longer tried to imitate others and how they learned. I came up with my own ways to learn. This was a relief. This was true success. I could learn, achieve, and smile all day. Through seeing my efforts pay off, I gained self-esteem. My learning disability was no longer disabling; I'd finally found ways to learn that worked for me. I was different, but it was something to be proud of—it was a true talent! I have my own mind and no one else's.

Because of my experiences, I will now begin college knowing that it won't be easy but I am up to the challenge.

Aaron Samouelian graduated from the Roeper School for the Gifted in 1995. He is attending college in Michigan.

Find Out More   To learn more about giftedness and LD, read:

Bireley, Marlene. *Crossover Children: A Sourcebook for Helping Children Who Are Gifted and Learning Disabled.* Second Edition. Reston, VA: The Council for Exceptional Children, 1995. Although this book is written for educators and parents, it contains information that may be helpful to "twice exceptional" students.

You might also contact the following for information about young people who are gifted and LD:

Nielsen, Elizabeth, and Dennis Higgins, Principal Investigators. University of New Mexico, 3098 Mesa Vista Hall, Albuquerque, NM 87131-1286; (505) 277-6652. "The Twice Exceptional Program: Project REACH."

Intelligence

Nearly 60 percent of our survey respondents said they'd like to know more about intelligence, including the latest findings and definitions. Almost 50 percent wanted help knowing how to explain giftedness to their friends. And two-thirds of our survey respondents reported that they regularly downplay their abilities and intelligence in order to fit in with their peers.

> **"GIFTED KIDS TEND TO HIDE THEIR INTELLIGENCE, AS WELL AS THEIR TALENTS, FOR A VERY SIMPLE REASON: CONFORMITY."** CLAUDIA, 16

> **"IF YOU ASK ME ABOUT MY INTELLIGENCE, I TRY TO CHANGE THE SUBJECT."** ALAN, 13

That's unfortunate, because when you deny your intelligence, you deny an essential part of yourself. And you prevent yourself from being all that you could be.

Think About It, Talk About It

● Have you ever denied your intelligence in order to fit in with your friends and peer group? Did you actually fit in better as a result? Was it worth it?

● What do you think are the short-term and long-term effects of downplaying your intelligence and abilities?

● Is it ever okay to choose to be "less" than your true self? Why or why not? What happens if you do this often? (Can being "dumb" become a habit?)

One way to come to terms with your intelligence—and start using it for all it's worth—is to understand more about it: what it is, where it comes from, what it's good for, what it means.

Intelligence has always been a survival skill. If our long-ago ancestors couldn't outwit as well as outrun predators, they didn't get a second chance. Later, as people began to master their environment and its resident beasts, the benchmarks for intellect changed. The ability to lead, plan ahead, come up with an efficient and safe way to build a fire or cross a stream—these traits also became desirable. Our predecessors started to realize that certain members of their tribe had more of something than others, and that something was intelligence.

Over the ensuing millennia, intelligence was perceived in different ways by different people and cultures. It still is. For example, who would you rather have along on a safari—a seasoned traveler who knows the terrain and its dangers, or the student who sits next to you in biology and always gets A's on his lab reports? Obviously, you'd prefer the company of someone whose intelligence is related to the situation at hand. Which leads to an important if baffling point: In schools, intelligence is often linked to something that doesn't matter much once you graduate: true-false, fill-in-the-blank tests. Unless your goal in life is to be a *Jeopardy!* champion, school-type intelligence won't get you very far if it isn't accompanied by something else. . . .

Intelligence

Courage. Specifically, the courage to accept the fact that you're bright and to use your intelligence in ways that will make other people say, "Hmmmm . . . I never thought of that." The courage to create something new, to voice a reasoned opinion with confidence, and to stand up and say no when everyone else is saying yes (or vice versa). The courage to come to terms with yourself, your abilities, and your potential.

Identifying and Supporting Intelligence: A Timeline

- More than 2,000 years ago, the Chinese instituted large-scale testing to determine which of their young people would make the best leaders.

- In A.D. 800, Charlemagne urged the state to finance the education of promising young children found among the common people.

- Around A.D. 1373, the Ottoman Turks identified young men with superior physical appearance and endurance.

- Thomas Jefferson (1743–1826) proposed that youth with potential be provided with a university education at public expense.

- The launch of the Soviet satellite *Sputnik* in 1957 prompted Americans to get serious about education—and to start recognizing and supporting giftedness.

- In 1972, the U.S. Department of Education published a report stating that approximately 1.5–2.5 million children in the United States could be identified as gifted and talented—but only 4 percent of those children were being served by special programs.

- In 1990 and again in 1995, federal funds were awarded through the U.S. Department of Education, Office of Educational Research and Improvement, to a consortium including the University of Connecticut at Storrs; City University of New York, City College; Stanford University; the University of Virginia; and Yale University to support the National Research Center on the Gifted and Talented.

A Short Course on Intelligence Theory

Lewis Terman: Genius and Test Scores

In 1921, Lewis Terman, a psychologist at Stanford University, initiated a famous study that continues today through the work of his research descendants. He began by identifying 1,528 children who scored 140 or higher on an IQ test developed by French psychologist Alfred Binet, refined by Terman, and now called the Stanford-Binet Intelligence Scale. Terman dubbed the children "geniuses," then followed their lives for the rest of his career, observing their physical, intellectual, and emotional growth. He measured everything about them, from their amount of acne to the age at which they first grew body hair; from their rates of marriage and divorce to their rates of depression and suicide.

After more than 40 years, Terman concluded that these "gifted" children (he was the first to popularize that term) grew up to be pretty much like anyone else who experiences success and failure, elation and rejection as parts of everyday life. A few more interesting findings from Terman's long-term study:

- *He expected great things from his "geniuses" as they matured. Although he found that very few were unsuccessful in their careers, they still experienced the normal turmoils of growing up.*
- *The exceptionally able students who were kept within their age groups instead of being placed with intellectual peers tended to develop lazy work habits and underachieve.*
- *The most important companions to success were supportive parents or mentors, a built-in desire to excel, and self-confidence about one's ability to succeed.*
- *No one developed post-adolescent stupidity. This finding helped to erase the commonly held belief ("early ripe, early rot") that gifted children get less intelligent with age because they "use up" all of their brain power prematurely.*

Thanks in part to Terman and his colleagues, giftedness began to be perceived as a positive trait. Personal success and career satisfaction were associated with stability, not instability; with the absence, not the presence, of internal conflict; and with the support of others who also have above-average abilities—"in short," said Terman, "with well-balanced temperament and with freedom from excessive frustration."

Terman's study has often been criticized, and not without reason. Many people disagree with his premise that giftedness is synonymous with high IQ, arguing that intelligence is too complex to be measured by any test. Also, the subjects of Terman's study were predominantly white (although some of the Jewish children in his study spoke English as a second language, and he did make a concerted effort to find children of other races). In other words, his study wasn't perfect, but it was a start.

Four Conflicting Views of Intelligence

- **Alfred Binet believed that intelligence can be learned, expanded on, and improved.**

- **Italian physician and criminologist Cesare Lombroso offered "scientific proof" that highly able individuals were freaks of nature and prone to insanity.**

- **Around A.D. 1373, the Ottoman Turks identified young men with superior physical appearance and endurance.**

- **British scientist Francis Galton, the founder of eugenics (and Charles Darwin's cousin), believed that intelligence was 100 percent inherited. He suggested that those who didn't measure up "could find welcome and a refuge in celibate monasteries or sisterhoods."**

Howard Gardner: Multiple Intelligences

A couple of generations after Terman began his study, a man named Howard Gardner made some fascinating discoveries. In his work with adults who had suffered from strokes resulting in major disruptions in their brains and nervous systems, Gardner, a psychologist at the Harvard School of Education, found that many of these people could still do things that seemed remarkable. For example, even if stroke victims couldn't remember someone's name for more than 10 seconds, some of them could vividly recall events that had occurred 30 years before.

"The time has
come to broaden
our notion of
the spectrum of
talents. . . . We
should spend
less time ranking
children and
more time help-
ing them to
identify their
natural compe-
tencies and gifts,
and cultivate
those. There are
hundreds and
hundreds of
ways to succeed,
and many, many
different abilities
that will help
you get there."
Howard Gardner*

This finding led Gardner to propose that the brain couldn't possibly have all of its many capabilities measured by a one-time IQ test. He theorized that the brain actually contains many different intelligences. In his landmark book, *Frames of Mind: The Theory of Multiple Intelligences,* first published in 1983, he proposed seven intelligences: linguistic, musical, logical-mathematical, visual-spatial, bodily-kinesthetic, interpersonal, and intrapersonal. In 1995, he announced the existence of an eighth intelligence—naturalist. It's expected that his model will continue to expand and grow.

According to Gardner, the intelligences are relatively autonomous; they can operate fairly independently of each other but can also be combined in an infinite number of ways. Also, while it's possible to be gifted in one area and average or below-average in others, no intelligence is necessarily "better" or "worse" than any other. This means that a person who can take apart and reassemble a car without the help of an owner's manual is just as gifted as a person who can take the championship in a chess match. Both are exceptional, but in different ways.

Although Gardner's theory of multiple intelligences is becoming better known and more widely accepted, it still hasn't penetrated our schools. Here's what one educator has to say:**

"Typically, the two forms of intelligence schools deal with are those related to language and math. In these areas, special programs and kits are usually available for kids to follow. But for the other areas, there aren't any specific programs or materials, so it's pretty much hit-or-miss.

"If a teacher is interested in music, he or she will make time for some units on music. If the school system doesn't have money, one of the first things to go is anything related to the arts. Hands-on, manipulative materials aren't heavily used, even though they're crucial to the development of spatial skills, because schools tend to be paper-and-pencil oriented.

"Interpersonal and intrapersonal learning are discouraged rather than encouraged. Kids are told to sit down and shut up rather than urged to communicate. We tell bright kids to be quiet and think a problem through, but we don't allow them to express their thinking skills verbally."

---

* Quoted in *Emotional Intelligence* by Daniel Goleman (New York: Bantam Books, 1995), p. 37.
** Sally Yahnke Walker, *The Survival Guide for Parents of Gifted Kids.* Minneapolis: Free Spirit Publishing, 1991, p. 17.

IDENTIFYING YOUR INTELLIGENCES

Which of Howard Gardner's eight intelligences do you have?

Linguistic Intelligence. You enjoy writing, reading, listening, and speaking, and you do them all with ease. You enjoy memorizing information and building your vocabulary, and you may be an excellent storyteller.

Musical Intelligence. You can detect rhythms, patterns, and tempos in things that seem to have none at all—like chirping birds, crickets, and even some of the music your parents listen to. You can "hear" tone and pitch, and you may be talented at playing one or more musical instruments, either by ear or with instruction. You may appreciate many kinds of music.

Logical-Mathematical Intelligence. You instinctively put things in order and comprehend quantities—often in your head. Numbers and math concepts come easily to you, and you love brain-teasers, logic puzzles, games, and computers.

Visual-Spatial Intelligence. You readily notice when a building (or painting, or person) is not quite symmetrical. If you're an athlete, you can judge almost perfectly the angle needed to score a goal in hockey or a basket in basketball. You can mentally rotate complex forms, and you can draw whatever you see. You're good at taking things apart and putting them back together, and you love games.

Bodily-Kinesthetic Intelligence. You are good at handling and manipulating objects, and you move your body with grace and ease. You enjoy training your body to do its physical best, and you may be a great mimic. You may be talented at one or more crafts—carving, sewing, weaving, making pots.

Interpersonal Intelligence. You easily understand other people, perceiving their moods and feelings. You're a natural leader and a skilled mediator; you can break up a fight between two of your friends and still remain on each person's good side.

Intrapersonal Intelligence. You understand yourself very well; you're profoundly aware of your feelings, dreams, and ideas, and you're true to your goals. People may say that you "march to the beat of a different drummer." You enjoy journaling. (Are you keeping a journal while reading this book?)

Naturalist Intelligence. You feel a deep connection to the natural world and its inhabitants—plants and animals. You enjoy experiencing and observing the out-of-doors, and you may be a talented gardener and/or cook.

Robert Sternberg: Three Intelligences

Yale psychology professor Robert Sternberg is also a proponent of broadening our definition of intelligence. In his book, *Beyond I.Q.: A Triarchic Theory of Human Intelligence*, first published in 1985, he defines three types of intelligence: contextual, experiential, and internal.

● *Contextual intelligence* is the one you use when you adapt to your environment, change your environment, or choose a different environment that better suits your needs.

● *Experiential intelligence* is the one you use whenever you build on your experience to solve problems in new situations.

● *Internal intelligence* is the one you use to approach a problem, then evaluate the feedback to decide if you should change your approach.

In other words, according to Sternberg, knowledge is only one part of intellect. It's not enough to store and remember information; you also need to be able to solve problems. (Some people call this "street smarts"—the ability to know what to do in most situations.)

EXAMPLE #1: Let's say that you're reading a book and you come across the word *rapprochement.** You've never seen it before and you don't know what it means. Can you figure it out from the context—the words and concepts that surround it? If so, you're using a different form of intelligence than is usually measured on IQ tests.

EXAMPLE #2: You arrive home from your date two hours past curfew. You forgot to call your parents to tell them you'd be late (time flies when you're having fun). You know you're in trouble, but instead of panicking or going on the offensive, you try to assess the situation by listening to your parents' complaints. Then, based on what they say, you take the direct approach:

> **Dad says:** "You blew it. I trusted you with the car, I trusted you to be home by curfew, and what time is it? Two in the morning! Did you forget that I have to be up by six tomorrow?"
>
> **You say:** "I'm sorry, I really am. I didn't mean to make you lose sleep because you were worrying about me."
>
> **Dad thinks:** "Well, I was young once, and I wasn't perfect either."

---

* **rapprochement:** The re-establishment of cordial relations; reconciliation. See Example #2.

Mom says: "I thought we had an agreement. You're supposed to be home by curfew. And if for some reason you're running late, or the traffic is heavy, or there's an emergency, you're supposed to call. I've been worried sick for two hours."

You say: "I should have called, and I'm sorry. I forgot, but I know that's no excuse."

Mom thinks: "She knows she was wrong, and it sounds as if she's learned her lesson."

Nobody argues, everyone stays calm, and you all go to bed with smiles on your faces. Maybe your parents come back to you the next morning and say, "That was a clever way to get out of being grounded." If this happens, you can respond, "Hey, I was just using my highly developed metaprocessing skills in the area of social relationships!" That's what Sternberg might say, and it sounds good, doesn't it? (Sometimes it pays to be smart.)

Sternberg further believes that intelligence is a mental activity—a process—that can be taught. In other words, it's not something you either have or don't have.

Emotional Intelligence

In 1996, a book about yet another type of intelligence became a national bestseller. In *Emotional Intelligence: Why It Can Matter More Than IQ*, Daniel Goleman spotlights several qualities that add up to "a different way of being smart": self-awareness, impulse control, persistence, zeal, self-motivation, empathy, and social deftness. Goleman, a Harvard Ph.D. who writes about the brain and behavioral sciences for *The New York Times*, based his thesis on research being done by Peter Salovey at Yale University and John Mayer at the University of New Hampshire, among others. What Goleman calls "emotional intelligence" is also related to the "personal intelligences" (interpersonal and intrapersonal) described earlier by Howard Gardner.

People with emotional intelligence are able to manage their feelings. They know what they feel, they handle their feelings in ways that are positive and helpful, and they make decisions about life—what jobs to pursue, what directions to take, who to marry— with greater assurance and competency than people with low or no emotional smarts. Their people skills make them more adept at relationships, cooperation, negotiation, leadership, and teamwork. They learn more, they learn more quickly, and they are less likely to engage in antisocial, at-risk, or criminal behaviors.

Goleman believes that emotional intelligence is on the wane in America, as evidenced by teen crime rates, escalating violence, and widespread rage and despair. But there's hope for the future, because emotional intelligence is not fixed at birth. We can all learn and strengthen these skills throughout our lives.

Think About It, Talk About It

● How would you rate your own emotional intelligence?

● What people in your life—parents, teachers, friends—do you see as being good role models for emotional intelligence?

● Where could you go, who could you ask, and what could you do if you wanted to boost your emotional intelligence?

Emotional Giftedness

Michael Piechowski, a professor of education at Northland College in Ashland, Wisconsin, has come up with another view of giftedness. After translating the work of Polish psychiatrist Kasmirez Dabrowski, Piechowski coined the term "emotional giftedness."* It suggests some intriguing new ways to view both giftedness and intelligence.

Dabrowski studied the mental health of intellectually and artistically gifted youth. He found his subjects to be extremely intense young people who lived life to its fullest, sometimes dangerously so, and experienced emotional highs and lows that caused exhilaration, conflict, pain, and what he called "overexcitability."

Piechowski developed an instrument called "The Overexcitability Questionnaire" to learn more about this characteristic. Gifted students ages 12–17 were asked nearly two dozen questions including:

---

* Don't confuse Piechowski's "emotional giftedness" with Daniel Goleman's "emotional intelligence." They sound similar, but they are not the same. Emotional giftedness is specifically about the range of emotions experienced by young gifted people.

● *"If you ask yourself, 'Who am I?', what is the answer?"*
● *"Do you ever think about your own thinking? Describe."*

A sampling of responses:*

> **Age 16:** "I am a very misunderstood person.... People think that my life is easy because I am talented, but I have a lot of problems of my own just because of these talents.... I am a very sensitive and emotional person. I get angered or saddened very easily. I can also get happy easily. I like this part of me. All these emotions somehow make me feel good about myself."

> **Age 17:** "When I take a stand on something, I later wonder why I did that. I think about how I came to that conclusion.... I think about my friends and other people I know and wonder if I really feel the way I let on, and if I am fooling myself by thinking things I really feel."

> **Age 14:** "I'm somebody no one else knows. Some people see one part of me, others see other parts. It's like I'm acting. The real me is the one inside me. My real feelings—those I understand but can't explain."

When young people are very aware of their moods and emotions—when they think deeply about everything and feel everything—this sometimes leads to problems. As Piechowski explains:

> "It is unfortunate that the stronger these overexcitabilities are, the less peers and teachers welcome them, unless they, too, are gifted. Children exhibiting strong overexcitabilities are often made to feel embarrassed and guilty for being 'different.' Criticized and teased for what they cannot help, they begin to believe something is wrong with them."

But there's *nothing wrong with them.* And if you share this intensity, there's nothing wrong with you. Don't be ashamed of your emotional giftedness. Simply accept that what's normal for you might not be normal for everyone else.

We asked Piechowski for advice on how to cope with emotional giftedness. In response, he wrote a letter to you.

---

* Reported in M.M. Piechowski and N. Colangelo, "Developmental Potential of the Gifted Child," in *Gifted Child Quarterly* 28 (1984), pp. 80–88.

Dear Young Friend,

When I was young and learning about music, I loved to go to concerts. My mother thought that my excitement about music was excessive. Sometimes I had to beg her to let me go to hear the symphony.

Has something like this ever happened to you? Do you ever get terribly excited about things? Perhaps you get so absorbed by what interests you that you lose all sense of time—and you get criticized for it. A friend of mine once said, "The trouble is not that some people get overly excited about things, but that most people don't." Would you agree?

Did anyone ever tell you that you are "too much" because you get too excited, or too absorbed, or too intense about things that matter to you? Perhaps when you imagine something, it appears so vivid and real that you can see the most minute detail. Someone once told me that he saw in his mind's eye children playing in a happy place. He would get so absorbed by what he "saw" that when someone interrupted him—this could happen in school—he felt a shock, and it made him angry to be so rudely awakened.

Perhaps you feel things so strongly that others tell you to "chill out." But you know this is impossible, because you are just made that way. Maybe the singing of birds makes you cry because it is so beautiful. What else brings tears to your eyes?

In *Dandelion Wine,* Ray Bradbury describes how 12-year-old Douglas suddenly realizes that he is truly alive:

> The grass whispered under his body. He put his arm down, feeling the sheath of fuzz on it, and, far away, below, his toes creaking in his shoes. The wind sighed over his shelled ears. The world slipped bright over the glassy round of his eyeballs like images sparked in a crystal sphere. Flowers were suns and fiery spots of sky strewn through the woodland. Birds flickered like skipped stones across the vast inverted pond of heaven. His breath raked over his teeth, going in ice, coming out fire. Insects shocked the air with electric clearness. The thousand individual hairs grew a millionth of an inch on his head. He heard the twin hearts beating in each ear, the third heart beating in his throat, the two hearts throbbing his wrists, the real heart pounding his chest. The million pores in his body opened.
>
> I'm *really* alive! he thought. I never knew it before. I never knew it before, or if I did I don't remember!
>
> He yelled it loud but silent, a dozen times! Think of it, think of it!

How sad it would be to live without a sense of wonder. Maybe you, like Douglas, have had a moment of profound awakening. Or maybe this is a daily awareness for you. Either way, I hope that you can celebrate your intensity, your excitability—your aliveness.

Warm regards,

Michael M. Piechowski

Born in Poland, Michael Piechowski came to America and earned two Ph.D.s, one in molecular biology and the other in counseling. He became interested in overexcitabilities when he and Kasmirez Dabrowski were both on the faculty of the University of Alberta, Canada. Michael's work on overexcitabilities continues to guide his personal research.

What This Means to You

When we combine these theories of intelligence with the definitions of giftedness in the preceding chapter, we can draw only one conclusion: There is no "right" way to view either intelligence or giftedness. What's best is to keep an open mind, to pick and choose from among the various ideas and findings and decide what's most meaningful to you at this juncture in your life. You may want to work on your problem-solving skills or focus on other intelligences you'd like to improve. (Enhance your visual-spatial intelligence; go shoot some hoops!) Or you may want to do your own research on intelligence, uncovering even more theories and definitions. Considering diverse ideas and viewpoints can be challenging and exciting.

> "The test of a first-rate intelligence is the ability to hold two opposed ideas in the mind at the same time, and still retain the ability to function."
> **F. Scott Fitzgerald**

The Top Ten Questions About Intelligence and Giftedness

These questions are the ones we most often encounter in letters from students, survey responses, and Q&A sessions after our speeches and workshops.

#1 Is intelligence inherited, determined by our environment, or do we pick it up on our own?

The next time your dad wants to give you "a piece of his mind," remind him that he already has! It's generally acknowledged that genes (from both sides of the family) do count for at least part of our intelligence. What's not clear is how much is hereditary (nature) and how much comes from our day-to-day interactions with the people and things around us (nurture).

Here's what we believe: There's nothing you can do to change your DNA, but there's a lot you can do to enhance your environment. So read that book, attend that ballet, enroll in that computer class at school (or that cooking class at your community education center). Get on the Internet and explore the Louvre or the Smithsonian.

Dr. Marion Diamond, a California scientist, has done work with rats that suggests some interesting possibilities. When a group of older rats was treated to an enriched environment, they grew more brain cell connectors. Dr. Barbara Clark, author of *Growing Up Gifted,* has said that a stimulating environment can cause changes in our neurons' chemical makeup. Recent research is finding that young children's brains are "wired" for music, math, language, and emotion by early experiences. It doesn't take a brain surgeon to figure out that the more you're exposed to and the more you learn, the smarter you become.

#2 If I don't use my intelligence, will I lose it?

Anyone who plays tennis, basketball, or chess can probably answer this question, because except for a few shining stars who never had

> "With a good heredity, nature deals you a fine hand at cards; and with a good environment, you learn to play the hand well."
> Walter C. Alvarez, M.D.

to work at it, the keys to strong performance in a game of sport or strategy are practice, practice, and more practice. If you don't use your abilities on a regular basis, they won't disappear, but they will weaken. The same goes for brain power. If the most strenuous thinking you do all day is to choose between MTV or VH-1, don't be surprised if your mind clamps up during next week's American History test.

> "To keep a lamp burning we have to keep putting oil in it."
> **Mother Teresa**

Although your intelligence won't ooze out of your ears some night when you're asleep, your mind *is* like a muscle. It's best prepared for challenge when you exercise it on a regular basis.

#3 Are some ethnic groups more intelligent than others?

Simply asking this question might lead some people to think that you're prejudiced. But there's nothing wrong with a question about bias—if you're open to hearing an honest answer. And the honest answer to this particular question is no. Ethnicity does not determine intellectual prowess.

> ● **"GIFTED STUDENTS WHO FALL INTO SO-CALLED**
> ● **'MINORITIES' MAY HAVE A HARD TIME GETTING THE**
> ● **HELP THEY NEED FROM PREJUDICED TEACHERS."**
> ● **GIRL, 12**

So why is the question asked at all? Because of our history, our culture, and our methods for determining intelligence. For example, some kids have the privilege of not worrying about where their next meal is coming from. They are free to focus on schoolwork and social activities that introduce them to a world beyond their own neighborhood. When an intelligence test question asks them to define a "gazelle" or a "gazebo," they can recall that they once saw the former at the zoo or the latter in a friend's backyard. This gives them an intellec-

> ● **"A GIFTED STUDENT SHOULD BE ABLE TO SEE BEYOND**
> ● **SKIN COLOR."** **ERIN, 13**

tual "edge"—or so it would appear on a paper-and-pencil test.

But if you asked them what a "joggling board" is, or how to deal with a bull moose you meet on your way home from school, or how to prepare a cedar log for carving, or how to use the stars to navigate their way across the ocean, you would probably be met with vacant stares.

Intelligence is not doled out to some ethnic groups any more frequently than it is to others. It's just that the way many people measure intelligence has a distinctly middle-class, middle-American tone. Blacks, Hispanics, Asians, Whites, Inuits: each group has its own traditions, wisdom, and areas of expertise; each has something to teach the others. Smart people of all ethnic persuasions would be wise to listen and learn.

#4 Can a person be gifted and not do well in school?

Can a person be hungry after getting up from a table full of food? The answer is yes, and to continue with this analogy, here's the reason: Schools offer a "menu" from which you can dine, academically speaking. The nutritional value of any course of study is directly proportional to how much you "eat." In other words, if math doesn't interest you, or if your English class is so bland that it has no taste, you may choose not to partake of much in those courses. As a result, you may earn grades that are lower than gifted kids are "supposed to get," prompting your teachers and parents to wonder if you're really as smart as they thought you were.

Only rarely will adults consider that the problem may not be you, but the too-easy courses you're enrolled in, or the unappetizing textbooks you're expected to read. Only rarely will they choose to change the curriculum instead of trying to change you.

#5 Can gifted people also have LD?

Yes. Some gifted people do have learning disabilities (or "learning differences," the term we prefer). Tom Cruise was considered "dumb" because he had difficulty reading and writing in school. Winston Churchill was considered "slow" as a child. Ann Bancroft, the first woman to reach the North Pole, was held back in school. Today we have a phrase that describes individuals like these: "twice exceptional." They clearly have gifts, but they also have difficulties with learning. (For more on this topic, see pages 22–24.)

On the other hand, some gifted students are incorrectly labeled LD because their behaviors are similar to those of students with learning differences. They may have trouble paying attention, daydream excessively, squirm in their seats, stare off into space, challenge authority, refuse to do their schoolwork, and so on, leading some adults to (wrongly) assume that they have attention deficit disorders (ADD or ADHD). The problem is not necessarily with the students, but with the system. Here's what two experts on education have to say:

> **Susan Winebrenner:** "If these students are mistakenly identified as having LD, ADD, or ADHD, the danger is that their giftedness will go unnoticed because the deficit label usually takes precedence over other learning exceptionalities."*

---

* Susan Winebrenner, *Teaching Kids with Learning Difficulties in the Regular Classroom*. Minneapolis: Free Spirit Publishing, 1996, p. 27.

Thomas Armstrong: "I'm reminded here of the canaries that were kept by coal miners deep in the mines. If the level of oxygen fell below a certain level, the canaries would fall over their perches and die, warning the miners to get out fast. It's possible that children who have been labeled ADD are the canaries of modern-day education; they may be signaling us to transform our nation's classrooms into more dynamic, novel and exciting learning environments. ADD may, then, be more accurately termed ADDD: Attention-to-Ditto Deficit Disorder."*

#6 Can intelligence get in the way of having a good time?

Sometimes gifted people are accused of always being "on": always thinking, questioning, explaining, and being too intense. Although these behaviors were probably considered cute when you were two, they might drive people insane now that you're a teenager. Unfortunately for you, trying to keep your mouth (and your brain) shut might be as difficult as putting toothpaste back in the tube. You might not be able to distinguish between topics that light up the room and those that turn it into a dungeon of drudgery.

If this is a problem for you, consider the following options:

1. Slow down, talk less, and listen more. (It's possible that you do talk too much. This isn't a crime, but it can make it difficult for others to get a word in edgewise.)

2. Take a look at the people you're spending time with. Maybe you need to find another group of friends—people who appreciate your vocabulary and your intelligence.

3. Lighten up. Leave room in your life for jokes, humor, spontaneity, goofing off, and having fun.

> "SOME PEOPLE THINK THAT ALL GIFTED KIDS ARE FAR-OUT BASKET CASES. THAT ALL WE DO IS READ BOOKS AND STUDY. I WAS LIKE THAT FOR AWHILE. . . . WHEN I WAS IN 7TH AND 8TH GRADE, ALL I DID WAS STUDY. I GOT TIRED OF MY IMAGE. ALL PEOPLE KNEW ABOUT ME WAS THAT I GOT ALL A'S AND READ A LOT OF BOOKS. I DECIDED THAT I WAS THE ONLY ONE WHO COULD CHANGE THINGS, SO I TRIED OUT FOR A SCHOOL PLAY AND GOT A PART. I REALIZED THAT I COULD GET UP ON A STAGE AND PERFORM. I GOT INVOLVED IN CHOIR. NOW MY GRADES AREN'T STRAIGHT A'S BUT I'M LEARNING MORE THINGS THAT ARE FUN AND WILL BE HELPFUL LATER IN LIFE."
> HOLLY, 15

#7 Are gifted people gifted in everything? Can I be gifted if there are some things I'm not very good at doing?

Think back on Howard Gardner's work on multiple intelligences (see pages 29–31). If it's true that intelligence itself can take many forms, then it also makes sense that giftedness can come in varying degrees. As an audience member observed during one of our presentations, "It's almost as though you have to have valleys in order to also have peaks of high ability."

---

* Thomas Armstrong, "ADD as a Social Invention." *Education Week*, October 18, 1995.

Consider your friends, a group that probably includes a fair number of bright, creative people. Are some better at math, others at art, and still others at mediating disputes or pursuing personal goals? Not everyone is equally accomplished at everything.

But you already know that. So why are we belaboring the obvious? Because even though you understand this *intellectually*, understanding it *emotionally* is another matter. And if you don't understand it emotionally, you may find yourself trapped in the "Bottom of the Top" syndrome.

Here's how it works: You know that you're smart. After all, you've been in honors math since seventh grade. But when you look around, you start comparing your performance to that of the other students. Since someone in the class has to be the *least* smart, you figure that it might as well be you. What you don't know is that at least one-third of your classmates have the same opinion of themselves. They're just as fearful of ending up at the "bottom of the top."

This syndrome affects many gifted students when they start college. They're used to being the high school stars—high honor roll, dean's list, advanced classes, valedictorian, National Honor Society, National Merit Scholar, the whole package. Suddenly—especially if they attend a highly selective college—they're surrounded by hundreds of other students whose abilities are equal to or even superior to theirs. Naturally, this shakes their confidence. No longer at the top of the academic heap, they start wondering if they belong at all.

If Gardner is right—and we believe that he is—then you can stop comparing and start enjoying who and what you are.

#8 Why do people call me a "nerd" just because I'm gifted?

As psychologist Sylvia Rimm points out, "Very bright students have been called 'eggheads,' 'nerds,' 'bookies,' 'geeks,' 'weirdos,' 'schoolies,' 'teacher's pets,' and a long list of other odious labels long before the term 'gifted' was used for school programming."*

Why? Take a look at our culture and the way it depicts gifted people. Consider Margaret, the brilliant, bespectacled classmate of Dennis the Menace; Zelda, the smart but socially

"**KIDS RAG THEIR CLEVER AND INTELLIGENT SCHOOL-MATES. I KNOW SOME EXAMPLES FROM MY PRIMARY SCHOOL WHEN MY SCHOOLMATES RAGGED TWO FRIENDS OF MINE UNTIL THEY BROKE THEM. THEY TRIED TO BREAK ME TOO, BUT THEY COULDN'T BECAUSE MY PARENTS SUPPORTED ME. BUT IF GIFTED KIDS LIVED IN A SYSTEM WHERE EVERYBODY SUPPORTED THEM AND EVERYBODY LIKED THEIR INTELLIGENCE, THEY WOULD HAVE NO REASON TO DENY IT." URBAN, 14**

---

* Sylvia Rimm, "Is Popularity Worth Pursuing?" in *The Best of Free Spirit.* Minneapolis: Free Spirit Publishing, 1995, p. 184.

inappropriate friend of Dobie Gillis (check out late-night Nickelodeon); and the King of the Geeks, Steve Urkel of *Family Matters*. The media have long portrayed intelligent young people as stereotypes—awkward, unathletic, out-of-synch dipsticks with bad clothes, thick glasses, and pocket protectors. These goofy images of gifted kids may make us laugh, but when they're applied to you, they're not funny anymore.

The truth is that Western society is more than a bit uncomfortable with the idea of giftedness. After all, we're all supposed to be equal, so when some people (especially kids) seem more equal than others in the brain power department, others look for ways to artificially "equalize" them. When the highly intelligent boy is portrayed as a basketball team reject, or the gifted girl sits home alone on prom night, this knocks them down a rung on the social ladder, making them appear more "average" and less special.

To counter the "gifted geek" image, consider trying actions, not words. Instead of protesting that "smart kids like sports, too," join a team—varsity, intramural, or neighborhood. Rather than insisting that "I have plenty of friends—you're just not one of them," go on group dates once in a while or frequent the popular hangouts. Take a risk, be seen, be noticed, participate, and eventually you may hear people saying, "I didn't know he/she was in the gifted program—he/she's pretty cool." Also . . . be patient. In college, the "gifted geek" image is virtually nonexistent.

#9 Why are some teachers intimidated or threatened by gifted students?

You'd think that they would know better. After all, they're the teachers, you're the students. They're the authorities, you're the subjects. They assign the grades, you have to earn them. Still, there have been, are, and always will be teachers who don't respond well to gifted students and, in fact, may seem to enjoy making your life miserable.

This often has more to do with the teachers' self-confidence and self-esteem than it does with your intellectual abilities. Certain teachers simply can't accept the fact that certain students may be smarter in some areas than they, the teachers, are. (Notice that we say "some areas," not "all." You may be the world's greatest genius, but your teachers will always have something you don't: life experience, maybe even wisdom.) What can you do if you end up in one of their classrooms? Be courteous; be respectful; be willing to learn. If there's a specific problem you need to address, see our "Ten Tips for Talking to Teachers" on pages 155–56. And if nothing you do seems to make any difference—if you're still feeling ignored, picked on, and put down after your best efforts to fit in and work things out—talk to your parents, the school counselor, or another adult you trust. Maybe they can help, or maybe you'll just have to live with the situation the way it is. You won't be in that class forever.

Knowing how to teach gifted students takes something that not every teacher is willing to reveal: vulnerability. Good teachers of gifted kids can accept being corrected (occasionally) by their students; they can face the fact that some kids have knowledge they don't have; they can listen to different points of view with an open mind. But it isn't easy. As one gifted education teacher said, "I get asked all sorts of questions just because I teach gifted, such as 'How many eggs do loons lay?' Now why would I necessarily have the vaguest idea how many eggs loons lay?" Another question teachers often have is: "What am I supposed to do with students who already know much of what I'm about to teach?"

You might take a moment to think back on those teachers who have welcomed you, encouraged you, and changed your life for the better—the ones who have treated you with respect and kindness, understanding, and even appreciation. Most gifted students have at least one wonderful teacher in their past and/or present. Perhaps you could add your own story to these:*

> "Starting with second grade and on through high school, there have been nine teachers I've admired. I admired them because their own strength and natural rapport with students in turn demanded our respect. Kindness, sensitivity, and intelligence were among their many qualities and virtues. Most importantly, they made each student feel significant, as if each of us had a part of them in reserve. You knew they cared. With all their other responsibilities, they always took time out to personally talk with you, to discuss problems, and to offer suggestions."

> "As an only child, I really hadn't had many experiences playing group games and participating in physical activities. The teacher recognized this, and encouraged my mother to teach me to jump rope and catch and throw balls. What I'm trying to say is that as a five-year-old gifted child I was like any other child. I needed to have standards imposed upon me so that I could develop the habits that are necessary for successfully continuing my education."

---

* American Association of Gifted Children, *On Being Gifted*. New York: Walker and Co., 1978, pp. 54–55, 61–62.

"In a high school of 1,800 students, I really did not expect to receive very much individual attention; in fact, my whole attitude was pretty bad. My counselor visited with me about my ability and about the importance of really working in high school. His interest in me persisted until I began to believe that I could go to him with any problem or question. He has assisted me in various applications for scholarships and has written countless recommendations for me."

If you have one of these teachers now, consider thanking him or her for the ways he or she invites you to learn. If you had one of these teachers earlier in your life, think about writing a short note of gratitude. (The school secretary can help you find the teacher's address; school secretaries can find anything!) We can honestly (and modestly) admit that we've received a few of those letters in our lifetime, and they mean a great deal to us. Go ahead; make someone's day!

#10 _____

(your question here)

There are so many questions about intelligence and giftedness that we've left room for you to add your own. Unless this is your personal copy of this book, please jot down your question in your journal or on a piece of paper, since librarians get upset (and rightly so) when people write in books. Then begin your quest for an answer.

If someone else you know is also reading this book, you might sit down together and discuss your question. As another alternative, take it to your school counselor or psychologist. (He or she will probably love it, since the only question most kids ask school counselors/psychologists is usually "Who are you and what do you do here?") Or seek out a gifted education teacher. Or head for the library (you know how to use it). Or write to us. You'll find our address on page 6, and we do answer the letters we receive from our readers.

Find Out More

To learn more about intelligence and intelligence theory, read:

Armstrong, Thomas. *7 Kinds of Smart: Identifying and Developing Your Many Intelligences.* New York: Plume, 1993.

Gardner, Howard. *Frames of Mind: The Theory of Multiple Intelligences.* 10th Anniversary Edition. New York: Basic Books, 1993.

Goleman, Daniel. *Emotional Intelligence: Why It Can Matter More than IQ.* New York: Bantam Books, 1995.

Sternberg, Robert. *Beyond I.Q.: A Triarchic Theory of Human Intelligence.* New York: Cambridge University Press, 1984.

IQ, Tests, and Testing

Seventy-two percent of our survey respondents wanted to know what IQ and achievement test scores do—and don't—mean. Because so much emphasis is placed on tests and testing throughout a student's school experience, we've devoted a whole chapter to this topic.

IQ tests first came into use in the early 1900s, thanks to psychologists Alfred Binet and Theodore Simon. Interestingly, the original IQ tests were developed to identify kids who were "too dull" to be educated in ordinary schools. During the 1920s, Lewis Terman took the Binet-Simon test, revised it as the Stanford-Binet test, used it to identify the "geniuses" for his study (see pages 28–29), and the era of more widespread IQ testing was born.

Your IQ (Intelligence Quotient) is calculated by a simple mathematical formula:

$$\frac{\text{mental age}}{\text{life age}} \times 100 = IQ$$

For example, let's say that your life age is 13. When you take an IQ test, the examiner computes your score by comparing your answers to those given by thousands of other people of various ages. If your responses are both accurate and sophisticated (that is, if you used logic or elaboration), chances are your thinking will be revealed as more like that of a 16-year-old. Thus, your mental age will be higher than your life age. And here's what happens to the formula:

$$\frac{16 \text{ (mental age)}}{13 \text{ (life age)}} \times 100 = 123 \text{ IQ}$$

IQ Overview

IQ Score	Classification	Approximate Incidence in Population
160	Very superior	1 in 10,000
150	Very superior	9 in 10,000
140	Very superior	7 in 1,000
130	Superior	3 in 100
120	Superior	11 in 100
110	Bright	27 in 100

P.S. A score of 132 on the Stanford-Binet qualifies you for membership in Mensa, the International High IQ Society. For more information on Mensa and test scores they accept, write or call: American Mensa, 1229 Corporate Drive West, Arlington, TX 76006-6103; telephone 1-800-666-3672. Or check out the Mensa Web site: http://www.mensa.org/

Since the average IQ is 100, a score of 123 puts you above average. Translated into percentiles, it ranks you at about the 92nd percentile, meaning that you scored higher than 92 out of 100 13-year-olds who took the same test.

Some people cite 140 as the cutoff between smart and genius. Very generally speaking, an IQ around 130 indicates the presence of solid intellectual muscle. (Of course, just because it's *there* doesn't mean it's being *exercised.*)

What IQ Really Means

Almost everyone believes that IQ bears a one-to-one relationship with being gifted—that someone with an average IQ can't possibly be gifted. But that's simply not true.

IQ scores by themselves mean very little. They don't measure creativity, leadership, or communication ability. A high IQ does not guarantee success or high grades. It won't make you president of your class or captain of your track team; it won't win you the lead in the school play; it can't even predict whether you'll pass or fail this year's classes.

What a high IQ does mean is that you have the *potential* to do well at *intellectual pursuits.* Potential unrealized is useless. There are many gifted people wasting away in prisons or working menial jobs because they haven't used their abilities in productive ways.

Consider Gerald Darrow. He was one of the Quiz Kids, young people of the 1940s who astonished radio and TV audiences with their brilliance. Darrow died at age 47 after spending most of his final years on welfare and in poor health.

Willie Sidis, another child prodigy, graduated from high school at age 8 and lectured at Harvard at 11. As an adult, he became the target of much resentment by the press. He blamed his father for treating him as an exhibit and grew to reject intellectualism of any sort. He worked by choice at menial tasks and collected streetcar transfers as a hobby. He died at age 46 in a rented room near Boston.

There are many more equally compelling examples. The point is not to alarm you, but to put things into perspective. Some people with high IQs experience great successes; others experience failures. On the other hand, countless people with average and below average IQs have done very well. Some people have said—and we agree—that I Can is more important than IQ.

> "Only the curious will learn and only the resolute overcome the obstacles to learning. The quest quotient has always excited me more than the intelligence quotient."
> Eugene S. Wilson

Should You Know Your IQ?

Most teachers and parents aren't in favor of sharing IQ scores with students. They worry that you'll use this information inappropriately. There does appear to be an "IQ mystique" that leads people who know their scores to set their expectations accord-

> "WHEN I WAS IN FIRST GRADE I HAD A SERIES OF TESTS THAT OTHER CHILDREN DIDN'T TAKE. MY SCORES WERE SENT HOME ONE DAY AND MY MOTHER SHOWED ME MY IQ AND TOLD ME MY SCORES AND THAT I WOULD BE IN A SPECIAL CLASS BECAUSE I WAS SMART." BOY, 11

ingly. For example, if you learned that your IQ was a "mere" 117, you might decide that your potential was forever limited to just above average—that you're smart enough to get by, but not to achieve significantly or make a difference in the world. Conversely, if you learned that your IQ was 157, you might conclude that you're so smart you never need to study. Either way, you'd be mistaken.

James and Shelagh Gallagher, a prominent father-daughter team in gifted education, have this to say:*

> "In an era when our lives seem to be controlled and regulated by numbers—social security, telephone, or credit card—a special place is reserved for the IQ score. It has been said that once a person has received information about his or her IQ score, that number becomes indelibly etched in his cortex as if it had been burned there with hydrogen fluoride."

We're acquainted with several adults who don't want to know their IQ scores. They would rather not get mired in the mystique. As one said, "What if I found out that my IQ was higher than I thought? Would I be disappointed with my life so far? Or what if I learned that it was lower than I hoped? Would I feel as if I had been fooling myself and everyone else?"

On the other hand, there are adults who believe that kids should know their IQ scores. Often these are people who know *their* IQs, and they point to themselves as examples of how to behave. There are also adults who place far too much emphasis on IQ. Some parents of gifted kids spend a lot of time talking about (and comparing) their children's scores; it's the modern-day equivalent of bragging about whose kid walked first, talked first, and brought home the best report card.

In the end, much of the sound and fury over IQ may signify less than we think. Critics of IQ testing and scores cite plenty of reasons to de-emphasize their importance. The tests are increasingly under fire for being racially and culturally biased; many school systems no longer give them. But if you've taken an IQ test and you really want to know your score, ask your school counselor or parents. If they choose to tell you, store it away under "fascinating facts" in your mental file cabinet and get on with your life. If they won't tell, you have two choices:

1. Wait until you're 18, and if you're still curious, ask to see your school files; or
2. Take an adult version IQ test (check your library or favorite bookstore) and score yourself.

Either way, don't let *any* score shape your opinion of yourself or your plans for the future.

> "Test scores should never 'define' a person, no matter what they may reveal about his or her intellectual or achievement potential. No single test can assess the broad range of traits and abilities that help to make a person successful and productive in society, a wonderful person to be around, or even a person of eminence. All tests are imperfect measurers."
>
> Jean Peterson

---

* J.J. Gallagher and S.A. Gallagher, *Teaching the Gifted Child.* 4th edition. Boston: Allyn and Bacon, 1994, p. 18.

Six More Possible Meanings for the Acronym IQ

I Quit

Some people believe that an average IQ predicts a life of menial jobs and dreary relationships. Wrong! IQ is only *one* way to measure intelligence, and it's by no means the last word. No one should be sentenced by a test score.

Inane Questions

When you look closely at some IQ tests, you can't help wondering if the people who wrote the questions are really nitwits disguised as experts. Who wants to be judged on the basis of whether they can define "uxoricide"? Puh-leeze! (If you must know, "uxoricide" is the murder of one's wife. Now there's a word that belongs in every student's vocabulary.)

Individual Quirks

In one IQ test, you are asked to find the "best, most sensible" word to complete this sentence: "The foundation of all science is _____." Your choices are "observation," "invention," "knowledge," "theory," and "art." Which do you feel fits best? The test developers have a particular word in mind. If your opinion differs, no point for you.

Insufficient Quantity

Some IQ tests last only 20 minutes, which doesn't leave much time for revealing your specific strengths and weaknesses. If you're going to be selected for (or barred from) a gifted program on the basis of your IQ, you deserve more than 20 minutes to show what you know.

Intense Queasiness

Tests have been known to make people anxious. The typical IQ test is administered in a situation that is stressful and constrained by time limits. "Brain drain" isn't uncommon. You may forget everything you've ever learned—only to recall it all five minutes after the test ends.

Impressive Quality

Although IQ tests are criticized, the fact remains that people with high IQs often do very well in life. The tests appear to do an adequate job of locating overall intelligence; a score of 150 usually isn't an accident or a fluke. But do the tests fail to identify some smart people who just don't perform well on tests? The evidence points to yes.

Tests and Testing: A Glossary of Terms

Achievement Test. A test developed by either a company or a teacher to determine how much you know about a certain broad subject (like math) or a specific topic (such as the Vietnam War).

Aptitude Test. A test designed to gauge your potential to perform certain tasks. IQ tests fall into this category, as they measure your potential in general intellectual pursuits. Other tests can measure your aptitude for mechanical activities, musical gifts, physical tasks, etc.

Battery. A collection of related mini-tests that are given over a period of one or more days to measure your overall achievement in a particular area.

Bias. Some tests, especially standardized tests, have been found to be culturally biased. They don't do a good job of measuring the skills and abilities of minority and low-income students, who often have different languages and dialects, thinking styles, and cultural experiences than the white middle- and upper-class students the tests are based on.

Diagnostic/Prescriptive. These terms follow a medical model. When you go to the doctor, he or she tries to diagnose your ailment. Once this is done, the doctor gives you a prescription (medication, bed rest, more exercise, or whatever) that ties in directly to the diagnosis. Theoretically at least, it's the same in education: once your academic needs are determined ("diagnosed") by a test, your curriculum should be "prescribed" in relation to these test results.

Percentile. Different from "percent," this statistic shows how well you did in comparison with others who took the same test. Thus, a result at the "98% ile" means that you did better than 98 percent of the people who took the same test; a result at the "2% ile" means that 98 percent of the test takers did better than you.

Pre-Tests/Post-Tests. These terms have to do with timing. A pre-test is given before you study a topic to gauge what you already know about the topic. A post-test is given after you've had instruction and tells how much you've learned due to instruction. A big difference in your pre- and post-test scores shows that you learned your lessons well. A high pre-test score indicates that you probably don't need the lessons that will be taught on that topic (although you may have to sit through them anyway).

Reliability. The likelihood that you'd get a similar score on a test the second time you took it. "High reliability" means that those who did well the first time also did well on a retake, and those who failed the first time would likely fail it again. (If a test doesn't have reliability, it's doubtful that it's a good test.)

Standardized. A term used by test developers to indicate that their test has "been tested" on many people prior to your taking it. Thus, your results can be compared against those of a larger group. Standardized tests often are used to show how well you did in comparison with a national sample of students.

Validity. How well a test measures what it's supposed to be measuring depends on its validity. For example, a math test that asks you to translate "binomial theorem" into Portuguese isn't measuring your math skills and therefore lacks validity.

Achievement Tests

The Iowa Test of Basic Skills, the Comprehensive Test of Basic Skills, the Stanford Achievement Test, the Scholastic Assessment Test, the National Assessment of Educational Progress, the Metropolitan Achievement Test, the National Achievement Test . . . you've heard of them, and you've probably taken one or more at some point during your school career. These tests and others like them are designed to measure your level of accomplishment in major subject areas such as math, reading, and science. If you do exceedingly well, this shows that you're learning what you're supposed to be learning in school. It also indicates that you're a good test taker.

Your individual scores are compared to those of hundreds of other students nationwide who took the same tests at an earlier time. Your final scores are based on the results of those comparisons—your performance in relation to that of the group.

Interpreting Your Scores

For example: You're in the 8th grade. Over a span of three days in October, you take a series of tests on various subjects. These tests are then scored by a computer, and your results are compared against those of other 8th graders. A score of 8.2 indicates that you are performing "on grade level" for that subject. The "8" refers to your grade placement; the "2" to the second month of the school year, October.

A grade equivalent (G.E.) score of 5.4 would imply that in comparison with the nation's 8th graders, your level of achievement in that subject is far below your grade level—approximately where an average 5th grader would be by December of the school year. On the other hand, a G.E. of 11.5 would suggest that you are far ahead of the typical 8th grader in that particular content area.

Let's say that your scores come back reading mostly in the double digits. For example:

- *Science: G.E. 11.5*
- *Social Studies: G.E. 10.4*
- *Reading: G.E. 12.1*
- *Math: G.E. 9.4*

On the surface, these scores are impressive. In fact, you may be surprised to discover how smart you are in certain subjects—especially if you've been struggling with them in school.

Most students have questions about their test scores. Unfortunately, the answers don't appear anywhere on the profile. Following are some typical questions and possible answers, using the test scores above as a model.

"How can I be reading at a senior high level when I sometimes have trouble with my 8th grade literature books?"

The G.E. score of 12.1 doesn't mean that you've mastered each and every reading skill up through the 12th grade. It means that compared to other 8th graders, your reading ability is high. A reading test only asks you about a small sample of all the possible items related to the skill of reading, so it would be misleading to think that you should be able to comprehend any book written for high school seniors. If you're having trouble with your 8th grade literature books, it may be because you haven't yet mastered all of the 8th grade level reading skills. Or perhaps you don't like the book you're reading.

"Since my math score is so low compared to my other scores, does this mean that I'm underachieving in this subject?"

No. To believe that you'll be "superior across the board" in all subject areas is to assume that you're equally good at every subject. Few people are. Plus math, unlike reading, is an area where you may need direct instruction on a particular concept before you understand it fully. (With reading, it's easier to "pick up" skills just by being exposed to words and books.)

"This is the second year in a row that I've scored 11.5 in science. Didn't I learn anything between last year and this year?"

The culprit here isn't you or your last year's science teacher, but the test itself. All tests have ceilings—top scores you can't exceed, regardless of your knowledge and capabilities. If the ceiling on a particular test is too easy for you, you'll score at the uppermost limit, which in this case is probably 11.5.

"My test scores say I'm above grade level in all subjects, but my school grades are lousy. What's up?"

There's no easy explanation for this problem. But since it's unlikely that your test scores are high due to divine intervention, it may be that you and your school aren't seeing eye-to-eye. You may need to improve that situation before your grades can come up to your test scores.

Creativity Tests

Creativity tests are relatively new and not nearly as popular as aptitude or achievement tests. They are useful for identifying divergent thinkers—students who can come up with many different responses to a problem or question.

If you take a creativity test, you'll have the opportunity to solve a variety of interesting and challenging problems. Your answers will be graded in four ways:

- for *fluency* (the number of responses—the more the better)
- for *flexibility* (the ability to change your mindset),
- for *elaboration* (the amount of detail you include in your answers), and
- for *originality* (how unique your answers are when compared with other students' answers to the same questions).

Have fun!

When Tests Fail

Several years ago, all school children in England were required to take tests at the end of the 5th grade. These tests were called the "11-plus exams," and they were used to determine who would eventually go on to college—and who wouldn't. Students who did well were placed on the "honors track." Those who did so-so were assigned to classes where not much was expected of them because they were "average." And those who did poorly went to a trade school.

Jonathan had always been an above-average student. But during the time of the 11-plus exams, he was under the weather. Sick, in fact, with a cold that made him feel as if he were hearing and seeing the world through a mattress. His concerned mum gave him antihistamines. As a result, Jonathan couldn't think straight. All of the questions seemed to run together on the page. His mouth felt dry and his head buzzed. He did poorly on the exams. His destiny? Trade school.

Helen was an extremely creative student. Her short stories won prizes, and she played the oboe beautifully. Unfortunately, Helen was not a teacher-pleaser. Rather than answer the questions on the exam, she decided to form a pattern of interconnected dots on her answer sheet. The results were graphically interesting but less than satisfactory scorewise. Helen's fate? Average classes, with the recommendation that she become a nanny.

Reggie had been a winner from way back. His mother had read to him when he was still in the womb, and by the time he was three years old, he was reading on his own. Naturally, he practiced for the 11-plus exams. He was the first student in his class to finish, and he earned the highest score. His future? Anywhere he wanted to go—as long as he chose college. And anything he wanted to be—as long as he decided to become a professional.

What conclusions can we draw from these cases? That none of these students got what they deserved—not Jonathan, not Helen, not even Reggie. Jonathan and Helen were told that they couldn't succeed; Reggie was told that he had to succeed. Jonathan and Helen were denied opportunities; Reggie was forced to take them, whether he wanted them or not.

The 11-plus exams are no longer given, because someone finally figured out that the only students gaining access to the honors track were those who already had certain advantages such as wealthy parents and high social status. The exams were creating an upper-class elite. Also, the trade school teachers resented being perceived as the dregs of the educational system. They knew that they (and their students) had talents, too, in mechanical, technical, and/or artistic areas.

Four Reasons Why Tests Can't Be Trusted

1. Test questions may have more than one correct response, depending on the test-taker's perspective.

"Eliminate the word that doesn't belong in this group: cricket, football, billiards, hockey."

In fact, each one can be eliminated. Cricket is the only one of British origin. Billiards is the only one played indoors. Football is the only one whose object is not to put a ball into a net. And which type of hockey is meant, field or ice?

Thus the *real* answer is "all of the above." But that's not a response option. Which raises an interesting point: Can you be *too* smart and think *too* deeply to score high on some tests?

What If You're Not Sure of Your Answer?

You read a test question and quickly enter an answer you *think* is right. But you're not *positive* it's right. What should you do?

Many people would say, "Leave it; your first impression is best." But University of Michigan professor Frank Whitehouse says, "Change it."

Dr. Whitehouse did a study on tests turned in by more than 1,000 of his students over a period of 10 years. He looked for eraser marks and other signs that students had changed their answers. He found that students changed from wrong to right answers 2.5 times as often as they changed from right to wrong.

After you answer a question, you may find that other questions contain clues to the first question. Or you may remember an important fact later in the test. Or you may think twice about your first answer and feel strongly that you should change it. Don't let superstition about "first impressions" hold you back.

2. Tests can discriminate against people from poor, minority, or disadvantaged backgrounds.

> *"Compare and contrast Truman Capote and Norman Mailer for their portrayal of the male figure in the novel."*

Many tests, including IQ tests, have a high "verbal load"—that is, they require a good working knowledge of vocabulary, ideas, and situations that are part of life in white, middle-class, advantaged America.

You may know quite a bit about Capote and Mailer. Or you may not, but if anyone asked, you could talk at length about the novels of Gabriel Garcia Márquez, which you've read in the original Spanish.

Which raises another interesting point: Would more students perform better on tests if the tests asked more of the right questions?

> "If the Aborigine drafted an IQ test, all of Western civilization would presumably flunk it."
> **Stanley Garn**

3. Test scores can be wrong.

There are times when tests are in error, meaning that the score you get doesn't reflect the knowledge you have. A test score that is lower than it should be is called a "false negative." A false negative can have a variety of causes, all unrelated to the subject on which you're being tested. For example, if you're ill on the day of the test or extremely nervous during the test, or if the test itself isn't valid, you could end up with a score that has no relation to what you know.

This is not to say that a low test score is always wrong. Sometimes you just don't know the subject matter, or you chose not to study. But if you do know the subject matter and you did study and you still get a lower score, it might be a false negative.

Incidentally, there is almost no chance of getting a "false positive." You don't score 140 on an IQ test or 99 percent on a math exam because you faked it or got lucky. You earned it.

4. Tests don't accommodate different learning styles.

Almost every test you will take in school will be a paper-and-pencil test. You'll fill in blanks, color in circles, write answers, compose essays, check true-false boxes, and so on. You probably do well on paper-and-pencil tests—but maybe you would do even better if the tests were different, or the testing environment was more conducive to your individual learning style.

For example: You do your best studying and learning at home while lying on your bed, eating Doritos, and listening to music. On test days, you're forced to sit at a desk, you can't even chew gum, and the room is silent (except for the usual pencil-scratching, squirming, and coughing noises from your classmates). Clearly these aren't the optimal test conditions for you.

You might not be able to do much about this, but it's worth discussing with your teacher, especially if he or she is knowledgeable about learning styles. You may find that the testing environment can be made more flexible in certain circumstances.

Before Taking Any Test . . .

1. Find out what type of test it will be. Remember that an aptitude test measures your potential and ability; an achievement test measures what you know and have learned. A multiple-choice or true-false test requires a different mindset than an essay test.

2. Find out how (and whether) you can study for the test. In general, don't bother trying to study for an aptitude test. But it might be worth practicing for an achievement test by reviewing course notes or taking a sample test, if available.

3. Find out what the test results are supposed to prove and what they will be used for. How will the test be scored? Who will see your test results? What does a high score "mean"? What does a lower score "mean"?

Your teacher (or the test administrator) should be able to answer these questions for you. Getting the answers may help to alleviate test anxiety and give your confidence a boost.

Tests and Testing: The Bottom Line

You know that tests are important; you're aware that test scores can help to determine whether you're accepted into a gifted program or the college of your choice. So you probably take tests seriously, and that's good. (For test-taking tips from an award-winning teacher, see pages 61–64.) But before you decide that tests are the be-all and end-all of your educational experience—and before you let your self-esteem rise and fall along with your test scores—read this:

Beginning in the 1960s, a lot of research has shown that tests fail to predict success in settings outside of school. In fact, some researchers have found that society's most productive people are *not* those who scored in the top five percent on standardized tests. For minority populations, standardized tests fail to predict student success either inside or outside of school. As reported in *Gifted Child Quarterly*:*

---

* C. June Maker, "Identification of Gifted Minority Students: A National Problem, Needed Changes and a Promising Solution." *Gifted Child Quarterly*, Vol. 40, No. 1 (Winter 1996), p. 42.

"Intelligence and achievement tests once were thought to be tools for predicting which children could become successful contributors to society. However, the failure of these tests to predict success in other than academic settings is widely recognized. . . . [Joseph] Renzulli (1979) concluded research 'clearly indicates that vast numbers and proportions of our society's most productive persons are not those who scored at the 95th+ percentile on standardized tests.'"

This happens to be consistent with our own experiences—with our students, our lives, and in our observations of a number of adults we know who didn't do very well in school. The bottom line is: Tests and test scores matter, but there's a whole world beyond school where their importance rapidly diminishes. If you're a good test-taker, that's definitely a benefit now, and your scores will likely affect the opportunities that are made available to you. If you're not a good test-taker, be patient. Before too long, it simply won't matter.

Think About It, Talk About It

● How many people do you know who lead satisfying, successful lives yet didn't do especially well in school?

Once you have identified two or three people, spend time talking with them. (If you can't think of anyone who fits this description, ask your parents and/or teachers for suggestions.) Afterward, consider these questions:

● What are the people doing now that you consider significant and/or remarkable?

● What is their perspective on school vs. the "real world"?

● What can you learn (what have you learned) from their experiences?

12 Test-Taking Tips

Randy McCutcheon

"Do you happen to know how many tassels a Restoration Coxcomb wore at the knee? Or the kind of chafing dish a bunch of Skidmore girls would have used in a dormitory revel in 1911? Or the exact method of quarrying peat out of a bog at the time of the Irish Corn Laws? In fact, do you know anything at all that nobody else knows or, for that matter, gives a damn about?" S.J. Perelman

Research demonstrates that your grade point average is affected more by your test-taking skills than any other factor. *It's not how much you know that counts, but how well you use what you know.* So when you want to be "in the know" at test-taking time, consider the following:

1. Memorize. Fortunately for you, few tests require that you do much thinking. Despite continuing efforts to reform testing procedures, few changes have been made in the classroom. What this means for you is that your achievement is still measured by your ability to memorize massive amounts of largely irrelevant information. Therefore, to make the best of a bad situation, refine your cramming techniques.

Initially, you need to be very selective about what you try to remember. Force yourself to choose only the most important elements that were covered in class. Drill on those items. If you attempt to memorize all of the material, your brain will probably malfunction from overload. Take a gamble on your judgment and drill, drill, drill. Recite aloud the important elements over and over and over and over and over again. Make use of mnemonics.

If you are conscientious in your drilling, then you will benefit from the "Vaccination Theory of Education." Neil Postman and Charles Weingartner, authors of *Teaching as a Subversive Activity*, used this theory to explain how once students have taken a course and passed the test, they are "immune" and will never again have to demonstrate any real learning in that subject.

2. Use your time wisely. Most teachers talk at a rate of about 100 words per minute. Believe it or not, you are able to think about four times that fast. Use that "extra" time to make sense of what is being said. Do that and you will significantly reduce the need for long hours of studying later.

3. Be note-worthy. Richard P. Gallagher, an educational consultant in Pennsylvania, recommends that you take notes only on the right-hand half of the notebook pages. Save the other half for your own comments and the teacher's. Mr. Gallagher is on to something. Teachers are constantly giving clues to potential test questions by repeating a fact several times, by writing it on the board, or by subtly saying that it will be on an upcoming exam.

4. Break away. When you are reviewing for a test, be sure to take many breaks. After an hour or two of studying, people reach a point of diminishing returns. Pushing beyond your natural limits will not increase learning; it will merely decrease desire. The quality of study time is the critical factor in being adequately prepared. Therefore, study the most difficult material first, while you are most alert. Furthermore, do not form a "study group" unless you plan to study. You may end up with a social group that gets together to avoid the loneliness of *not* learning.

5. Know thy teacher. Surprise. . . . Students whose work is most similar to that of their instructors get the best grades. Author Clark McKowen explains that although students who get the best grades learn the least, they are better able to look like the expectations of their teachers. Remember, your teachers are not likely to change, so you must adapt your learning style to their teaching style.

6. Watch your test. Before you begin any test, examine it. Allocate your time wisely. Assign a certain number of minutes per section; answer easy questions first to gain momentum; save some time at the end for review. You *always* need to review in order to catch silly mistakes and obviously wrong answers.

7. Haste makes waste. The classic error in test-taking is *not reading the directions* (or any question) *carefully*. Next time, pretend that you are attempting to disarm an atomic bomb.

8. Play games. The late actress Ruth Gordon once said, "Never give up, and never face the facts." Good advice for the passive test-taker who wants to improve grades. Too many students assume that if they don't know the answer right away, then they never will. Expecting to fail, they do. Instead, you should make test-taking into a game. Be positive. Practice possible questions and answers before the exam. Drill yourself. Try to outguess the teacher. During the test, restate difficult questions in terms that you can understand. And when all else fails . . . think.

9. Know the M.O. A test-maker, like any other criminal, has a *modus operandi*—a method of operating. Entire books have been devoted to discussing clever ways to outsmart these test-makers on objective exams. Skip those books and instead obtain old tests given by your teacher. Most teachers are ambitious enough to continually create new questions, but there will always be patterns that you can decipher. For example, in true-false questions, the teacher will probably favor one over the other. In multiple choice questions, sentence structure or answer length are often repeated even if the exact questions are not. One imagines that Sherlock Holmes, as a schoolboy, let no detail, however small, go unnoticed. Do the same.

10. Write to learn. Write neatly, be brief, and be clear. Grading short answer and essay questions can be largely a subjective exercise—don't give a "burned out" teacher a reason to take out frustrations on you. Many educators suggest that you should practice writing answers to essay questions you yourself make up. Another strategy is to use mnemonics or some other memory devices to retain factual information on the day of the test. Finally, when answering essay test questions, you will have greater success if you follow a specific structural approach. In short, be organized.

11. Reach out. In times of quiet desperation, when you suddenly realize that you are facing a major exam and you have no idea how to prepare, pay a visit to the teacher. You will be surprised at how much valuable information can be acquired if you are both direct and tactful.

Here is how one student demonstrated the good that can come of such a visit.

He was dismayed to discover that his semester grade in "Introduction to Political Science" would be determined by only two hour-long exams and a final. Following a D+ on the first exam and a B– on the second, dismay turned to depression. At the last moment, reason triumphed over reluctance and he set up an appointment with the professor.

The conversation went something like this: "I have always been an A student. But in your class I have been disappointed with myself. I have worked very hard (expecting lightning to strike) but evidently in vain.

"I do not want any special favors . . . I am willing to do all the work, but could you give me some ideas on what to study for the final?"

The Gifted Kids' Survival Guide

The professor then handed him a sheet of paper that contained a list of ten questions. She informed him that the three questions on the final would be taken from the list.

Twelve hours later, the student had prepared ten compelling arguments with specific supporting material for each question. Fortunately, he didn't blank out the next morning. He scored an A+ on the final and received an A in the course.

It is important to note that not all teachers will help in this way. Not all would have given the benefit of the doubt when it came to final grades. But what if this student, for fear of rejection, hadn't asked?

12. Correct old tests. When most students are handed back their tests, they glance at the grades and discard the remains. Wrong. You should analyze each incorrect answer for future reference. You may never be tested over the same material again, but *you will be tested again*. Anyone can make a mistake. Successful students try to avoid repeating the same kinds of errors.

Here is a sample examination question to test your mettle, as well as your mental abilities.

> **Question:** A man is walking down a road at four miles per hour. Another man is perfectly motionless but is holding five apples and four oranges. If gravity equals seriousness, and if x is the 24th letter of the alphabet, then how much wood can a woodchuck chuck?*

Randy McCutcheon teaches English and is Director of Forensics at Albuquerque Academy in New Mexico. He is a former Nebraska Teacher of the Year and National Forensic League National Coach of the Year.

* If you failed to answer, "As much wood as a woodchuck could chuck if a woodchuck could chuck wood," then you are easily distracted by extraneous information. We suggest that you reread this section.

Taking Charge of Your Life

Although there are many things in your life you can't control—such as where you live, who your parents are, the legal driving age, the weather, and your math teacher's questionable taste in clothes—there are certain things you *can* control or at least influence. This chapter focuses on some of these and suggests ways for you to take charge—by deciding what you want and need, being yourself, and building life skills.

> **"I BELIEVE THAT EVERYTHING WE DO, AND EVERYTHING THAT HAPPENS TO US, HAS SOME KIND OF EFFECT ON US LATER IN LIFE."** HEATHER, 16

Great Expectations

Fifty-eight percent of our survey respondents wanted to know how to deal with other people's expectations. Try as you may, you can't escape from the planners, plotters, prodders, predictors, strategists, and dreamers in your life. Parents, teachers, friends, neighbors, siblings, and strangers will try to tell you what to do (and not to do) with all that potential you have.

"MANY PEOPLE HAVE UNFAIR EXPECTATIONS OF US. THEY EVEN SAY, 'IF YOU'RE SO GIFTED YOU SHOULD KNOW THIS, OR YOU SHOULD HAVE GOTTEN AN A.'"
GIRL, 11

"SOME KIDS DOWNPLAY THEIR ABILITIES BECAUSE THEY'RE AFRAID TO BE MADE FUN OF, OR BECAUSE PEOPLE WILL THEN EXPECT TOO MUCH OF THEM."
BOY, 14

"HOW CAN PARENTS HELP GIFTED STUDENTS? BY LOWERING THEIR EXPECTATIONS. THAT WAY THEY ARE ALWAYS SURPRISED!" JONATHAN, 12

Potential. It's a word to love . . . and loathe. It implies that you have something to offer, so in that sense it's positive. But it can also be a burden, a drag, a voice urging you to try harder, work smarter, do better, go farther, and achieve more. As in:

YOU	THE VOICE
"I want to be an artist."	"You have the brains to be a surgeon."
"My grade point average is 3.4."	"It could be higher if you applied yourself."
"I made the J.V. soccer team."	"You should have tried out for varsity."
"I'm going to graduate in the top one-fifth of my class."	"You could have been valedictorian."

The voice that diminishes your goals and achievements is seldom the voice of experience. It's the voice of *expectation.* Sometimes it comes from other people; often it comes from within your own mind. If you listen too closely, you can end up making decisions and choosing paths that aren't right for you.

Expectations aren't all bad. They can provide us with goals to strive for, aims to achieve. But if you're a gifted teenager, they can also create demands that are difficult or impossible for you to meet. To make things worse, it's often the case that the harder you try to please adults, the more you alienate your friends. You've heard the names kids call each other: "teacher's pet," "brown nose," "Mama's boy (or girl)." What's the solution? Should you defer to adults who insist on planning your future and determining your direction? Should you resist? Should you start doing less than you're capable of so the adults in your life will lower their expectations and your peers will accept you more readily?

It's not just the adults you know personally—your parents, other family members, and teachers—who put the pressure on. Our world is full of messages that exhort us to be #1. You've seen them on T-shirts and in advertisements: "If you can't win, don't play." "Second place is for the first loser." The athlete who earns Olympic gold is literally put on a higher pedestal than the silver and bronze medalists. At high school graduations, the valedictorian gives the commencement address and wears a different colored robe than the salutatorian, whose GPA might be within .003 of a point (we're not making this up; see "A Tale of Two Sisters" below). Awards, honors, salaries, promotions, and success seem to depend on being the smartest, fastest, strongest, most beautiful, most popular, etc. Although there's nothing wrong with extolling the accomplishments of winners, there is something wrong with believing that first place is the only place worth being.

> "I don't know the key to success, but the key to failure is trying to please everybody."
> **Bill Cosby**

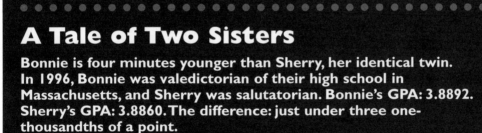

A Tale of Two Sisters

Bonnie is four minutes younger than Sherry, her identical twin. In 1996, Bonnie was valedictorian of their high school in Massachusetts, and Sherry was salutatorian. Bonnie's GPA: 3.8892. Sherry's GPA: 3.8860. The difference: just under three one-thousandths of a point.

How can you deal with this attitude when it's thrust upon you by others? Here are three suggestions:

1. Listen selectively.

There are probably people in your life who feel that they, and they alone, know what's best for you, now and in the future. They'll warn you that "colleges are getting more choosy," so you must earn straight A's in everything but lunch. They'll insist that the career you want to pursue may not be challenging enough for "someone with your talents," so you'd be better off with cardiology or corporate law. They'll pay you $10 for each A on your report card but 25 cents for B's. In countless other direct and subtle ways, they'll try to convince you to strive for their standards of success.

Fortunately, nature has given you two ears. What goes in one can fall out the other.

Are we proposing that you ignore these people? Yes . . . and no. If you truly respect their knowledge, experience, and opinions, then by all means listen. If you don't, nod enthusiastically (the better to dislodge their words from your brain and ease their exit), then excuse yourself as soon as you can.

2. Speak up.

Even people whose opinions you value can sometimes go too far. Out of deference to their age or position, you may remain as mute as a ventriloquist's dummy. Or, since you're no blockhead, you may decide to speak up. For example:

> **Mom says:** "Your grades are good this time, but I noticed you dropped down a grade in French."
> **You say:** "The final was a killer."
> **Mom says:** "Maybe if you studied more. . . ."
> **You say:** "I did study. I did the best I could."
> **Mom says:** "I believe you, but I'm concerned that these lower grades will become a pattern."
> **You say:** "Mom, can I be honest with you?"
> **Mom says:** "Of course!"
> **You say:** "Promise you won't get mad?"
> **Mom says:** "I'll try."
> **You say:** "Okay. . . . When you say you're concerned that my grades will keep dropping, I feel that you think I'm just fooling around and not being responsible."
> **Mom says:** "That's not what I mean!"
> **You say:** "But that's how I feel! Believe me, I want to do well in school, too. But there will be times when I'll do better . . . and times when I'll do worse. Just trust that I'm still the responsible kid you thought I was last grading period."
> **Mom says:** "And if you need help . . . ?"
> **You say:** "I'll ask you for help—except in French, since you're clueless in that department. *N'est-ce pas?*"
> **Mom and you:** Smiles all around.

In this scenario, Mom learns that the message she means to send ("I'm concerned about you") can easily be interpreted as "Why aren't you working up to your potential?" or "You're not good enough." Your willingness to talk things over shows maturity and affirms that you and she aren't adversaries after all.

3. Find allies.

When you're being assailed by others' expectations, you need someone who will be on your side. Find a sympathetic friend, a supportive teacher, an understanding neighbor or family member—anyone who will listen and encourage your efforts without trying to direct them.

What if you can't find allies? Barbara Sher, author of *Live the Life You Love*, suggests that you develop an *imaginary* support network.* Think of historical figures you find inspiring, or admirable characters from fiction, then mentally enlist them as your advocates. Imagine them praising you and cheering you on. It may be all in your head, but it's a start. In time, Sher says, "leaning on your imaginary allies will also show you how to get the help you need from real people."

GIFTED PEOPLE SPEAK OUT

Abigail L. Hing, 18

Dear Smart Student,

I can sympathize. Being known as gifted was fun in third grade, when everyone was impressed by my speed in classroom games like "Around the World" and "Memory." But after a few years, I started to feel more pressured than impressive. It seemed that all my teachers expected me to achieve high. I was supposed to understand the reading; I was supposed to be able to explain the lab to my partners. At times I felt almost resentful that they demanded more of me than they did of my classmates. Later I realized that it was partly my own inner desire to succeed that caused me to interpret my teachers' attitudes in this way. Today I am grateful that I was able to channel my resentfulness into positive efforts.

Mastering my teachers' expectations was difficult, yet I found it even harder to deal with being considered smart by my peers. Though they claimed to be "just kidding," their frequent cracks about my mistakes (and we all make them!) grated on my nerves. I had to struggle to maintain an "I-don't-care" smile when faced with their mock astonishment: "I thought you were supposed to be smart!" And then, of course, in junior high and the beginning of high school, I had to tackle the current trend—it was definitely "not cool" to be smart.

---

* Barbara Sher, "Proven Ways to Get the Most out of Life," in *Bottom Line Personal*, June 1, 1996, p. 9.

Why are academic smarts considered a "gift"? It seems that the only people who like and admire you are teachers (and yes, a few friends), leaving you with a new name of "Suck Up." People automatically assume that you spend every evening studying hard in your room. Even though you can get away with minimal studying, it's not easy to convince your peers that you really don't work that hard—and it usually just makes things worse. But why should you have to justify your grades? And why are other people so curious about your free time? I've seen too many students betray themselves by downplaying, concealing, or (worst of all) neglecting their talents. To avoid being labeled "nerds," they deliberately don't study, sass back at teachers, and party over-hard. Saddest of all, to satisfy their parents' and teachers' expectations, as well as to maintain a cool image, they sometimes resort to cheating. But this "evil teenager" personality is generally not genuine. Furthermore, other people eventually see right through it. "Be yourself!" advise Mom and counselors. And they're so right. If you won't be yourself, who will? Being gifted certainly makes you different from everyone else, but so does being tall, good-looking, or charismatic. It's just a special characteristic that makes you uniquely yourself. In the end, you will respect yourself more (and so will your peers) if you openly accept who you are.

Good luck!

Abigail L. Hing

Abigail L. Hing is a Presidential Scholar from Solon, Ohio. She attends Harvard-Radcliffe University and enjoys dancing, debating, singing, and playing the piano.

The Perfectionism Plight

Forty-six percent of our survey respondents wanted help learning how to give themselves permission to fail sometimes—to be more gentle with themselves and not set their own expectations so high. As demanding of you as other people are, you may be even harder on yourself. Consider these questions:

1. Are you ever satisfied with being adequate?
2. Can you accept getting an average grade on a test or paper?
3. Do you ever do the minimum that's required of you?
4. Are you comfortable with an occasional failure?
5. Are you pleased with your past accomplishments?

If you answered no to any of the above, you may be suffering from perfectionism.

Psychologists and educators have long argued about how and where perfectionism begins. Is it self-inflicted or other-inflicted? (Do people choose to be perfectionists, or are perfectionists "made" by their parents, teachers, etc.?) Whatever its source, perfectionism can block your way to success and threaten your peace of mind.

If you can never settle for anything less than first place, you're in for a lot of disappointment. Perfection simply isn't possible. And even when you do reach the top, you may find that holding on isn't worth the effort. Fortunately, there's help for perfectionists. What it takes is the will and ability to put things into perspective. Examples:

> **"I PERSONALLY NEVER FELT LIKE ANYTHING I DID WAS GOOD ENOUGH."** ANGELA, 17
>
> **"MANY GIFTED KIDS ARE PERFECTIONISTS, AND THEY ALWAYS THINK THEY CAN DO BETTER."** ADRIANE, 12
>
> **"THEY EXPECT THEMSELVES TO BE PERFECT IN ALL AREAS OF STUDY, THEREFORE WHEN SOMETHING GOES WRONG THEY UNDERMINE ANY PRIOR SUCCESS."** SONJA, 13

EXAMPLE #1: You see yourself as an A student—until the day you get your first B+. You're shocked, stunned, and furious with yourself. ***But wait:*** What did you get that B+ in? Rotation Biology II? Advanced Placement Medieval Literature? A course in which all of the material was new to you or especially challenging? It makes a difference.

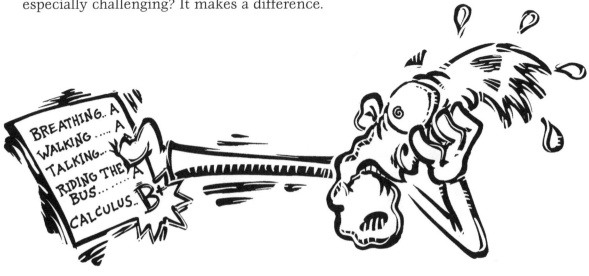

BREATHING.. A
WALKING ..... A
TALKING...
RIDING THE
BUS.... A
CALCULUS.. B+

EXAMPLE #2: For years, everyone has been telling you what a terrific athlete you are. You start high school expecting to letter in every sport you participate in, from football to jujitsu. **But wait:** Do you know any athletes who are good at everything? Even Olympic athletes tend to specialize in one sport. Have you ever heard of an ice skater who was also a sumo wrestler? Or a championship swimmer who went from the pool to the soccer field with equal ease? What happened when Michael Jordan tried to switch from basketball to baseball?

EXAMPLE #3: You're nominated for Student Council President—and you lose the election. You feel dejected, rejected, and embarrassed. **But wait:** Out of the dozens or even hundreds of students in your class, you were among the two or three whose names appeared on the ballot. That's something to be proud of. There's a big difference between "I lost" and "I came in second (or third)."

It's all a matter of attitude. What's yours? Do you tend to look on the dark side of everything, or are you one of those individuals who can see the sun shining through the thickest clouds? (Find out by taking the Attitude Adjustment Quiz on page 73.)

There is a healthy alternative to perfectionism. It's called the Pursuit of Excellence. Here are three important ways in which the two differ:

1. Perfectionism means thinking less of yourself because you earned a B+ instead of an A. **The Pursuit of Excellence** means thinking more of yourself for trying something new.

2. Perfectionism means being hard on yourself because you aren't equally talented in all sports. **The Pursuit of Excellence** means choosing some things you know you'll be good at—and others you know will be good for you or just plain fun.

3. Perfectionism means chastising yourself because you lost the student council election. **The Pursuit of Excellence** means congratulating yourself because you were nominated, and deciding to run again next year—if that's what you want.

How can you become a Pursuer of Excellence? By:

- *determining the sources of your perfectionism,*
- *reassessing your feelings about failure and success,*
- *standing your ground against people who pressure you to be perfect, and*
- *learning ways to be easier on yourself so you're free to take risks and try new things.*

Attitude Adjustment Quiz

1. **The glass is**
   a) **half empty**
   b) **half full**

2. **The sky is**
   a) **partly cloudy**
   b) **partly sunny**

3. **The man is**
   a) **half bald**
   b) **half hairy**

4. **Your favorite ending for the word "hope" is**
   a) **-less**
   b) **-ful**

5. **At middle age, life is**
   a) **half over**
   b) **half begun**

SCORING:

Give yourself **1 point** for every **"a"** answer and **no points** for every **"b"** answer.

INTERPRETING YOUR SCORE:

0–1: You are an Eternal Optimist, a Pollyanna who sees everyone and everything in a positive light.

2–3: You are a Rampant Realist, forever weighing pros and cons. And you're hesitant to take people or things at face value.

4–5: You are a Permanent Pessimist, someone who sees everyone and everything in a negative light.

Where does your perfectionism come from?

Maybe your parents are always pushing you to stay at the head of your class. Maybe your teachers are constantly reminding you to "keep up the good work." Maybe your classmates frequently say things like, "We know you'll win the district essay contest." And maybe you often tell yourself that being the best is the only way to go.

Any and all of these influences can drive you to perfectionism. In fact, it may seem as if you don't have any choice. What's the price you pay for not being perfect? You risk disappointing everyone around you—and yourself.

It's wonderful when your parents, teachers, and classmates are supportive of your talents and efforts. It's terrific when they believe in you. It's great when you have confidence in yourself. But any and all of these positives can be carried too far, and when that happens, you suffer. (See "Problems of Perfectionists" on page 75.)

Ask yourself: Who are the people in your life who seem to want you to be perfect? Who are the people who like and accept you "as is"—for all that you are, and for all that you are not?

> "**DISTINCTIONS [BETWEEN PERFECTIONISM AND EXCELLENCE] ARE SO IMPORTANT IN ORDER FOR KIDS TO FEEL GOOD ABOUT THEIR ACCOMPLISHMENTS. OTHERWISE THEY GET BURNED OUT. . . . EVEN JUST HAVING PERMISSION TO TRY NEW THINGS WITHOUT HAVING TO WORRY ABOUT 'SUCCESS' OR 'FAILURE,' AND EXTERNAL PRESSURE TO PERFORM. I ALSO THINK IT'S IMPORTANT TO DEVELOP OTHER INTERESTS AND ENJOYABLE ACTIVITIES AS A PART OF DISCOVERING WHO YOU ARE. SO OFTEN GIFTED KIDS ARE DEFINED BY THEIR SMARTNESS, WHICH IS NOT THE ONLY ASPECT OF YOUR PERSONALITY.**" PAULITA, 18

> "When you aim for perfection, you discover it's a moving target."
> George Fisher

How do you feel about failure?

Gifted people are often driven to perform and excel. To them, "fail" is a four-letter word. Taken to the extreme, the fear of failure can halt your forward motion and trap you in boring, non-challenging classes and tasks. Why take Honors Math if you know you'll get an A in the regular class? It's safer to stick with the sure thing.

The most successful people are those who have figured out how to face failure, live with it, take it in stride, and learn from it. They realize that the road to achievement is paved with mistakes. They trip over them, pick themselves up, and move on.

Ask yourself: How do you feel when your performance is less than flawless? What can you tell yourself the next time you don't do as well as you hoped you would? How can you develop a healthier, more positive attitude toward the possibility—and the reality—of imperfection?

> "The principal mark of genius is not perfection but originality, the opening of new frontiers."
> Arthur Koestler

How do you feel about success?

The fear of success is closely related to the fear of failure. After all, once you succeed at something, people will expect you to keep on

Problems of Perfectionists

Perfectionists sometimes or often . . .

... set unreasonable, impossible goals for themselves

... can't be satisfied with even a great result and may, in fact, be chronically dissatisfied

... have difficulty enjoying the present moment because they are preoccupied with overcoming the next "hurdle"

... are not risk-takers (academically and/or socially) because they fear "failing," "not being the best," and "not doing it well enough"

... have an "all-or-nothing" view: "If I can't do it perfectly, there's no point in doing it at all"

... are highly self-critical and preoccupied with their own and others' expectations

... are critical of others

... are highly competitive and are constantly comparing themselves to others

... experience stress and anxiety

... are afraid of making mistakes

... are afraid of revealing their weaknesses or imperfections

... procrastinate because of their need to do something "perfectly"

... are prone to depression

... have difficulty in relationships because they expect too much of themselves and others

... feel that their self-worth depends on "performance," and therefore are very sensitive to criticism and are afraid to just "be"

... cannot accept that love can be unconditional

... are compulsive planners

... have difficulty seeing situations, performances, and projects in terms other than "good" or "bad"

... are dissatisfied with situations and relationships that are not "ideal."

succeeding . . . and what if you don't? The higher you climb, the farther you have to fall.

Imagine this scenario: Your history teacher asks you to direct a class play on the U.S. Constitution that will be performed at a PTA meeting in two months. You're thrilled to be asked—you enjoy bossing people around, which is what directors do—so you say yes. You're enthusiastic, you work hard, and the play is a hit.

And that's when the trouble begins. The drama teacher approaches you and invites you to join the drama club. They need a good director, and you've proven that you can more than handle the job . . . or so she says. You, on the other hand, are not so sure. Maybe the class play was a fluke. Maybe you got lucky. Maybe your success was due to the fact that you knew a lot about the Constitution from the start. Maybe the PTA was easy to please, but the drama club is uncharted territory. Deciding that it's better to quit while you're ahead, you decline the invitation.

How can you resist those who pressure you to be perfect?

There are times when brains can be a burden. Such as when people tell you how smart you are—and how smart they know you could be and should be. They mean well, but that's no excuse. You'd like to tell them to _____ (fill in the blank). Actually, it's okay to tell them how you feel, but it's best to do it diplomatically and succinctly. Examples:

> "I USUALLY WIN A PRIZE IN OUR SCHOOL SCIENCE FAIR. BUT THIS YEAR I WAS BUSY WITH A LOT OF OTHER THINGS AND DIDN'T SPEND AS MUCH TIME ON MY PROJECT. ALL MY SCIENCE TEACHER SAID WAS, 'WHAT HAPPENED? YOU USUALLY DO SUCH A GREAT JOB.'" KEVIN, 14

> "MY FRIENDS ARE ALWAYS ASKING ME FOR HELP WITH THEIR HOMEWORK. THEY ACT AS IF I ALWAYS KNOW EVERYTHING, AND WHEN I SAY I DON'T KNOW SOMETHING, THEY THINK IT'S BECAUSE I DON'T WANT TO HELP THEM." DANETTA, 12

> "EVEN MY GRANDPARENTS BUG ME ABOUT BEING GIFTED. WHENEVER I SEE THEM, THE FIRST THING THEY SAY IS, 'HOW'S OUR SMARTEST GRANDCHILD?' IT DRIVES ME CRAZY!" CHARLES, 15

To your parents:

"I know you like it when I get A's, but I need you to understand that I worked just as hard for that C in Russian—maybe harder."

"I probably could have gotten an A in regular biology, but we all agreed that I should try the honors course. I think I'm learning a lot, and I want to stay in it even though my grades aren't as high. I need your support."

To your teachers:

"I wish you wouldn't always call on me and expect me to know the answers. I feel pressured to perform all the time."

"Your pre-calculus course is a lot tougher than I thought it would be. I know it's worth the effort, but I feel like you always expect me to be the star student."

Do You Fear Success?

Find out by taking this quiz. For each statement, give yourself 3 points if you *strongly agree*, 2 points if you *somewhat agree*, and 1 point if you *disagree*.

1. Other people enjoy my successes more than I do.
2. People expect too much of me.
3. Other people are generally more satisfied with my work than I am.
4. I'm worried that my successes are due to luck, and someday my luck will run out.
5. I'm not really as smart as people think I am.
6. Success can be a burden.
7. I seldom reach a level of performance that makes me happy.
8. I'd rather do something I know how to do than try something new.

INTERPRETING YOUR SCORE:

19–24: Whose life is it, anyway? Are you more interested in making other people happy than you are in pleasing yourself? Once those "other people" are no longer involved in your daily life, you'll still have to live with yourself and your choices. It's time to start making your own decisions—ones that are right for you.

14–18: It seems as if you're still struggling with the question of which goal should be your top priority—pleasing others or pleasing yourself. That's okay, as long as you maintain a balance between the two.

8–13: Some people would you call you "self-assured," while others might label you "arrogant." Still, it does appear that you are your own person, and you're relishing your successes. Congratulations!

"I've learned that nobody's perfect, and I don't expect myself to be perfect anymore."
Carly Simon

To your friends:

"Just because I'm a good student doesn't mean I spend every weekend with my nose in a book or my eyes glued to a computer screen."

"You're right, my grades were pretty good this period. Let's go shoot some hoops."

Be assertive, not aggressive; honest, not arrogant. Most people who are pressuring you may not be aware of how you feel.

Ask yourself: Is there someone you need to talk to about your perfectionism?

Ten Tips for Combating Perfectionism

1. Be average for a day. Allow yourself to be messy, late, incomplete ... imperfect. Then celebrate your success.

2. Get involved in activities that are not graded or judged—activities that focus on process, not product.

3. Take a risk. Sign up for a course with a reputation for being challenging. Start a conversation with someone you don't know. Do an assignment or study for a test without overdoing it. Alter your morning routine. Start a day without a plan.

4. Give yourself permission to make at least three mistakes a day.

5. Stop using the word "should" in your self-talk. Remove "I have to" from your conversation.

6. Share a weakness or limitation with a friend. Recognize that he or she doesn't think any less of you as a result.

7. Acknowledge that your expectations of yourself might be too high, even unrealistic.

8. Savor your past accomplishments. Write about how good they made you feel.

9. Ask your friends to help you "cure" your perfectionism. Perhaps they can give you a sign or a word when they notice you are being a perfectionist.

10. Join the human race. It's less lonely when we accept our own and others' imperfections and feel part of life.

If you need more help combating your perfectionism, talk with your school counselor, psychologist, or social worker. Explain your situation and ask for suggestions.

Find Out More

To learn more about perfectionism, read:

Adderholdt-Elliott, Miriam. *Perfectionism: What's Bad about Being Too Good?* **Minneapolis: Free Spirit Publishing, 1987.**

The Value of Mistakes

Question: What do these six things have in common?

- cheese
- chocolate chip cookies
- Coca-Cola
- penicillin
- Post-It Notes
- Silly Putty.

Answer: All six were discovered or invented by mistake. According to Mark Twain, "accident" is the greatest inventor who ever lived. In *Mistakes That Worked*, author Charlotte F. Jones points out that accident (not necessity) is the mother of invention.

Failures or . . . ?

Thomas Edison tried 1,500 different filaments for the lightbulb before finding the right one. After the final experiment, an assistant asked, "Mr. Edison, how do you feel about having 1,500 failures to your credit?" Edison replied, "They weren't failures. We now know 1,500 lightbulb filaments that don't work."

Here are five more reasons why misteaks are grate:

1. Mistakes are universal. Everybody makes them, from preschoolers to presidents. They give you something in common with the rest of the people on our planet.

2. Mistakes show that you're learning. Whether you incorrectly apply a geometry theorem or say something foolish in front of someone you're trying to impress, a mistake is a point of information that inspires you to do better the next time you're in a similar situation.

3. Mistakes show that you're trying something new or different. It's rare that you (or anyone else) will accomplish something perfectly on your first attempt. If you had spent your whole life doing only those things you could master on the first try, you never would have learned to walk, read, or ride a bicycle.

One of the biggest problems of perfectionism is that, over time, we become less willing to take chances. As a result, we miss out on some of the best things in life because risks often lead us to something (or someone) new and exciting. Our lives are richer when we're open to serendipity.

"The greatest mistake you can make in life is to be continually fearing you will make one."
Elbert Hubbard

"We don't make mistakes. We just have learnings."
Anne Wilson Schaef

The Five Stages of Making a Mistake

Stage 1: The Deed. You goof, err, blow it, slip up, screw up, stumble, bumble, or otherwise make a mistake.

Stage 2: Embarrassment. You blush, cry, cover your face with your hands, withdraw, or run away. You are absolutely convinced that people will remember your mistake for the rest of your life.

Stage 3: Denial or Downplay. You refuse to acknowledge your mistake ("I could have gotten 100 percent on that math test; I just didn't want to set the curve too high for the rest of the class"), or you blame your mistake on some convenient other (your sister, your teacher, your dog), or you proclaim your indifference to the fact that you flubbed ("So what? I'm only human"). But deep down inside, where no one else can see, you hold onto the self-appointed title of "World Champion Dolt."

Stage 4: Laughter. This usually occurs anywhere from one minute to one year following your mistake. It all depends on the mistake. You can overcome minor infractions (a lower-than-usual test grade, a stupid remark made at a party) within a week. For bigger blunders (destroying someone's ego, getting caught doing something expressly forbidden by your parents or teachers) it can take many months before you're able to crack a smile. Even then, the laughter doesn't minimize the seriousness of your mistake; it's just a step in the healing process.

Stage 5: Acceptance. Again you proclaim, "I'm only human," only this time you really mean it. You know that you messed up in a minor or major way, but you also know that mistakes are a part of life ... thank goodness.

4. Mistakes allow you to see your own improvements.
If you had videotaped your first attempt at the backstroke, then videotaped yourself after three months of swimming lessons, you'd notice a significant change for the better.

5. Mistakes allow you to learn from others.
Often, gifted students are reluctant to seek help from others, believing that asking for help is tantamount to admitting failure. That belief, need we point out, is mistaken.

Find Out More

To learn more about the value of making mistakes, read:

Jones, Charlotte F. *Accidents May Happen: 50 Inventions Discovered by Mistake.* New York: Delacorte, 1996.
— *Mistakes That Worked.* New York: Doubleday, 1991.

Roberts, Royston M. *Serendipity: Accidental Discoveries in Science.* New York: John Wiley & Sons, 1989.

SEVEN CARDINAL MISTAKES OF SELF-ESTEEM
Sol Gordon

Everybody has *tzuris* (that's Yiddish for "troubles"), but people who feel inferior seem to have more than their share.

Eleanor Roosevelt once said, "No one can make you feel inferior without your consent." Why, in fact, so many people give their consent is an enduring mystery.

Everybody is unique—special—and has a particular mission in life. One of our sages is reported to have said on his deathbed, "God will not ask me why I was not like Moses. He will ask me why I wasn't like myself."

We have identified Seven Cardinal Mistakes of Self-Esteem. Are you a person who is making some or all of these mistakes?

I. Comparing yourself unfavorably to others. There will always be people who appear to be handsomer, prettier, richer, luckier, and better-educated than you. What's the point of comparing? We are all created equal. We are all created to serve in a special way.

2. Feeling you won't amount to much unless. . . . Choose your favorite ending to this sentence: a) someone falls for you, b) someone marries you, c) someone needs you, d) you earn a lot of money, e) your parents are satisfied with your achievements. In fact, you have to be someone to be attractive to someone else. You have to be self-accepting before you can please someone you care about. If you don't amount to anything before someone wants you, you won't amount to much afterwards, either.

3. Thinking you must please everyone. You must first please yourself . . . and thereafter, only people you care about. Those who try to please everyone end up pleasing no one.

4. Setting unreasonable goals for yourself. Lower your standards to improve your performance. You can always advance beyond today—tomorrow is always another day.

5. Looking for THE meaning of life. Life is not a meaning, it is an opportunity. You can only find the meaning of life at the end of it. Life is made up of meaningful experiences—mainly of short duration, but repeatable.

6. Being bored. If you are bored, then it is boring to be with you. If you are bored, don't announce it. It is especially unattractive to bemoan how you don't like yourself, or that you have "nothing to do." If you have nothing to do, don't do it in company.

7. Deciding that your fate is determined by forces outside yourself. Mainly, you are in control of your life.

People who feel good about themselves are attractive to others because they don't exploit others and they are not available for exploitation. They also share some of the following characteristics. They:

are enthusiastic,
have a sense of humor,
have interests,
like being helpful,
are unselfish,
don't make fun of anyone,
have a sense of their own
special mission,

can begin again,
turn their mistakes into lessons,
are optimistic,
are energetic,
are willing to take risks,
know how to listen, and
exude self-confidence.

How can you achieve these qualities? You can start by creating your own miracle. Here is one way to go about it:

Recognize that you are unique. Do not compare yourself to anyone; believe that you are good enough to stand on your own merits. You will be fine, especially if you are open to new ideas.

Do mitzvoth—good deeds. There is nothing more energizing and enlivening of the spirit than being helpful to others.

Do keep in mind that failure is an event, not a person. Someone else's power cannot define who you are. Only you can do that, for yourself.

Sol Gordon, Ph.D., has been a professor of Child and Family Studies at Syracuse University and director of the University's Institute for Family Research and Education. He is the author of When Living Hurts, The Teenage Survival Book, *and many more books for adults and young people.*

GIFTED PEOPLE SPEAK OUT
Olecoy Robinson, 17

Throughout my years of middle and high school (primarily those of high school), I experienced points in time where I never could see myself at the top of the scale. I always saw myself as nothing more than someone who was in between the bottom and the middle of the scale. I couldn't seem to find anything that made me a true artist.

But with the encouragement of teachers and peers, I finally came to realize that, indeed, I had talents—also, I found that I had more capabilities than I ever thought I had. I made an assertive effort to involve myself in every activity possible, whether it was academic or social. By doing so, I found out that you can do anything you want to—and do it well, all at the same time. In my case, I found that I excelled in doing dramatic interpretations of literature. I was able to reach out to an audience and touch the hearts of people with words that came from the voice of someone who wasn't all that confident in herself.

I have this advice for anyone who lacks self-confidence: Get involved in as many activities as possible. Not so many that you come to the point of being totally stressed, but to the point of where you don't limit your chances. Not only will you gain new experiences, but you will meet new people, build new relationships, and find new ways to challenge yourself.

In terms of academics, I had a great desire to learn throughout high school, so I was able to make the best of subjects that were extremely challenging for me. I said to myself, "If I can excel in easy subjects, why not everywhere?" Sure, there were subjects I couldn't master, but as long as I knew that I tried my best, that was all that really mattered.

As I look back at my last couple of months of high school, I sometimes wish someone would have shown me an easy way to build my confidence. But then again, if someone had shown me an easier way, I don't think I would be as strong minded as I am today. So, in essence, finding the way to build up my own self-confidence did me quite well.

Olecoy Robinson is attending Wayne State University.

Successful Goal Setting

When University of California performance psychologist Charles Garfield researched 1,200 high-achieving adults, he found that they shared these characteristics:

- *They were able to transcend previous accomplishments.*
- *They solved problems instead of placing blame.*
- *They took risks confidently, but only after laying out the worst consequences beforehand.*
- *They rehearsed coming events mentally, using imagery.*
- *They were guided by internal goals.*
- *They were able to set goals for themselves.*

"DON'T GIVE UP YOUR DREAMS BECAUSE OF WHAT OTHER KIDS SAY. STICK WITH YOUR GOALS BECAUSE YOU HAVE TO LIVE WITH THEM." GIRL, 14

Only a small percentage of the gifted students we've worked with have been committed goal setters. Most of the others seem to believe in doing what they're told or what is expected of them—no more and no less. As a result, many have not yet learned to take charge of their lives.

Initially, setting goals may seem like a lot of work. You may wonder, "How can I set goals when I don't know what I want to do with my life?" Or you may ask, "Why bother?" Here are five real and immediate benefits of becoming a goal setter:

1. Setting goals and acting on them gives you independence. You no longer have to wait for someone else to decide your life for you.
2. Setting goals and acting on them gives you a sense of accomplishment—more than if you simply follow someone else's orders.
3. Setting goals and acting on them allows you to make things happen instead of waiting and wishing for them to happen.
4. You begin to manage your time more effectively and, as a result, you get more done.
5. People who make plans and do things aren't bored, and they aren't boring.

"Goals determine what you're going to be."
Julius Erving

Getting Started

To begin setting your goals, you'll need four things:

- *a period of uninterrupted quiet time*
- *a place where you can think and work comfortably*
- *something to write with*
- *something to write in or on.*

Walk in the woods, find a quiet corner at the library, or go to your room, hang a "Do Not Disturb" sign on your door, and take the phone off the hook. Now follow these steps:

1. Write down all of the things you'd like to accomplish during the next 10 years. These are your *long-range goals*. Be specific and thorough.
2. When you have completed your list of long-range goals, prioritize them. Select the 3–4 that are most important to you.
3. Write down all of the things you'd like to accomplish during the next 3–5 years. These are your *intermediate* (medium-range) *goals*. Prioritize them; select the top 3–4. IMPORTANT: Your intermediate goals should help you to achieve your long-range goals.
4. Write down all of the things you'd like to accomplish within the next year or so. These are your *immediate* (short-range) *goals*. Prioritize and select the top few. IMPORTANT: Your immediate goals should relate directly to your intermediate goals.
5. Write your prioritized lists in a small spiral-bound notebook and date them. Carry your notebook with you and consult your lists regularly—once a day (best) or once a week (minimum). When you reach a goal, write down that date in your notebook.

Many young people and adults have a general idea of where they might like to be in 5, 10, or 20 years from now. But they don't have the discipline to do the *daily planning* that enables them to accomplish the "little things" on the way to achieving their long-range goals. If you can train yourself to do this—and you must *do it for yourself*—then you truly will be taking charge of your life.

> "The way to success: First have a clear goal, not a fuzzy one. Sharpen this goal until it becomes specific and clearly defined in your conscious mind. Hold it there until it seeps into your unconscious. Surround this goal constantly with positive thoughts and faith. Give it positive follow-through. That is the way success is achieved."
> Norman Vincent Peale

CAUTION

Please don't dismiss this process because it seems too simple. It is remarkably powerful and effective. Everyone we know who has taken the time to think about, write down, and consult their goals reports that *this really works*. Try it and see for yourself. TIP: Make an initial commitment to do this for at least three weeks. By then you'll have a good idea of whether this process works for you. A day, two days, or even a week isn't long enough to experience the benefits.

12 Goal Setting Guidelines

1. Make your goals specific.

If someone asked you to list your goals for the upcoming year, what would you say? Chances are your list might look something like this:

- To try harder in school.
- To stop procrastinating.
- To get along better with my siblings, classmates, parents, etc.
- To study regularly.
- To be more responsible.
- To have more fun.

Each of these goals sounds good, but each has the same problem: It's impossible to achieve. Not because it's a "bad" goal, not because you're unwilling to work at it, but because it's *too vague*.

Instead of saying . . .	Try saying . . .
"I'll try harder in school."	"I'll take careful notes every day and ask the teacher when I don't understand something."
"I'll study regularly."	"I'll go to swimming practice and then have dinner. Then I'll study for at least an hour before turning on the TV."
"I'll stop procrastinating."	"When I know I've got a project due, I'll make a calendar so I can finish it at least two days ahead of schedule."

Instead of saying . . .	**Try saying . . .**
"I'll get along better with my siblings."	"When Jessie interrupts me while I'm trying to study, I'll promise to play with her after I'm done."
"I'll be more responsible."	"I'll clean my room twice a month, and I'll mow the lawn every Saturday unless it rains."
"I'll have more fun."	"I'm going to set aside every Saturday night and make plans by the Thursday before to do something special with friends that evening."

The more specific your goals are, the more likely you are to achieve them—and to know when you've achieved them. How can you measure "being more responsible"? You can't—but you can measure whether and how often you clean your room and mow the lawn. And even if you don't enjoy those chores, you can relish the satisfaction of reaching your goal.

2. Keep your goals realistic.

Don't promise yourself (or your parents) that you'll get straight A's when you don't even know what your classes or teachers will be like. It's more realistic to say, "I'll try to improve my grades in at least two courses."

3. Include enjoyment among your goals.

When most people think about goal setting, they usually limit themselves to serious pursuits—school performance, self-improvement, personal responsibility, life direction. Make sure to leave room on your lists for hobbies, interests, passions, friends, and fun. These shouldn't be "rewards" for reaching your "real" goals; they should be goals in and of themselves.

4. Don't set too many goals at once.

It's a cliché but true: Rome wasn't built in a day. Try not to juggle more goals at a time than you can reasonably expect to achieve.

5. Be prepared to achieve some of your goals but not all of them.

Generally speaking, we have the *most* control over our immediate (short-range) goals and the *least* control over our long-range goals. It's very unlikely that you will achieve all of the goals you set for

> "When I was growing up, I always wanted to be somebody, but I see now I should've been more specific."
> **Lily Tomlin**

yourself. Give yourself permission to let go of some without feeling like a failure.

6. Free yourself to revise your goals as circumstances change.

Obviously, if one of your goals is to go to the library every Saturday and you later find out that the library isn't open on weekends, something has to give. It's pointless to pursue impossible goals—or to stick with goals that aren't right for you. Something that's important to you today may no longer be important six months or a year from now.

7. Be honest with yourself.

Learn to recognize the dishonest and deceptive ways of thinking that will conspire to prevent you from reaching your goals. Examples:

The Lie	The Truth
"I can't."	"I don't want to try. I'm afraid."
"I don't have time."	"I choose not to make time."
"Why me?"	"Why not me?"
"School/life is boring."	"I'm bored with school/my life. What can I do to make things better?"

8. Trust your intuition.

When in doubt—is a particular goal right for you? should you pursue one goal over another? should you take someone else's advice?—go with your gut feeling. It can set you straight when circumstances are especially challenging, uncertain, or unclear.

9. Practice, practice, practice.

It's been said—and behavioral studies have shown—that it takes 2–3 weeks to form a new habit or break an old one. To make goal setting part of your life, practice it every day (including weekends) for at least 14 days and preferably 21. Consult your lists; make any necessary revisions; choose a short-range goal for the day and just do it.

10. Share your goals with a friend.

Identify a support person; this might be one of your first immediate goals. Ask if he or she would be willing to hear about your goals and offer support and constructive criticism. Dreams become more real when you air them; problems more manageable when you share them; achievements more enjoyable when you have someone to celebrate with.

11. Be prepared to hold fast to your convictions.

Are you confident enough to proceed with your plans even if others (parents, teachers, peers) don't approve? Standing firm in the face of pressure to change can be difficult, lonely, even scary. (Another good reason for #10 above.)

12. Don't compare yourself to anyone but yourself.

What's right for one person might not be right for another. What's achievable for one person might be impossible for another. Avoid the trap of comparing your goals and accomplishments to anyone else's. What matters most is what *you* think of yourself.

> "It does not matter how slowly you go so long as you do not stop."
> Confucius

If you're plagued by insecurities and self-doubts, try this revealing exercise: Do a net worth analysis on your life. Adults figure out what they're worth financially by listing their *assets* (what they own) and subtracting their *debits* (what they owe). Their *net worth* is what remains. To do a net worth analysis on your life, start by enumerating your strengths—in the areas of school work, relationships, extracurricular activities, character, and anything else that has value to you. Then list your weaknesses in those areas. Compare your lists to find out how "solvent" you are. Do you have too many weaknesses/debits? Consolidate them into a self-improvement plan for positive change. You might also ask another person—someone you trust who knows you well—to do a net worth analysis on you. Then examine the two analyses closely. Did your list of assets omit some of your strengths? Did your list of debits omit some of your weaknesses?

Find Out More

To learn more about goal setting, read:

DuBrin, Andrew J. *Getting It Done: The Transforming Power of Self-Discipline.* Princeton, NJ: Peterson's Pacesetter Books, 1995.

Kramer, Patricia. *Discovering Personal Goals.* New York: Rosen Publishing Group, 1992.

Managing Your Time

"It is possible that for persons who use their time well, knowledge and experience increase throughout life."
Michel de Montaigne

French essayist Michel de Montaigne (quoted at left) lived from 1533–1592, which only goes to show that time management is a timeless topic. In fact, 62 percent of our survey respondents wanted help learning how to manage their time more effectively.

Because time management usually isn't taught in school, you'll probably need to learn and practice this important skill on your own. Fortunately, whole books are devoted to this subject; two of our favorites are listed on page 92. You might want to start by visiting a library or bookstore. Look through some books on time management and see which ones appeal to you. As you'll discover, there are many different approaches, and some are more detailed and/or concrete than others. Explore several before making your choice. (Obviously it's a *waste* of time to try something that seems too complicated, unrealistic, demanding, or dull.) You might also benefit by asking people around you—people you view as productive and efficient—how they accomplish so much. It's likely that they have developed a series of habits and attitudes about time use, and they may have helpful suggestions for you.

Certain time-honored tactics (setting goals, handling papers only once, making and prioritizing to-do lists, not procrastinating, etc.) are worth trying even if they don't seem very exciting. But the degree to which you improve your own use of time will largely be determined by your internal beliefs, not by mechanical steps or routines. These internal beliefs or values are what give you the power to do what needs to be done. Remember that what works for someone else might not work for you, keep trying various techniques you read about or hear about, and stay focused on your values until you find one or more methods that are a good fit with your learning style, personality, energy level, intellect, and needs.

Think About It, Talk About It

● If we all have the same number of hours in a day, why do some people accomplish so much more than others?

● How do you define "accomplishment"? What does "effective time management" or "good time management" mean to you personally?

● What are some of the things that "steal" time from you? (Think about external and internal influences, interruptions, and distractions.) What can you do to keep your time from being "stolen"?

● Describe a day in which you managed your time exceptionally well. What specific actions made it possible for you to achieve your goals for that day?

Don't be afraid to experiment with methods that aren't specifically recommended by the "experts." (They might know a lot about time management, but they don't know anything about *you*.) We manage to accomplish a lot in our lives, and we don't always follow the rules. Our motto is "Whatever works!" and here's what works for us:

Judy: I'm a piler. I know I'm "supposed to" file things in an organized and orderly fashion, but that particular time management technique just doesn't work for me. Piling things where I can see them helps me to keep track of the many projects I have going on at any given time. If I file things away or store them in a cabinet, I have a tendency to forget them, even if I make lists about them. Sometimes I put my most important projects on the floor of my office so I have to step over them to get to the door. Those projects take on (literally) elevated status by virtue of their inconvenient location, and ultimately I give them priority. It may be a silly sort of game, but it's effective for me. I take solace in knowing that Einstein was a piler, too; I once saw a photograph of his office, and it was more of a mess than mine. (P.S. At home, I'm meticulous!)

Jim: Somewhere during my lifetime, I learned a very important lesson: People don't waste *hours*, they waste *minutes*. For example, if I have 20 minutes between office appointments, or when I had 30 minutes between college classes, I didn't (and don't) just hang around waiting for the next event to happen—I write a letter, return a phone call, pay a bill, or read ten pages of a book. These little smidgens of time add up to several hours each week, and by using them efficiently, I save time in the end for other things I want to do. Also, everyplace is a workplace for me: an empty classroom, an airport lounge, a doctor's waiting room. By using my spare minutes wisely wherever I am, I've been able to keep on top of most projects (like working on this book, for example). One more trick: Whenever you talk on the phone, do it standing up. You'll be surprised at how short your conversations turn out to be!

As you start making better use of your time, here are a few more thoughts and suggestions to keep in mind:

● *In our fast-paced culture, it's easy to believe that more + faster = better. But sometimes you can accomplish more by doing less and slowing down. When you spread yourself too thin, the quality of your work suffers. You don't enjoy it as much, and you make more mistakes, which take time to fix.*

> "Time is life. It is irreversible and irreplaceable. To waste your time is to waste your life, but to master your time is to master your life and make the most of it."
> **Alan Lakein**

"Only you can know how much you can give to every aspect of your life. Try to decide what is the most important."
Barbara Walters

● If you feel caught in a time trap, you'll need to make the time (sorry!) to figure out your goals and priorities—the ones that matter to you. Start by eliminating some of your obligations so you can give the others the best of your attention. Most of us are terrific time managers when we're doing what we really want to do.

● Learn to say no (to others and yourself) to things that diminish your ability to manage your life well.

● Give yourself permission to be human. No one is efficient, organized, and productive every waking hour of every day. We don't have any survey results to support this belief, but we suspect that many gifted teens who told us they wanted help with time management are actually quite productive. You probably have high expectations of yourself, and you may be too hard on yourself. It's important to know how to manage your time and be disciplined, but it's also important to know how and when to relax, goof off, and be a little irresponsible. In our experience, some of our most productive periods have been preceded by spontaneous, unstructured hours, days, even (too rarely) weeks. To lead a healthy, creative, satisfying life, you need to strike a balance between planned accomplishment and free time.

Find Out More

To learn more about time management, read:

Bliss, Edwin C. *Getting Things Done: The ABCs of Time Management.* New York: Scribners, 1991.

Lakein, Alan. *How to Get Control of Your Time and Your Life.* New York: Signet, 1973.

Being Assertive

Taking charge of your life requires planning, commitment, energy—and courage. In order to make positive changes and get what you want and need, you must be willing to stand up for your rights.

What are your rights, exactly? For starters, they include:

● the right to think for yourself
● the right to express your views and opinions

- *the right to say no*
- *the right to act as you choose, as long as you don't hurt yourself or others*
- *the right to have your needs taken seriously*
- *the right to respond to violations of your rights.*

In addition to these basic rights, you also have other rights related to being gifted and talented. Specifically:

1. You have the right to attend classes that are interesting and challenging for you.

2. You have the right to do your best work when you want to and less than perfect work when you don't.

3. You have the right to have friends who understand and support you.

4. You have the right to pursue relevant and meaningful schoolwork at your own speed.

5. You have the right to be treated with respect by your friends, teachers, and parents.

6. You have the right to be different.

7. You have the right to choose your life's direction.

8. You have the right to be concerned with life on earth and ways to make it better.

It's not likely that you will be handed your rights on a silver platter. Instead, you're going to have to ask for them and, at times, fight for them. In order for this to happen, you need assertiveness skills.

Many gifted teens have difficulty being assertive. Perhaps they don't understand the rights they are entitled to, or they're uncertain about what their rights mean. Or they aren't sure what they want and need. Or they fear seeming "stupid" or unreasonable, pushy or obnoxious. Or they have tried to be assertive, have been shot down, and are reluctant to take the risk again. Or they confuse assertiveness with aggressiveness, alienating other people and making it even harder to exercise their rights.

Before you can be assertive, it helps to know what assertiveness is. Here's a definition that makes it perfectly clear:*

> "Assertive behavior promotes equality in human relationships, enabling us to act in our own best interests, to stand up for ourselves without undue anxiety, to express feelings honestly and comfortably, to exercise personal rights without denying the rights of others."

"I was thought to be 'stuck up.' I wasn't. I was just sure of myself. This is and always has been an unforgivable quality to the unsure."
Bette Davis

"You must learn to say no when something is not right for you."
Leontyne Price

"Wishing is okay . . . asking is faster."
Anonymous

---

* Robert E. Alberti and Michael L. Emmons, *Your Perfect Right: A Guide to Assertive Living*. San Luis Obispo, CA: Impact Publishers, 1995, p. 46.

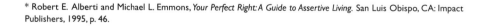

Learning to be assertive doesn't happen overnight. It takes time, patience, and practice. If you feel that you haven't been sufficiently assertive in your dealings with friends, family members, and/or teachers, these do's and don'ts will get you started.

DO:

- *Think about a situation you'd like to change—a case in which one of your rights is being denied. Start with a small, simple one to maximize your chances of success.*
- *Identify the person you perceive as denying your right. Try to see the situation from his or her point of view, and consider his or her position.*
- *Observe others around you who behave assertively. Analyze their approach. How do they act? What's their body language, their facial expression, their tone of voice? What words do they use? What are their keys to success?*
- *Consider what you'd like to tell the person, and also what you'd like to request from him or her. Create a "script" and go over it mentally, or role play it with a friend. Visualize yourself having a respectful and positive interaction with the person.*
- *Anticipate what might happen if your conversation takes a different direction. Be prepared with backup statements and requests; be willing to compromise if necessary.*
- *Choose the best time to approach the person and give it a try.*
- *If you're successful, review the experience later in your mind. Store it away so you can draw on it the next time you need to be assertive.*
- *If you're not successful, try to figure out what went wrong. What could you have done differently?*

**"Be bold in what
you stand for
and careful what
you fall for."
Ruth Boorstin**

DON'T:

- *Procrastinate. The longer you wait to assert your rights, the harder it is to gather your courage to change what has now become the status quo.*
- *Place blame. This puts the other person on the defensive and makes him or her less willing to listen.*
- *Get off track. Instead, stay focused on your purpose. Don't bring up unrelated issues or allow yourself to be distracted.*
- *Refuse to compromise. You're asking the other person to make a change. If you give a little, you may get a lot.*
- *Make threats. This backs the other person into a corner.*
- *Attack. This is aggressive behavior, not assertive behavior. It makes you feel powerful, but it disrespects the rights of the other person.*
- *Stay silent or withdraw. This is passive behavior, and it leads to feelings of anger, anxiety, disappointment, and depression.*
- *Get even. This is a form of passive-aggressive behavior. It's covert, insincere, and ineffective.*
- *Give up. If you won't fight for your rights, who will?*

The ASSERT Formula

The ASSERT Formula is a simple mnemonic that can help you to frame assertive responses on the spot. It's ideal for times when you don't have the luxury of developing a thoughtful assertiveness strategy.

A stands for "Attention"

Before you can address a problem you're having with another person, you first have to get his or her attention. Make sure that the person is willing to hear what you have to say. *Example:* "Dad, I need to talk to you about something that's on my mind. Is now a good time?"

S stands for "Soon, Simple, and Short"

Speak up as soon as you realize that your rights have been violated. ("Soon" may be a matter of seconds, hours, or days.) Look the person in the eye and keep your comments brief and to the point. *Example:* "I'm having a problem with something you said in front of my track team today."

S stands for "Specific Behavior"

What has the person done to violate your rights? Focus on the behavior, not the person. Be as specific as you can. *Example:* "I didn't like it when you told that old story about the time I ran away from home."

E stands for "Effect on Me"

Share the feelings you experienced as a result of this person's behavior, such as: "I get angry when . . ." or "I get frustrated when. . . ." *Example:* "I got embarrassed because everyone laughed at me. I'm already the youngest member of the team, and I felt like a little kid."

R stands for "Response"

Describe your preferred outcome, what you'd like to see happen instead, and ask for some feedback on it. *Example:* "Would you be willing to keep that story private from now on—just in our family? It is pretty funny, and I don't mind if we all laugh about it at home."

T stands for "Terms"

If all goes well, you may be able to make an agreement with the other person about how to handle the situation in the future. Or you may "agree to disagree" or simply come to an impasse. *Example:* "I appreciate your hearing me out. So it's okay to tell it to family members, but not to people I go to school with. Do we have a deal?"

Find Out More

To learn more about assertiveness, read:

Alberti, Robert E., and Michael L. Emmons. *Your Perfect Right: A Guide to Assertive Living.* San Luis Obispo, CA: Impact Publishers, 1995.

Multipotential: An Embarrassment of Riches

Jim, 33: "I ended up teaching at a university, but not until I'd toyed with the fields of psychiatry, pediatrics, and forestry."

Leah, 36: "I got my B.A. in psychology, worked for an orchestra, went to business school for my M.B.A., and now I'm vice president of a software company. I may have arrived by an indirect route, but I like where I am."

Tania, 30: "I work in advertising. I enjoy it, and I'm good at it, but I also take flying lessons on the weekend and I wonder—is it too late to apply to astronaut school?"

"You have brains in your head. You have feet in your shoes. You can steer yourself any direction you choose."
Theodor Seuss Geisel (Dr. Seuss)

Charlie Brown, speaking to his friend Linus on the meaning of life, once lamented, "There is no heavier burden than a great potential." When you are bright and capable of many different things, it becomes very easy to disappoint those people who have your future all planned out. Perhaps Mom has always wanted you to be a doctor, while Dad dreams about you taking over the family business. Your high school chemistry teacher might be pushing you toward a degree at M.I.T., while the school counselor is urging you toward Harvard or Yale. And if you're female, you may even be hearing from well-intentioned (but out-of-touch-with-reality) relatives that finding a husband should be your primary goal.

What to be? What to become? Where to go? Where to turn? And how to convince everyone to let you make up your own mind?

For more than 30 years, researchers at the University of Wisconsin studied the problems encountered by gifted teens seeking answers to career-related questions. They used interviews, questionnaires, and follow-up surveys with hundreds of young adults in the hope of clearing up some of the fuzzier facets of career selection and satisfaction. One of their most important findings was this: Gifted teenagers are often interested in—and have the potential to succeed at—many career options. Today this characteristic is commonly referred to as *multipotential*.

While it sounds wonderful, multipotential can be a burden. However, complaining about it won't elicit much sympathy from others. "I'm so good at so many things that I just can't make up my mind what to do" is not the sort of comment that wins friends and influences people.

It helps to know that you're not alone. The dilemma posed by multipotential is shared by many gifted persons. Here's how one describes his predicament:

> **Mike, 17:** "I participated in three semesters of a mentorship program. In one placement I worked with a physician who does research at the university. In a second setting I worked with an attorney, and in the third a computer expert. I had great experiences in all three settings and felt like I could be successful in any of those professions. I guess I'm not any closer to knowing what I want to do in the future. Maybe I'll have to figure out a way to combine all three of those areas into a 'custom designed' job."

Multipotential is clearly a mixed blessing, but recognizing it is a positive step toward living with it—and making the most of it. Even when you do decide on a career, you don't have to stay with it forever. Most people switch careers once, twice, and even more often before they retire—going back to school for degrees in other fields, changing companies, starting their own businesses.

According to the Bureau of Labor Statistics, about 10 percent of the American work force switches occupations every year. In *Change Your Job, Change Your Life*, Ronald L. Krannich writes that "if you are like most other Americans, you will make more than 10 job changes and between 3 and 5 career changes during your lifetime." Some career counselors today are using the word "role" instead of "career" or "job" because people entering the workforce are expected to perform many different functions in the years ahead.

Multipotential may mean occasional headaches. But it also means *choices*—enough to last a lifetime. What's the secret of success? Making *informed* choices.

> **"If I didn't start painting, I would have raised chickens."**
> **Grandma Moses**

> "When individuals have several abilities and options, other aspects than ability should be considered, such as personality, personal needs, dreams, and even values."
> Jean Peterson

Making Informed Choices

What do you want to be when you grow up? That seems like a silly question these days. It makes more sense to ask, "What are all of the things I'd like to do and try in life, and how can I set goals and organize myself to make the most of my varied interests?"

Assume that you have a general idea of the direction you think your life should take. For example, you've assessed your talents and abilities, and you have some notion of what might suit you. The point is not to specialize early or sign up only for those courses that fit your eventual goal, but to find out as much as you can about what it will take to get there.

What do you need to learn? Do? Become? Who should you talk to? Which colleges or universities should you start thinking about? What will you need to put your plan into action? When and where should you begin? Following are three suggestions for you to consider along the way.

Try Before You Buy

Often, when deciding on a college major or a career focus, gifted teens make up their minds too soon. Listen to people who have been there, done that:

> **Andrew, 26:** "I was sure from the day I started high school that I wanted to be an English teacher. All the way through college, I took as many English courses as I could and the bare minimum in all other subject areas. The summer before I was supposed to go to graduate school, I got a part-time job at a bank. I liked it so much that I never left. Now, five years later, I wish I knew more about math and economics."

> **Gina, 30:** "If I had it to do over, I'd probably take courses in art history, philosophy, and music—subjects I neglected because I was sure I wanted to be a doctor. I got on the pre-med track too soon, and now I wish I had studied other subjects in more depth."

Imagine that you're 14 and you want to be an allergist someday. Ask yourself: What is it about that particular profession that interests you? The money? The prestige? The independence? The challenge? A career as an allergist is nothing to sneeze at; how thoroughly have you examined the pros and cons? Can you see spending more than eight years in college and over $120,000? (And this is even allowing for $40,000 in scholarships.) What is an allergist's life really like?

**Taking
Charge of
Your Life**

It's not hard to find answers to these questions and more. Check with your school counselor; ask your family doctor to contact an allergist for you and see if he or she would be willing to share insights and information. Search your local library or the Internet. You might even find an allergists' newsgroup where you can post your questions and collect responses from people all over the world. It's possible that a professional allergists' association might even have its own Web site.

Will busy allergists want to spend time answering your questions? Some won't, but many will. If a student on the verge of seventh grade walked up to you and said, "Come on, tell me about junior high—what's it *really* like?" wouldn't you be flattered? And wouldn't you be willing to offer your perspective on food fights, jammed lockers, and getting along with teachers? Most adults enjoy talking about themselves and their experiences, especially to young people who are seriously interested in what we have to say. You may want to conduct several fact-finding interviews—in person, by phone, by mail, or by E-mail.

Or consider an internship, if available. Many businesses offer them during the summer and part-time during the school year. An internship gives you the chance to sample a profession before making a commitment. It may not pay much (or anything) in terms of dollars, but it will give you experiences and insights you can't buy.

> **Bob, 28:** "I think the most important thing I learned during my internship is that one's job doesn't have to be something that is only endured. It can also be pleasurable and fulfilling. When I first started working as an intern in an office, I had the notion that the rest of my life would be filled with jobs which I would take simply because I needed to pay my bills. I knew that some jobs would be better than others, but that the differences would be small because they were all work. I learned, by the example of the people I worked with, that this concept was wrong. I learned that people can care a lot more about work than how much money they make. I learned that a person's work is an extension of their mind and soul, and that the rewards are more than money. I learned that an office can be more than a workplace; it's a community of people. Work can be fun and interesting in ways I never could have imagined."

Another way to "try before you buy" is through a mentorship. In Minnesota, a program called The Mentor Connection matches high school students with mentors—professionals in the business and academic communities who are willing to work with them, guide them, answer their questions, and help them to explore possible careers through real on-the-job experiences.* Before being placed with their mentors, the students participate in a guidance lab to learn advanced research skills, decision making, self-awareness, and career awareness. Accelerated and enriched learning are the natural consequences of mentorships.

There may be a similar program in your school district or community, or you may need to find your own mentor. Ask your principal; ask the gifted education coordinator in your school district; check with your parents, other relatives, neighbors, local business owners, etc., to see if they might want to mentor you or point you toward someone who will.

Randy, 17 (placed in research and design with a computer corporation): "I gained a broader horizon of insight in human experience. The diversity of people who worked at my site is staggering. Trying to meet and get along with all these new people was very exciting."

Paula, 18 (placed at the YWCA): "I was very pleased with my mentor; we related very well to each other. The people at the YWCA accepted me with open arms. The most beneficial part of the experience was getting out into the working world and finding out what it's really like."

Find Out More

To learn more about internships and mentorships, read:

Princeton Review: America's Top 100 Internships. New York: Random House, updated often.

Princeton Review Internship Bible. New York: Random House, updated often.

Reilly, Jill M. *Mentorships: The Essential Guide for Schools and Business.* Dayton, OH: Ohio Psychology Press, 1992.

* Although The Mentor Connection is only for students in Minneapolis/St. Paul, Minnesota, you can request information that may help you to initiate a similar experience where you live. Write or call: The Mentor Connection, ATTN: Jeanie Davis Pullen, Northeast Metro School District 916, 3300 Century Avenue North, White Bear Lake, MN 55127; telephone: (612) 415-5454.

Consider Creating Your Own Career

If early specializers are at one end of the spectrum, the opposite end is crowded with people who can't make up their minds. You've probably met someone—you may be someone—who wants to be everything: psychologist, rock star, architect, poet, boutique owner, missionary, frozen-foods distributor, engineer, pilot.

Trying to fulfill just one of these ambitions seems as pointless as going to a smörgasbord and eating only mashed potatoes; the selections are so varied and look so appealing that you want a little taste of each. Many gifted persons who fit this description decide to focus on one career for a while and use their free time to explore other options.

> **Ron, 28:** "Right now I'm teaching courses in special ed while taking courses in archaeology. This summer I'll go on a dig to Mexico as part of my master's degree program."

> **Therese, 19:** "I couldn't choose between careers in medicine and art; I enjoy both areas. So I'm studying both in the hope of becoming a medical artist for anatomy textbooks."

These two individuals have "married" their vocations with their avocations. And each is in the process of creating a career rather than fitting into preexisting ones.

If your multipotential has you confused about what to do and be, ask yourself these two questions:

1. What would you *like* to be doing ten years from now?
2. What do you think you *will* be doing ten years from now?

If your responses differ (and they probably will), sit down and consider how you can merge them into a future of your own devising. It's not that uncommon these days to strike out on one's own. More and more people are choosing the entrepreneurial route—starting their own businesses, inventing their own jobs. Countless occupations exist today that weren't even imagined a decade ago—aquaculturist, hotline counselor, E-mail technician, information broker, robot trainer, artificial intelligence technician, computer network manager, solar energy consultant, etc. Why not add to the list?

You'll probably encounter a few naysayers who will urge you to quit goofing off and get serious about a career. And at times you may question the validity of your decision, especially since you may not have much company along your eclectic way. Don't be diverted by doubters or self-doubts. Times change, needs change, and you'll

> "To love what you do and feel that it matters—how could anything be more fun?"
> Katharine Graham

change, too. With the right blend of foresight, intelligence, ambition, and aplomb, you may find yourself shifting directions several times before you're ready to retire . . . *if* you retire. In other words, a career choice doesn't have to be a life sentence.

Marybeth, 32: "I've spent the past 11 years as a freelance writer, and it's only been in the last year or so that my parents have stopped asking me, 'When are you going to get a real job?' "

Dexter, 25: "My parents and my brothers and sisters all work 9-to-5 jobs. I think they resent it that I have my own business and don't work for anyone else. What they don't realize is that I put in 12, sometimes 14 hours a day. The big difference is, I work for me."

Take the Road Less Traveled

To choose "the road less traveled" (in the words of poet Robert Frost) or to "boldly go where no one has gone before" (to quote Captain Jean-Luc Picard of the starship *Enterprise*) is to leave yourself open to criticism and a chorus of "I-told-you-so's" in the event of a setback or failure. But if your reason for selecting pottery over podiatry, or nursing over nuclear physics, stems from your own genuine interest and the belief that it's right for you, that's all you need to heed.

Listen to Colin, who grade-skipped his way to a Ph.D. at age 21, then went on to be a college professor of economics:*

> "The only thing people can rightfully demand from you is excellence—or at least an honest effort—in whatever you decide to do. In fact, the only reason you owe excellence in exchange for your gift is that you owe it to *yourself*. 'That's impossible' and 'That's too wild an idea' are the favorite chants of the narrow minded."

"When you come to a fork in the road, take it."
Yogi Berra

Find Out More

To learn more about making career choices, read:

Bingham, Edmondson, and Stryker. *Challenges: A Young Man's Journal for Self-Awareness and Personal Planning.* **Santa Barbara, CA: Advocacy Press, 1993.**
— *Choices: A Woman's Journal for Self-Awareness and Personal Planning.* **Santa Barbara, CA: Advocacy Press, 1993.**

Bingham, Mindy, and Sandy Stryker. *Career Choices and Changes: A Guide for Discovering Who You Are, What You Want, and How to Get It.* **Santa Barbara, CA: Academic Innovations, 1994.**

Combs, Patrick. *Major in Success: Make College Easier, Beat the System, and Get a Very Cool Job.* **Berkeley, CA: Ten Speed Press, 1995.**

Terkel, Studs. *Working.* **New York: Ballantine Books, 1985. (CAUTION: If** *Working* **was a movie, it would be rated R for language. But if you don't mind the strong stuff, it's well worth reading.)**

---

* From *Gifted Children Speak Out* by James R. Delisle. New York: Walker & Co., 1984.

GIFTED PEOPLE SPEAK OUT
Jonah Klevesahl, 16

For some reason, the idea of flipping burgers or bagging groceries never appealed to me. I wanted something different. Consequently, when my mother suggested that I get a job a couple of summers ago, I didn't wander into the local fast-food joint or supermarket. I took the skill I knew and loved the most and ran with it—computers.

It all started a few years back when I returned from a trip to California to find a new Macintosh computer sitting on my mother's desk. She told me that she wasn't going to be using it for a while and I could tinker with it until she wrapped up some projects on her old PC. Now, I had previous experience on some older computers, but when that class ended in grade school I pretty much lost interest. The uninterrupted three weeks I had on my mom's new Mac rejuvenated my eagerness to learn everything I could about computers.

Soon I was hooked, and I decided that if I was going to get a job, it had to be in the field of computers. I became discouraged, however, to find that just about every computer-related job listed in the newspaper said something like "3 years previous experience required" or "College degree required." I was 15, with no work experience and no college. But I didn't let that stop me.

My mother knew someone who sold computers, and I started by interviewing with that company. I prepared a portfolio and scheduled an interview. The owners of the company spent more than an hour grilling me. I didn't get the job, but I did gain valuable experience in surviving a tough interview.

My second interview was with one of the partners in a graphic design firm, also someone my mother knew. She let him know that I was looking for a job, but the rest was up to me. I had to call and set up the interview and prepare for it. I got the job, and I spent that summer and the following school year working part-time. I did a lot of image scanning and color correction, as well as some minor editing and layout on the computer. I also got a crash course in System Administration—fixing software and hardware problems, chasing down bugs in the network.

When summer rolled around again, I anticipated new challenges. Although I had the opportunity to learn some new database and Internet software, I still spent a lot of time doing image scanning, which by now had grown monotonous. I decided that it was time to look elsewhere.

My father knew an executive at Northwest Airlines, and I called him to request an interview. We met and chatted for over an hour. I didn't get the job, but once again I gained experience—and a major connection for the future.

Then one afternoon I decided to stop by a local computer dealer/service center on my way home from my scanning job. I started talking with a salesperson about what kind of computers my school should get for our new Technology Center, and our conversation quickly moved from business to casual. He asked to see my résumé. I dropped it off the next day, thinking that it would probably get lost in a sea of others just like it. Instead, the manager called me and asked me to come in for an interview.

So I went into the interview, and once again I got grilled. Every possible question that could be asked was asked. The conversation became very technical, but I found myself knowing many of the answers. When I didn't know an answer, I was honest and said so. I was hired the next day as a service technician.

That was almost a year ago. Today my responsibilities include servicing computers, taking customer calls, troubleshooting, helping other technicians (who seem to come to me with all of their Internet questions), and learning everything I can. Each day, I go home knowing about ten times as much as I knew the day before. It's endlessly interesting, exciting, and challenging.

Here's my advice if you're looking for a job and want to go beyond burgers and bags:

- *Figure out what you really want to do, then go for it. Don't let fears, uncertainties, and inexperience stand in your way. Remember—you're intelligent and a fast learner. Those are qualities many employers value.*

- *Take advantage of your parents' connections. Tell them what you'd like to do, then ask if they know anyone in your chosen field (or fields) who might be willing to talk to you. They probably will.*

- *When someone turns you down for a job, don't view it as a personal rejection. Instead, thank the person for the interview, then stay in touch (I do this by E-mail). If someone was willing to talk with you in the first place, chances are he or she won't mind hearing about your progress. Who knows—this could lead to a job offer in the future.*

- *Take chances; take risks. What have you got to lose?*

- *Don't give up. If you don't find the perfect job this month (or this summer), keep trying.*

Jonah Klevesahl is a junior at Benilde-St. Margaret's High School in St. Louis Park, Minnesota, where he is also the Systems and Network Administrator for the school's Technology Center.

Gender Issues

How many househusbands do you know? What about male nurses? How many state governors are women? How many CEOs of major corporations wear skirts to work? People talk about how our society is becoming less sexist, and in some ways it is. But equality is a long, tedious process that frequently slows and stalls.

We may be a generation beyond the time when a woman's

> "**SEXISM IS PREVALENT IN TODAY'S SOCIETY, NO MAT-TER HOW MUCH WE TRY TO DENY IT.**" BRIAN, 18

place was in the home and men provided the family's sole financial support, but sexism still exists, and it continues to affect both males and females. We'd like to believe that men and women can do the same jobs equally well (for equal pay), but the myths linger on, and male preschool teachers are still as rare as women firefighters.

Gender stereotyping can be conscious (refusing to consider a woman doing a "man's job") or unconscious (being surprised at finding a man doing a "woman's job"). The effects are the same either way: limited choices, narrowed horizons, truncated potential, frustration. Men are criticized for wanting to spend more time with their children; women are censured for having careers. Girls are "supposed" to wait for boys to call them (or risk being branded boy-crazy tramps); boys are "supposed" to be sexually aggressive (or risk being labeled wimps). And every gender stereotype has two sides. If girls are "supposed" to be loving and affectionate with children, then boys

● ● ● ● ● ● ● ● ● ● ● ● ● ● ● ●

Can You Solve This Riddle in Three Seconds or Less?

There was a major automobile accident in which a boy was critically injured and his father killed. When the boy was rushed to the emergency room, the attending physician exclaimed, "I can't operate on this boy—he's my son!" How is this possible?*

*If you took more than three seconds to figure out the answer to this riddle, you may be guilty of gender stereotyping. The answer, of course, is that the attending physician was the injured boy's mother.

● ● ● ● ● ● ● ● ● ● ● ● ● ● ● ●

"should be" less so. If girls are "supposed" to be emotional, then boys "shouldn't" cry. If girls are "supposed" to be nurturing wives and mothers, then boys "should" grow up to become the family breadwinners. All stereotypes have this in common: They rob us of our freedom and our right to make choices.

You might ask, "Who came up with these rules?" That's a good question, and you could spend a lifetime searching for the answers. Or you might use your time and energy more efficiently and work for change. Suggestions:

- *Don't let sexist comments slide by. When someone denounces a male or female for exercising his or her right to be an individual, a simple statement like, "Hey, if it makes them happy, why should you care?" will identify you as someone who celebrates diversity and free expression.*

- *Don't tell sexist jokes.*

- *Learn about other teenagers and adults who have encountered and overcome gender stereotypes. For starters, see "Find Out More" on page 112.*

- *Examine your own attitudes. How do you treat the women in your life? The men? The girls? The boys? How do your expectations differ, if in fact they do?*

- *Look for role models in your school and community—people who exemplify fairness in their treatment of others, regardless of gender.*

- *Practice what you preach. If you say that gender stereotyping is hurtful and wrong, make sure that your actions speak as loudly as your words.*

- *Be true to yourself and your goals. Aim for what you want to be, even if it doesn't match other people's expectations for your gender.*

> **"The test for whether or not you can hold a job should not be the arrangement of your chromosomes."**
> Bella Abzug

Both males and females deserve to know that they are valuable and capable. To dismiss a person's achievements because "you're only a girl" is as ignorant and shortsighted as saying, "I expect you to do well because you're a boy." Or vice versa. It's patently unfair to be judged on the basis of something you can't control—whether you were born a boy or a girl. We can all benefit from letting go of the idea that gentleness or genius is determined by gender.

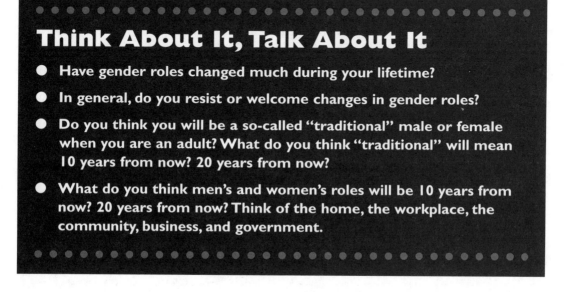

Think About It, Talk About It

- Have gender roles changed much during your lifetime?

- In general, do you resist or welcome changes in gender roles?

- Do you think you will be a so-called "traditional" male or female when you are an adult? What do you think "traditional" will mean 10 years from now? 20 years from now?

- What do you think men's and women's roles will be 10 years from now? 20 years from now? Think of the home, the workplace, the community, business, and government.

Focus: Gifted Girls*

Forty percent of our survey respondents thought that gifted girls had to deal with special problems. They identified the following as the top three dilemmas facing gifted girls today:

1. sexism/discrimination/sexual harassment,

2. dealing with males who are intimidated by intelligent girls and won't date girls they perceive as smarter than they are, and

3. high expectations.

Author and psychologist Barbara Kerr specializes in guidance for gifted females. In researching the attitudes and ambitions of gifted teenage girls, she has found some disturbing results and a few encouraging ones. Examples:

An attorney addressing the Supreme Court: "I would like to remind you gentlemen of a legal point." Justice Sandra Day O'Connor: "Would you like to remind me, too?"

"Of my two 'handicaps,' being female put many more obstacles in my path than being black." Shirley Chisholm

"**YOUNG WOMEN WITH ABOVE-AVERAGE INTELLIGENCE ARE TOLD THAT MEN FEEL THREATENED BY THEM; THUS, WE SHOULD HIDE OUR BRAINS OR WE'LL NEVER GET MARRIED.**" GIRL, 14

"**HIGHLY INTELLIGENT GIRLS ARE OFTEN NOT ENCOURAGED AND ARE VIEWED AS 'WEIRD.' OTHER GIRLS FEEL THREATENED BY THEM, AS DO BOYS, WHICH SEVERELY STUNTS DATING RELATIONSHIPS AND EVEN NORMAL FRIENDSHIPS.**" SARAH, 15

"**EVEN NOW, SOME MEN BELIEVE THAT WOMEN CAN NEVER MEASURE UP TO THEM. THEY STILL BELIEVE THAT WOMEN SHOULD STAY HOME, CLEAN THE HOUSE, COOK, TAKE CARE OF CHILDREN, AND LOVE IT!**" GIRL, 12

"**THERE IS, OF COURSE, THE STEREOTYPE THAT FEMALES DO NOT DO WELL IN MATHEMATICS. I ENJOY PROVING THAT WRONG.**" TACO, 13

- *Highly gifted girls often do not receive recognition for their achievements.*

- *Gifted girls take less rigorous courses than gifted boys in high school.*

- *Gifted girls' IQ scores drop during adolescence, perhaps as girls begin to perceive that giftedness in females is undesirable.*

- *Gifted girls are likely to continue to have higher academic achievement than boys, as measured by grade point average.*

- *Highly gifted girls attend less prestigious colleges than highly gifted boys, a choice that leads to lower status careers.*

- *Gifted girls fear having to choose between career and marriage, yet this "either/or" dilemma is not in fact a reality for many gifted women.*

- *Gifted girls maintain a high involvement in extracurricular and social activities during adolescence.*

Dr. Kerr analyzed the lives of several eminent women in an attempt to learn how they transcended the barriers to achievement that gifted women often face. She found that scientist Marie Curie, actress and activist Katharine Hepburn, agricultural worker and

---

* Some of the information in this section is from Barbara Kerr, *Smart Girls II*. Dayton, OH: Ohio Psychology Press, 1994. Used with permission of the publisher.

Indian Rights activist Rigoberta Menchu, anthropologist Margaret Mead, painter Georgia O'Keeffe, singer Beverly Sills, and writer, dancer, and political activist Maya Angelou had all or most of these factors in common:

1. As girls, they spent time alone, whether by choice or necessity.

2. They read voraciously.

3. They felt "different" or "special."

4. They received individualized instruction as children, often in their areas of future fame.

5. Many went to all-girls schools and/or all-women colleges, or benefited from participating in girls' activities.

6. They experienced embarrassing social awkwardness during adolescence.

7. Rather than defining themselves in terms of their relationships with others, they had a unique sense of self.

8. They took responsibility for themselves and their own lives.

9. They had the ability to fall in love with an idea; they had the capacity to be intensely interested in something and pursue it wholeheartedly.

10. They refused to acknowledge limitations of gender.

11. They had mentors—men or women who nurtured their talents and provided them with access to a profession.

12. Because they were impatient with mediocrity, they grew "thorns" (some became brusque, sarcastic, and sharp-tongued) or "shells" (others became shy and/or hid their private selves behind public personas).

13. They were able to integrate several tasks and roles—wife, mother, career woman, leader.

Dr. Kerr found that the most vulnerable stage for gifted girls—the time when juggling friends, school, and family seems like a never-ending struggle—often comes during junior high. Puberty sets in, and suddenly the feelings of comfort and security experienced during childhood are replaced by insecurity and emotional turbulence. She maintains that gifted females need special guidance and encouragement to believe that it's okay to be simultaneously feminine, intelligent, and competent, and to enjoy math and science as well as dating and sports. She suggests several ways that parents and teachers can help gifted girls to sustain their dreams over time. If you're a gifted girl, and if the adults in your life are willing to read Dr. Kerr's book, *Smart Girls II*, encourage them to do so. (See page 112 for publishing information.)

Meanwhile, there are several things you can do to help yourself. Following are suggestions based on a combination of survey information, interviews with gifted girls, our research, and Judy's personal experience.

> **"Choice is not an answer to the question of how life should be lived, only a condition for answering that question freely."**
> **Dorothy Wickenden**

Now and in the future, take advantage of educational opportunities that will give you the qualifications you need to explore a variety of careers.

Think of as many ways as you can to "open doors" for yourself (and keep them open). For most gifted people—both women *and* men—having choices is essential to a happy, satisfying life.

Be sure to take courses in science, math, and computer technology—preferably advanced courses. In the words of futurist Andy Hines, "Science and technology is the cornucopia of exciting new jobs. Massachusetts Institute of Technology economist Lester Thurow . . . cites seven critical technologies: microelectronics, biotechnology, materials, civil aviation, telecommunications, robotics and machine tools, and computers plus software. That is where the brains, jobs and money will be."* The 1996–1997 edition of the *Occupational Outlook Handbook,* published by the U.S. Department of Labor, notes that "the fastest growing occupations reflect growth in computer technology and health services."

Study career options and learn what's required to be successful in a variety of occupations. Watch for "emerging" careers and read about trends. If a futurist gives a speech at a local college, go and listen.

Learn to distinguish between friends (male and female) who bring out the best in you and those you're better off without.

People who are overly critical, sexist, and/or resentful of your abilities will only bring you down. Listen to your "inner voice"—your intuition about what's right and wrong in a relationship—and choose your friends accordingly.

Remember that decisions you make at this stage of your life will affect your future independence and freedom.

There will probably come a time in your life when you'll need to be self-sufficient. Maybe you'll be on your own when you graduate from college (or even high school). Maybe you see yourself getting married before too long, but marriage is no guarantee that you won't have to support yourself someday. Over half of all marriages end in divorce, and when that happens, the woman's standard of living usually declines by 27—30 percent or more.

If you never marry, or if you do marry and things don't work out, will you have the education and skills you need to sur-

"Senior high gifted girls need to complete four full years of math in order to assure all career options. If four full years of math are not available through the high school, try to find evening courses at a local community college."
Barbara Kerr

---

* Andy Hines, "Transferable Skills Land Future Jobs." *HRMagazine* (April 1993), p. 55.

vive on your own? And what if you have children? Most children of divorced parents live with their mothers—and many live in poverty. Whether or not you get married and stay married, whether or not you have children, the choices you make now are important to your future security and capacity to take care of yourself.

It's perfectly normal to want to fit in and be popular, but not at the expense of your talents and intellect.

If you're not part of the "in crowd," try not to take it personally or assume that there's something wrong with you. Instead, find at least a few people with whom you feel comfortable and can share a social life. Some gifted people have to work harder than others to make friends—perhaps because their goals and interests are unique, or because they're more mature than others in their peer group. Remind yourself that your worth is determined by how *you* feel about yourself, not by what others think of you. (For more about making friends, see pages 206-15.)

Seek out girls and women who are doing interesting things, and learn as much as you can from them.

What are their hobbies and interests? What are their careers, and how did they get where they are? What challenges did they face, and how did they overcome them? What were their growing-up years like, and how did they get through them? Did they date a lot? Why or why not? What do they like most and least about their lives?

Read biographies of women you admire; read biographies to discover more women to admire. Find a "femtor" (the female equivalent of a mentor) who can challenge and support you in your endeavors.

Assess your self-esteem.

How do you really feel about your intellectual, physical, social, and emotional self? If your positive feelings are few and far between, or if they fluctuate (a common experience for teenagers of both genders), turn back to pages 81–83 and read Sol Gordon's words again. Keep a journal and identify situations that foster and/or jeopardize the positive feelings you have about yourself. What can you do to fortify yourself against people or situations that leave you feeling insecure or "not good enough"? It takes confidence to pursue the best life has to offer—new experiences, new relationships, new challenges.

"No person is your friend who demands your silence, or denies your right to grow."
Alice Walker

"When women help women they help themselves."
Wilhelmina Cole Holladay

"It is no exaggeration to say that a strong, positive self-image is the best possible preparation for success in life."
Dr. Joyce Brothers

Make it a priority to know yourself and decide what's important to you.

Try not to worry so much about meeting other people's expectations. What is something that you would like to learn, practice, strive for, achieve? Ten years from now, where do you want to be? What do you want to be doing? How will you get there?

"To do good things in the world, first you must know who you are and what gives meaning in your life."
Paula P. Brownlee

Find Out More

To learn more about the challenges of growing up female, read:

Kerr, Barbara. *Smart Girls II.* Dayton, OH: Ohio Psychology Press, 1994. This groundbreaking book reports on Dr. Kerr's long-term study of the lives of gifted women, with suggestions and strategies for guiding gifted girls.

Pipher, Mary. *Reviving Ophelia.* New York: Ballantine Books, 1994. A psychologist who specializes in work with girls and young women tells about the ways in which our culture stifles the creativity, intellect, and self-esteem of adolescent girls. She quotes girls throughout and tells what adults can do to help. (CAUTION: This book contains strong language and frank portrayals of the dangers of being young and female.)

To learn more about career options and economic equity for women, read:

Godfrey, Joline. *No More Frogs to Kiss: 99 Ways to Give Economic Power to Girls.* New York: HarperCollins Publishers, 1995.

Lateef, Nelda. *Working Women for the 21st Century: 50 Women Reveal Their Pathways to Success.* Charlotte, VT: Williamson Publishing, 1992.

Focus: Gifted Boys*

Thirty-four percent of our survey respondents felt that gifted boys had to deal with special problems. They identified the following as the top three dilemmas facing gifted boys today:

1. being labeled a nerd and being teased about giftedness,
2. peer pressure to fit in; having to continually conform, and
3. high expectations, extra work, and/or more responsibilities.

Researchers are discovering that gender stereotyping and cultural conditioning affect gifted males in unique and specific ways. Examples:

1. Gifted boys raised in families that reinforce primarily "macho" values, roles, and relationships may be especially at risk.

> **"THERE'S PRESSURE ON BOYS TO BE ATHLETIC, MACHO, ETC., THAT CAN HURT THEIR POTENTIAL TO BE REAL PEOPLE, LET ALONE INTELLIGENT PEOPLE."**
> JAY, 17

> **"BOYS ARE SUPPOSED TO BE INTERESTED IN SPORTS AND CARS, NOT IN STUDIES, SCHOOL, AND SCIENCE."**
> ANDREJ, 17

> **"BOYS HAVE TO DEAL WITH KIDS WHO CONSIDER THEM UNPOPULAR OR NOT COOL BECAUSE OF THEIR BRAINS."**
> GARRETT, 13

> **"OFTEN WE HAVE TO DEAL WITH THE DISAPPROVAL THAT COMES IF YOU ENROLL IN TRADITIONALLY FEMALE-DOMINATED COURSES, SUCH AS FINE ARTS."**
> BOY, 14

The "macho man" is aggressive, competitive, insensitive, self-reliant, logical, and non-emotional. Highly creative or sensitive young people can experience extreme frustration and insecurity when they're expected to conform to this tough guy image. Boys interested in art, dance, or nurturing roles are punished for being different. When gifted boys are made to feel that they must be macho against their natures, they end up feeling self-alienated, guilty, and inadequate and suffer from poor self-esteem.

Everyone knows that "boys don't cry"—or, at least, they're not supposed to. Instead, they're taught to suppress their feelings, hide their vulnerabilities, and be strong. They are not given permission to express their emotions. For gifted boys in particular, this can limit the development of their creativity and intuitive side.

Some of the male violence in our society can be traced back to a culturally conditioned inability to vent and work through bottled-up emotions. But because gifted boys have a deeper appreciation for and understanding of life's complexities, they tend to have empathy for others and strike out against *themselves*. The results may range from a low self-concept to substance abuse, depression, and even suicide.

---

* This section is adapted from "Snips & Snails & Puppy-Dog Tails: The Plight of Gifted Boys" by Jim Alvino in *The Best of Free Spirit*, pp. 76–77.

2. Gifted boys seem to have special problems with their parents.

Their intense and earlier-than-normal need for independence leads to arguments at home. Sparks fly when highly divergent thinkers with off-the-wall, original ideas come up against authoritarian moms and dads.

The adolescent rebellion period may be even more painful for gifted boys. Not only are they dealing with growing up and forming a self-identity; they're also struggling with the development and expression of their superior abilities. Pressure from their parents to perform and achieve can turn them into "paralyzed perfectionists" so desperate to do things right that they can't act at all out of fear of failure. Their sense of self-worth and means of obtaining love and affection become tied to their accomplishments. It's hard for them to find and make friends. And often they end up feeling anxious and depressed, unworthy and inferior, burned out and lonely.

3. One study found that giftedness is an advantage for elementary school girls, but not for boys.

Part of this has to do with the reality of most elementary school classrooms—even gifted programs. Most teachers are women who tend to value conformity and obedience. Gifted boys are more likely than girls to rebel, question authority, and be the class troublemakers. Compounding this problem is the fact that boys are on a different developmental schedule than girls. In general, they mature more slowly, particularly in the verbal and reading areas. Bright and active boys may be designated hyperactive, distractible, or disorderly, and their giftedness may go unrecognized.

4. Gifted boys are haunted by the stereotype of the "nerd."

It's not enough to be academically able; for a boy to be accepted, he must also be athletic. And he must also endure more ridicule, name-calling, and bullying than non-gifted boys because he's different, and because others are threatened by his abilities.

Like all kids, gifted boys want to be part of a peer group, and they may decide to hide their talents in order to fit in. They choose to underachieve and deny their giftedness. They turn off and say no—and perhaps even end up as juvenile delinquents. A University of Denver study found that underachievement is the one thing most delinquents have in common, gifted or not.

Taking Charge of Your Life

If you're a gifted male, there are things you can do to make growing up easier on yourself. Suggestions:

- *Let yourself feel and express your emotions.*
- *Share your hopes, dreams, fears, and insecurities with your parents. They care.*
- *Educate yourself about gender stereotyping and expectations and how they limit you and girls.*
- *Find other adults or mentors who accept you as you are and can help you to make the most of your gifts—whatever they happen to be.*
- *Don't push yourself so hard. Remember that you're on a slower developmental schedule than girls.*
- *Learn to accept your strengths and your limitations.*
- *Follow your own interests. Try to make time to learn about things you want to know.*
- *Make friends with peers of similar abilities and interests.*
- *Respect and like yourself for who you are. Other people may have their own expectations of you, but it's your life.*

"True equality can only mean the right to be uniquely creative."
Erik H. Erikson

Ethnic Issues*

Thirty-two percent of our survey respondents felt that a gifted student's ethnic background could create special challenges. The gifted young people who took our survey identified the following as their top three concerns related to ethnic background:

"PREJUDICE CAN DISCOURAGE PEOPLE FROM DOING THEIR BEST." IRIS, 12

1. having to deal with discrimination, prejudice, and racism,
2. coping with stereotypes based on assumptions related to race or ethnicity, and
3. fitting in with other gifted students in light of being raised with (perhaps) different belief systems.

Gifted students from minority cultures have traditionally faced special challenges in school and in life. They have historically been underrepresented in gifted programs. A brief timeline:

---

* Some of the information in this section was compiled from the following sources: A. Harry Passow and Mary M. Frasier, "Toward Improving Identification of Talent Potential Among Minority and Disadvantaged Students," *Roeper Review*, Vol. 18, No. 3 (February/March 1996), pp. 198–202; C. June Maker, "Identification of Gifted Minority Students: A National Problem, Needed Changes and a Promising Solution," *Gifted Child Quarterly*, Vol. 40, No. 1 (Winter 1996), pp. 41–50; Linda M. Cohen, "Meeting the Needs of Gifted and Talented Minority Language Students," *Eric Digest* #E480, Reston, VA: ERIC Clearinghouse on Handicapped and Gifted Children; U.S. Department of Education, Office of Educational Research and Improvement; *National Excellence: A Case for Developing America's Talent*, Washington, DC: 1993; and Jean Sunde Peterson, *The Underrepresentation of Minority Children in Gifted Education: An Ethnographic Study*, Iowa State University, 1996.

In 1950, the Educational Policies Commission reported in *Education of the Gifted* that "lacking both incentive and opportunity, the probabilities are very great that, however superior one's gifts may be, he will rarely live a life of high achievement. Follow-up studies of highly gifted young Negroes, for instance, reveal a shocking waste of talent—a waste that adds an incalculable amount to the price of prejudice in this country."

In 1971, the U.S. Office of Education observed in *The Marland Report* that "existing services to the gifted and talented do not reach large and significant subpopulations (e.g., minorities and disadvantaged) and serve a very small percentage of the gifted and talented population generally."

In 1988, the Jacob K. Javits Gifted and Talented Education Act was created to give highest priority to gifted students who are traditionally underserved. In passing the Javits Act, Congress reasserted the conviction that gifted and talented children are found in all cultural groups, across all economic strata, and in all areas of human endeavor.

In 1993, the U.S. Department of Education released *National Excellence: A Case for Developing America's Talent,* which declared that "the United States is squandering one of its most precious resources—the gifts, talents, and high interests of many of its students. In a broad range of intellectual and artistic endeavors, these youngsters are not challenged to do their best work. This problem is especially severe among economically disadvantaged and minority students, who have access to fewer advanced educational opportunities and whose talents often go unnoticed."

In 1996, C. June Maker wrote in *Gifted Child Quarterly* that "changes in values, beliefs, and the demographics of American society have not been accompanied by consistent changes in definitions and practices related to the education of the gifted ... certain cultural, ethnic, and linguistic minority students continue to be under-represented in special programs."

In other words, experts have been saying for nearly half a century that the talents of minority students are being overlooked and wasted. Since the problem was identified so long ago, why is it still a problem? There are at least six reasons (and no doubt more):

1. We live in a racist culture. Countless people across the United States are working to change this, but it's a long, hard, and sometimes dangerous road to travel.

2. Educators and the general public continue to have negative stereotypes and inaccurate perceptions of the abilities of students from minority groups.

3. Most states use a definition of giftedness that has changed only slightly in the past decades, so it doesn't reflect current thinking about giftedness and intelligence.

4. Many schools and districts still use IQ scores as the sole criterion when identifying gifted and talented students.

5. When nominating students for inclusion in gifted programs, many teachers make choices based on mainstream values and their own self-interest—the "best" students are those who behave in teacher-affirming ways.

6. Although many states have enacted legislation encouraging local school districts to provide special opportunities for high-achieving and talented students, including minority students, the statutes are often contradictory. This creates confusion and prevents change.

Most gifted programs have a stated goal of providing full services to special populations including minority students, but these goals for the most part have not been reached. Either the recommended procedures aren't being used or they aren't working. Some hard facts:

- *In one large urban district in the Southwest, minority students make up about 48 percent of the total student population but only 25 percent of the students in the full-time elementary program for the gifted.*

- *In a large urban district in the Southeast, 81 percent of the students are African American and Hispanic, but only 50 percent of the students in the gifted program belong to those groups.*

- *Studies have shown that as many as 50 percent of gifted students of low socio-economic status enrolled in public schools are not identified by current identification procedures, mainly because they tend to score low on standardized verbal subtests.*

Even when minority students are identified for inclusion in gifted programs, they may not succeed once they get there. Their behavior may not fit with the teacher's beliefs about what giftedness means or how gifted students should behave. Examples:

- *Native American children are taught to value interdependence, not independence; in their culture, decisions are made collectively.*

- *Puerto Rican children learn to seek the advice of their family rather than act independently.*

- *Mexican American children are taught to respect their elders, the law, and authority, not individual competition, initiative, and self-direction.*

"Do not call for
black power or
for green power.
Call for brain
power."
Barbara Jordan

African American students may have mixed feelings about academic success. In one inner-city high school, high-achieving black students were labeled "brainiacs" and accused of "acting white"—of disavowing their ethnic heritage so they would be accepted by the dominant society.

Because the gifted curriculum is usually designed for students who are high achievers in the traditional curriculum, many minority students in gifted programs end up being mistaught, feeling frustrated, and either dropping out or being asked to leave.

> **"AFRICAN OR HISPANIC AMERICANS ARE KNOWN TO BIGOTS AS 'ILLITERATES' OR 'DUMB.' SOME KIDS SAY THINGS LIKE, 'WOW! A SMART BLACK!'"**
> JESSICA, 12

Asian students face a different set of difficulties. Because their traditional values—educational attainment, obedience to authority—support achievement in U.S. schools, more Asian students are identified as gifted than students from any other minority group. They are 2.5 percent of the school-age population, but 5 percent of the identified gifted population. These students may experience enormous pressures to perform and excel. Parents, teachers, and peers may *expect* them to be gifted.

> **"RACIAL STEREOTYPES CAUSE PROBLEMS AT TIMES. FOR EXAMPLE, ASIANS ARE PERCEIVED AS BEING MATH- AND SCIENCE-ORIENTED, WHICH ISN'T ALWAYS TRUE."** JAY, 15

Considering the scope of the problem and how deeply entrenched it is, can we really expect that things will change for the better? The answer is yes, and here are some reasons why:

- *The perception of giftedness is changing. No longer do most people assume that it's strictly a matter of scoring high on an IQ test. There's a growing emphasis on multiple intelligences, which requires new ways of measuring ability, achievement, and potential—ways that are more likely to identify minority students.*

- *As our culture grows more diverse, the differences among individual groups are becoming less "foreign" and more a part of our everyday lives. We are learning about each other, and this in turn leads to increased tolerance, acceptance, and recognition of each other's abilities, talents, and strengths.*

- *More schools are turning away from traditional assessment practices and using new tools to identify gifted students. For example, a program called DISCOVER allows students to express knowledge developed through direct experience as opposed to academic learning. The assessment is conducted in the student's first language (or in two languages, if that seems best), and part of it draws on the symbols and notational systems (writing, numbers, etc.) of the student's own culture.*

- During the early 1970s, there were very few programs for gifted and talented students. Today such programs exist in every state. (Unfortunately, many programs that got their start in the 1970s and 1980s have since been curtailed or had their funding cut because of budget crises.)

- The public is becoming more aware that gifted students have special educational needs, and more supportive of school programs that address those needs. In a 1992 Gallup poll, 61 percent of the respondents said that schools should do more to challenge the brightest children; 84 percent said that they would support special funding for gifted programs, as long as this did not reduce what was offered to average and slow learners.

A New Way to Identify Gifted Students

National Excellence: A Case for Developing America's Talent calls on schools to develop a system to identify gifted and talented students that:

- **Seeks variety** — looks throughout a range of disciplines for students with diverse talents;

- **Uses many assessment measures** — uses a variety of appraisals so that schools can find students in different talent areas and at different ages;

- **Is free of bias** — provides students of all backgrounds with equal access to appropriate opportunities;

- **Is fluid** — uses assessment procedures that can accommodate students who develop at different rates and whose interests may change as they mature;

- **Identifies potential** — discovers talents that are not readily apparent in students, as well as those that are obvious; and

- **Assesses motivation** — takes into account the drive and passion that play a key role in accomplishment.

"You're either
part of the solu-
tion or you're
part of the
problem."
Eldridge Cleaver

Is there anything we can do as individuals in our classrooms and schools to promote positive change and appropriate education for everyone? Again, the answer is yes. Suggestions:

● *If your school offers special education opportunities for highly able students and you're invited to participate, do. The more students who take part in these programs, the more school districts can "justify" keeping them and funding them. They may even decide to add options due to increased participation.*

● *When you take part in special education opportunities, be sure to let people in power (principals, school board members, your parents, etc.) know how you are benefiting from the experience. Make phone calls, write letters—do whatever it takes to document the important role your school is playing in meeting your educational needs.*

● *Support your school in offering challenges that accommodate a variety of intelligences and talents. Find out how your school identifies students for participation in special programs, and if you see inequities, talk to the gifted coordinator or principal to learn what can be done to make the process more meaningful and fair.*

● *If you aren't identified for a special program but you think you should be— because you would benefit from the challenge, and/or because you have abilities that match those of other students who have been identified—talk to the gifted coordinator or principal. Find out if you can participate on a trial basis for a period of time, with the understanding that you'll be allowed to continue if you are successful.*

● *If you know other students who, in your opinion, should be identified for special programs but are being overlooked, talk to the gifted coordinator or principal. Come prepared with specific examples to support your claim. Advocate for students who may not feel comfortable speaking up for themselves, for cultural or other reasons.*

● *Fight racism in your school. See page 121.*

We know a 14-year-old student from Thailand who has been in the gifted program at his school for several years. He offers these thoughts and suggestions:

> "In school I haven't felt any discrimination as a result of being in the gifted program, but I am called names and teased because I am Hmong. When I'm teased, I use avoidance—I ignore the person or walk away because to do anything else is a waste of time. I have a lot of patience, and I try not to get stuck in arguments with people. I also talk with teachers about what's happened, rather than talking with friends, because teachers understand more.

> "If you are teased because of your race, I recommend talking with an adult about it—a principal or a teacher. You could also contact the Department of Human Rights to learn more about minority cultures and what to do about discrimination."

EIGHT WAYS TO FIGHT RACISM IN YOUR SCHOOL

1. Don't put up with racism. Don't laugh at racist jokes or join in on racist taunts—but don't just ignore them, either. You might say something like, "I don't think that joke is very funny." Or, "Don't call Michael that word. Call him by his name." Take a strong personal stand against racism, and let your friends know how you feel. Set a good example in the ways you talk about and treat people of different races. At first, your friends may give you a hard time. But eventually some of them may follow you.

2. Learn to recognize racist biases. Do students from one racial or ethnic group seem to win most of the awards at school assemblies? Do they seem to get more positive attention in the classroom? Are they encouraged more to achieve? Do they receive other forms of special treatment? Do students from a particular group seem to get praised more highly—or punished more harshly—than others?

3. If you have a conflict with a student of another race, don't immediately assume it's a racial conflict. Try to determine the real reason you're not getting along. If you need help, ask an adult you respect and trust.

4. Find out your school's policy regarding racist behavior. What happens when one student makes a racist remark about another? When a teacher makes a racist remark? When racial tensions lead to fights between groups of students? What are the penalties for these behaviors? Are they fair? Do they work?

5. Widen your circle of friends to include people from many races and cultural backgrounds. Do you tend to hang out only with people from your own racial or ethnic group? Look for an integrated club or team you can join. As you get to know students from other groups, you'll feel more comfortable with them, and you'll start to see them as real people. (Naturally, this goes both ways.)

6. Learn about other cultures. Read books. Watch TV programs and movies. Listen to music. Sample ethnic foods at restaurants, or at home, using cookbooks borrowed from the library. The more you learn, the more you'll start to question your own prejudices and stereotyped thinking. Learn more about your own culture, too. Feel proud of who you are and where you come from.

7. Talk about your racist feelings. Even if we don't realize it or admit it, we all have racist feelings. Don't just ignore yours. Talk about them with an adult you respect and trust—a parent, teacher, counselor, religious leader, or friend. You might be surprised when the adult says, "Yes, I sometimes have those thoughts and feelings, too. Here's how I handle them. . . ."

8. Work for positive change. Paint over racist graffiti. Remove racist words from your vocabulary. Brainstorm a list of other ways you can fight racism in your school.

You don't have to like everybody, but *you can only like or dislike people you know*. When you give people a chance—when you knock down the barriers of racism, prejudice, and stereotyped thinking—you may find yourself with more friends than you can count. And you will make a difference in your school, your community—and the world.

GIFTED PEOPLE SPEAK OUT

Danita Salone, 21

I've been in gifted and talented programs all through school, beginning in about third grade. What I've experienced most in terms of discrimination has been in relationship to my peers within my own culture. Many black people would think I was trying to be white because I was in those programs and spoke differently, and that would really hurt. As a teenager, I was once confronted by a group of black girls who asked me, "What color do you think you are? What are you trying to be?" It was very tense—they literally blocked my path in the school hallway. I was scared, of course, especially since no one was around at the time. I worried that they could have been physically depending on my reaction—if I'd gotten mouthy. I told them that they might believe I was trying to be white, but it wasn't true, and that I didn't see myself as being any better than they were. I didn't react by getting physical with them. It was a difficult situation.

I enjoyed the gifted programs and having the opportunity to progress in school. But sometimes I would regret being in them from an acceptance standpoint within my own culture. I wasn't accepted by my peers, and I wished people could have understood how hard that was. Usually, out of a class of 30 students identified as gifted, there would be two or three black students. There would be few minority groups represented as a whole.

I didn't ever feel discriminated against by teachers in the gifted programs. That helped a lot, because even when I left the special class and returned to the regular classroom where gifted students might be considered "different" and it wasn't as comfortable for me, I knew I would be supported or consoled by my teachers from the gifted program. Throughout my schooling, I always counted on them for help with special problems.

In my experience, it really helps to talk about discrimination and to learn to accept various points of view. I encourage other students to talk about what's going on with them. I'm willing to explain differences between our cultures. That's how people learn about each other. Having family support is also very important, because they're part of the same culture. My family has always been very supportive of me. Friends can be consoling to some degree, but they may not understand fully what you're going through.

I'm not your stereotypical black. For example, people have told me that I don't talk "like a black person," and I think comments like that are odd. At times, I've tried to learn how to speak more like the stereotype of how a black person is "supposed to" talk, but I'm not comfortable doing that. Whenever I've tried to be different from who I am in order to fit in, it just didn't work. You can try to change, but you know that's not you, so it won't feel comfortable.

Even today, things aren't easy for me because I face the same problems. Sometimes I feel down and even cry. What helps me is to remember who I am inside and to keep building that up. People may make fun of you, but only you can decide if conforming is what you really want to do. I think it's important to build your personal foundation stronger so you can stand by your beliefs. Take time out—actually stop—and take notice of your surroundings, and ask yourself, "What do I want to do?" That helps me to recognize who I am, and it gives me direction. Look at yourself rather than looking at who or what others think you are.

Danita Salone is a senior at a university in the Midwest, where she is pursuing a double major in marketing and international business with a minor in communications. During the 1995–1996 school year, she was student body president. She speaks fluent Spanish and studied in Mexico while in high school and college.

Find Out More

To learn more about ethnic issues, discrimination, and tolerance, read:

Duvall, Lynn. *Respecting Our Differences: A Guide to Getting Along in a Changing World.* Minneapolis: Free Spirit Publishing, 1994.

Dresser, Norine. *I Felt Like I Was From Another Planet.* Reading, MA: Addison-Wesley, 1994.

Teaching Tolerance Magazine. This respected publication from the Southern Poverty Law Center is published "for" adults but offers a lot for teens, too. It's free to educators, so you might encourage your school librarian to subscribe. For more information, write to: Teaching Tolerance, 400 Washington Avenue, Montgomery, AL 36104.

Stress

Expectations, perfectionism, multipotential, stereotypes; these are some of the stressors experienced by many gifted young people. Gifted teens have also told us that they feel stressed when they:

- *suffer an excessive fear of failure*
- *don't fit in with their peers*
- *try to do too much*
- *feel that they have too many options and choices in their lives*
- *are stuck with dull, routine classes and schoolwork*
- *have difficulty finding friends who accept them as they are*
- *feel that they need to compete with their siblings or classmates*
- *have too few challenges in school*
- *are teased about being gifted and talented*
- *feel compelled to do their best at everything.*

"The process of living is the process of reacting to stress."
Dr. Stanley J. Sarnoff

Add to these the normal stressors of adolescence—school, family, and peer pressures, relationships, physical and emotional changes, sex and sexuality issues, worries about violence, concerns about community and world problems, the search for meaning, and so on *ad infinitum*—and it's no wonder you sometimes (or often) feel burned out, oppressed, and depressed.

"I'VE ALWAYS BEEN CONSIDERED A SO-CALLED GENIUS, BUT I REALLY LOST IT FOR A FEW YEARS. I COULDN'T UNDERSTAND WHAT WAS GOING ON, AND I COULDN'T FIND A WAY OUT OF MY RUT. I REALIZED THAT I'M BASICALLY A NORMAL TEENAGER BUT THAT I'M ALSO HIGHLY STRESSED AND ANXIETY-RIDDEN. REALIZING THIS, AND LEARNING HOW TO COMBAT IT, SAVED MY MIND." AMANDA, 15

"I HAVE WAY TOO MUCH ON MY PLATE." PAUL, 13

"PEOPLE'S UNREALISTIC EXPECTATIONS ABOUT MY PERFORMANCE, SOCIAL AWKWARDNESS, BEING STEREO TYPED BY PEERS, LONELINESS AND CONFUSION MAKE ME JUST WANT TO SHOUT, 'LEAVE ME ALONE!'" CHARITY, 17

Stress is your body's way of telling you that things aren't quite right in your life. Or perhaps you feel elated about a particular idea, project, or event; strange as it may seem, excitement is another form of stress.

It's important to recognize that not all stress is bad. In fact, a certain amount of stress enables us to improve our performance, increase our productivity, be more alert, and ultimately get more out of life. But if the stress you're experiencing goes beyond what might be categorized as "mild," or if even mild stress is prolonged, your physical and mental health may be compromised or jeopardized.

The consequences of intense or prolonged stress vary from individual to individual. Generally speaking, people without appropriate outlets for coping with undue anxiety or strain exhibit one or more of the following behaviors:

- nervousness
- excessive daydreaming
- apathy
- laziness
- withdrawal

- chemical abuse
- truancy
- vandalism
- hostility
- suicidal thoughts.

"Contemporary American society has struck teenagers a double blow. It has rendered them more vulnerable to stress while at the same time exposing them to new and more powerful stresses than were ever faced by previous generations of adolescents."
David Elkind

How stressed are you? One way to find out is by taking the "Measuring Emotional Stress" survey on pages 126–28.* Developed by the University of Minnesota Adolescent Health Program, this questionnaire is a subset of items taken from a larger statewide survey of teens in Minnesota.**

* Notice the permission to photocopy statement at the bottom of each page of the survey. If this book doesn't belong to you, please photocopy the survey before you start marking it. Even if this book does belong to you, making a photocopy now will enable you to take the survey again at a later date.

** The items on the survey are not copyrighted, and the authors encourage practitioners and researchers to use the questionnaire. Copies of the complete survey, as well as related monograph reports and a publications list, are available from the National Adolescent Health Resource Center, Box 721, UMHC, 420 Delaware Street S.E., Minneapolis, MN 55455; telephone (612) 624-8644.

For questions 1–14, check the box beside the statement that best represents your response.

1. How have you been feeling in general (during the past month)?

0 ❏ In an excellent mood
1 ❏ In a very good mood
2 ❏ My moods have been up and down a lot

3 ❏ In a bad mood
4 ❏ In a very bad mood

2. Have you been bothered by nervousness or your "nerves" (during the past month)?

4 ❏ Extremely so, to the point where I couldn't work/take care of things
3 ❏ Quite a bit

2 ❏ Some, enough to bother me
1 ❏ A little
0 ❏ Not at all

3. Have you felt in control of your behavior, thoughts, emotions, or feelings (during the past month)?

0 ❏ Yes, for sure
1 ❏ Yes, sort of
2 ❏ Not very much

3 ❏ No, and it bothers me a bit
4 ❏ No, and it bothers me a lot

4. Have you felt so sad, discouraged, hopeless, or had so many problems that you wondered if anything was worthwhile (during the past month)?

4 ❏ Extremely so, to the point that I have just about given up
3 ❏ Quite a bit

2 ❏ Some, enough to bother me
1 ❏ A little bit
0 ❏ Not at all

5. Have you felt you were under any strain, stress, or pressure (during the past month)?

4 ❏ Yes, almost more than I could take
3 ❏ Yes, quite a bit of pressure

2 ❏ Yes, some/more than usual
1 ❏ Yes, a little/about usual
0 ❏ Not at all

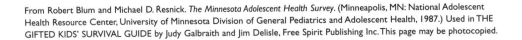

From Robert Blum and Michael D. Resnick. *The Minnesota Adolescent Health Survey*. (Minneapolis, MN: National Adolescent Health Resource Center, University of Minnesota Division of General Pediatrics and Adolescent Health, 1987.) Used in THE GIFTED KIDS' SURVIVAL GUIDE by Judy Galbraith and Jim Delisle, Free Spirit Publishing Inc. This page may be photocopied.

6. **How happy or satisfied or pleased have you been with your personal life (during the past month)?**

   0 ☐ Extremely happy, could not have been more satisfied or pleased

   1 ☐ Very happy
   2 ☐ Satisfied, pleased
   3 ☐ Somewhat satisfied
   4 ☐ Very dissatisfied

7. **Have you worried that you might be losing your mind or losing control over the way you act, talk, think, feel, or of your memory (during the past month)?**

   0 ☐ Not at all
   1 ☐ A little bit
   2 ☐ Some, enough to bother me

   3 ☐ Quite a bit
   4 ☐ Very much so

8. **Have you been waking up fresh and rested (during the past month)?**

   0 ☐ Every day
   1 ☐ Most every day
   2 ☐ Less than half the time

   3 ☐ Rarely
   4 ☐ None of the time

9. **Have you been bothered by any illness, bodily disorder, pains, or fear about your health (during the past month)?**

   4 ☐ All of the time
   3 ☐ Most of the time
   2 ☐ Some of the time

   1 ☐ A little of the time
   0 ☐ None of the time

10. **Has your daily life been full of things that were interesting to you (during the past month)?**

    0 ☐ All of the time
    1 ☐ Most of the time
    2 ☐ Some of the time

    3 ☐ A little of the time
    4 ☐ None of the time

11. **Have you felt sad (during the past month)?**

    4 ☐ All of the time
    3 ☐ Most of the time
    2 ☐ Some of the time

    1 ☐ A little of the time
    0 ☐ None of the time

From Robert Blum and Michael D. Resnick. *The Minnesota Adolescent Health Survey.* (Minneapolis, MN: National Adolescent Health Resource Center, University of Minnesota Division of General Pediatrics and Adolescent Health, 1987.) Used in THE GIFTED KIDS' SURVIVAL GUIDE by Judy Galbraith and Jim Delisle, Free Spirit Publishing Inc. This page may be photocopied.

12. Have you been feeling emotionally secure and sure of yourself (during the past month)?

0 ❏ All of the time   3 ❏ A little of the time
1 ❏ Most of the time   4 ❏ None of the time
2 ❏ Some of the time

13. Have you felt anxious, worried, or upset (during the past month)?

4 ❏ All of the time   1 ❏ A little of the time
3 ❏ Most of the time   0 ❏ None of the time
2 ❏ Some of the time

14. Have you felt tired, worn out, burned out, or exhausted (during the past month)?

4 ❏ All of the time   1 ❏ A little of the time
3 ❏ Most of the time   0 ❏ None of the time
2 ❏ Some of the time

For questions 15–17, circle the number on the continuum that best represents your feeling.

15. How relaxed or tense have you felt (during the past month)?

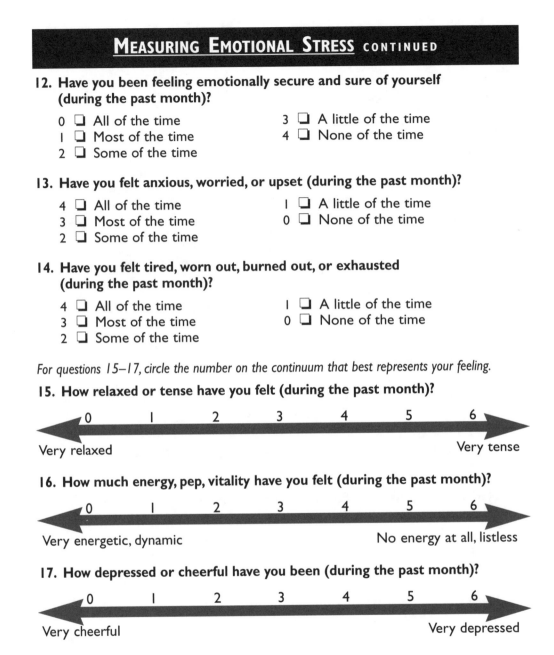

0   1   2   3   4   5   6

Very relaxed   Very tense

16. How much energy, pep, vitality have you felt (during the past month)?

0   1   2   3   4   5   6

Very energetic, dynamic   No energy at all, listless

17. How depressed or cheerful have you been (during the past month)?

0   1   2   3   4   5   6

Very cheerful   Very depressed

SCORING:

Add up the points beside the responses you checked for questions 1–14 and those you circled for numbers 15–17. The lowest possible score is 0; the highest possible score is 74.

There is no "good score" or "bad score" for this survey. What's important is to decide for yourself whether stress is a problem in your everyday life. Does your score represent a manageable level of stress for you? Or does your stress level seem excessive?

From Robert Blum and Michael D. Resnick. *The Minnesota Adolescent Health Survey.* (Minneapolis, MN: National Adolescent Health Resource Center, University of Minnesota Division of General Pediatrics and Adolescent Health, 1987.) Used in THE GIFTED KIDS' SURVIVAL GUIDE by Judy Galbraith and Jim Delisle, Free Spirit Publishing Inc. This page may be photocopied.

**Taking
Charge of
Your Life**

Handling Stress

The first step toward handling the stress in your life consists of identifying the specific things (people, events, circumstances, etc.) that you associate with feeling anxious or pressured. Take time to think seriously about this and make a list of your top 5–10 stressors.

**"Rule Number 1 is, don't sweat the small stuff. Rule Number 2 is, it's all small stuff. And if you can't fight and you can't flee, flow."
Dr. Robert S. Eliot**

The second step is taking responsibility for the stress you're experiencing. Many of the gifted teens we talk with about stress have difficulty with this step. They seem to think that "someone else" or "something else" is causing their stress—a certain teacher, parents, friends (or the lack of friends), school, the multitude of choices available to them, even the world at large. In fact, stress comes from the *inside,* not the outside. You control your perceptions; you are responsible for your feelings. Other people can do or say things that "trigger" certain feelings within you, but they don't *make* you feel a certain way.

Which leads to the third step: taking positive action. There are at least three alternatives available to you:

1. You can diminish or eliminate the problem you associate with your stress;

2. You can change your attitude toward the problem; or

3. You can lower your stress level by engaging in one or more stress-reducing activities.

For example: If being teased causes you to feel anxious, you can 1) try to convince the person(s) to stop teasing you; 2) change your attitude so the teasing doesn't bother you; or 3) accept the teasing and lower your stress by taking a brisk walk or a bike ride, listening to calming music, or talking about the problem with someone you trust and respect.

Another example: A young man named Todd B. told us that tests caused a great deal of stress for him. After thinking and talking about this for a while, he realized that the tests themselves weren't the problem—his degree of preparedness was. The less he prepared for a test, the more anxious he felt. Once he identified the real problem, Todd took control. He made sure to schedule time to prepare for tests, and to bring home the books and materials he needed. He learned new study skills, which made his test preparation more focused and efficient. Todd's "test stress" problem didn't solve itself; he greatly diminished it by taking positive action.

Through patience, willingness, and trial-and-error, you'll discover what works best for you. Other gifted students have shared their favorite stress reducers with us. You might try one or more of these:

- *go to a movie or watch a video*
- *take a nap*
- *talk to somebody you know and trust*
- *slug something (not somebody)*
- *go for a ride*
- *visit your church, synagogue, temple, or mosque*
- *wander through a bookstore*
- *call a relative on the telephone*
- *work on a hobby*
- *do something nice for another person (anonymously).*

EIGHT STRESS REDUCTION TIPS

1. Think back to other times when you have successfully coped with a difficult situation, person, or event. What did you say? What did you do? You may be able to recycle those winning strategies.

2. Learn how to handle stress without alienating the people around you. Don't take it out on your family, friends, or teachers, even if you (erroneously) believe that they "caused" your stress.

3. Find a sounding board—someone who will listen and, if you want, offer honest, respectful, and trustworthy advice.

4. If you don't know how to relax, learn how. (See pages 132–36 for suggestions.) Maintaining our physical and mental health requires that we spend at least part of each day slowing down.

5. Develop and maintain your sense of humor. Many gifted people have a tendency to focus on the serious side of life. Laughter is a terrific stress-reducer.

6. Compile a "library" of stress reduction techniques. If one doesn't work for a particular situation, you can always try another.

7. Don't give up. Handling stress is a learned skill and an ongoing endeavor. Few of us are taught it in school; either we learn it on our own, or we find "teachers" at various junctures in our lives.

8. Always remember that you don't have to go it alone. Even in your darkest, most stressful hour, there's bound to be someone or somewhere you can turn to for help. Suggestions:

- *a supportive adult*
- *a friendly neighbor*
- *a teen clinic*
- *a crisis intervention center*
- *an emergency hotline*
- *the public library*
- *a stress management class*
- *your favorite friend*
- *a counselor.*

Find Out More

To learn more about stress, stress management, and relaxation, read:

Ayer, Eleanor H. *Everything You Need to Know About Stress.* New York: Rosen Publishing Group, 1994.

Hipp, Earl. *Fighting Invisible Tigers: A Stress Management Guide for Teens.* Minneapolis: Free Spirit Publishing, 1995.

Moser, Adolph. *Don't Pop Your Cork on Mondays! The Children's Anti-Stress Book.* Kansas City, MO: Landmark Editions, Inc., 1988. Although this book is written for younger readers, we recommend it because it's a thorough (and somewhat comic) introduction to stress management. There's a lot to be said for "short, sweet, and to the point," especially if you have a stressful schedule!

Two Tried-and-True Ways to Really Relax
Earl Hipp

Knowing how to relax is essential to maximizing your potential and maintaining your brain in tip-top shape. Without periods of relaxation, you lose your abilities to think straight and concentrate—much less generate brilliant or creative ideas.

There are many different types of relaxation skills, but they all have these three characteristics in common:

1. Because they are skills, they must be learned and practiced often.
2. They result in noticeable, measurable physiological changes.
3. They invite you to focus your attention on something besides "thinking."

Basically, relaxation is *nondoing*—something a lot of people find difficult. The goal of every relaxation technique is to be physically still while maintaining an alert but neutral mental state.

Watching TV is *not* a relaxation technique because your brain is busy, your mental focus isn't neutral, and the TV is in charge. Reading a book is *not* a relaxation technique because your mental focus is on the printed page. Sleeping is *not* a relaxation technique because it isn't a controlled state and you're not alert during it. (Plus dreams—especially bad dreams—can cause physical and emotional stress.) Having a cup of coffee is *not* a relaxation technique for obvious reasons.

Following are two simple "nonactivities" for you to try.

Deep Breathing

Your body and mind function together. When you're nervous, excited, or angry, your breathing is more rapid than usual and tends to move up in your chest (short, shallow breaths). When you're calm and relaxed, your breathing is slow and regular and located further down (deep, regular breaths). Slow, deep, regular breathing is the physical expression of a peaceful mind.

It's possible to consciously manipulate your breathing to achieve a restful mental state—even during times of stress. Here's how:

- *Start by finding something comfortable to lie on or sit on. Loosen any restrictive belts or tight clothing. Lie on your back or sit comfortably so your hips and legs relax.*
- *Keeping your mouth closed, inhale and exhale deeply through your nose three times. Now place your right hand on your stomach, just above your belly-button, and your left hand at the top of your chest. Notice where in your body your breathing is coming from.*
- *Now take a long, slow, deep breath into your chest. Your left hand should rise, but your right hand should stay still. Pause briefly, keeping your chest full, then exhale slowly through your nose.*

Notice which muscles are involved, the sensation of fullness at the pause, and the feeling of relaxation that comes with the slow, deliberate release of air.

Repeat this "chest breathing" three times. In . . . pause . . . out, in . . . pause . . . out, in . . . pause . . . out.

- *Take a break. Stop controlling your breathing and let it find its own rhythm and location.*
- *Now take a long, slow, deep breath into your stomach. Your right hand should rise while your left hand stays still. (This "belly breathing" will feel awkward at first, but be patient.) Repeat three times, then take another break and let your breathing return to its natural state.*

> "Rest is not a matter of doing absolutely nothing. Rest is repair."
> Daniel W. Josselyn

Now, keeping your hands in place, combine all of these breathing movements into one slow, continuous, four-count exercise, like this:

1. Count "one" and breathe into your belly so your right hand rises. Pause for a mini-second.

2. Count "two" and breathe into your chest so your left hand rises. Pause for a mini-second.

3. Count "three" and begin a controlled, gradual exhalation from your stomach so your right hand lowers. Pause for a mini-second.

4. Count "four" and slowly release the remaining air in your chest so your left hand lowers. When you feel that you have completely exhaled, pause for a mini-second before you start the cycle again.

Repeat this slow, rhythmic breathing for two to three minutes. Remember to alternate between chest breathing and belly breathing. When you are done, take a minute to let your breathing return to normal.

With practice, these four movements will all blend together and become more-or-less automatic, and you'll be able to call on this relaxation skill whenever you need it.

Meditation

Just as your heart beats endlessly, day in and day out, your mind produces an endless stream of thoughts. Even when you try to stop thinking, it's impossible. That's because your brain is a regular thinking machine! Even when you try to create a quiet space, thoughts keep pushing their way in.

Because your thoughts contain all of your fears, worries, and concerns, *you can be one of your own worst stressors.* Although you can't control the flow of your thoughts, you can get some relief from them by skillfully focusing your attention somewhere else.

If you were asked to move your attention to the bottom of your right foot, you'd suddenly become aware of what was going on there. We can shift our attention fairly easily, but learning to shift our mental focus to neutral is *the* primary challenge of all relaxation skills and the heart of most meditation activities. The instructions that follow can help you learn this skill of detaching from your thinking machine.

- *Find a firm chair and a blank wall to look at. Sit on the chair facing the wall with your back relaxed but straight. (This position may feel uncomfortable at first, but it's easier on your back in the long run.) Your feet should be flat on the floor. Fold your hands in your lap or lay them palms-down on top of your thighs.*
- *Keep your head upright and pull your chin in a little to keep your neck straight. Keep your eyes open and look down at about a 45-degree angle. Don't tilt your head; just look down.*

Once you're familiar with this basic posture, you're ready to proceed. There are only three important rules to remember:

1. Don't try to control your breathing. Just let it come naturally.
2. Don't move your body. Remain absolutely still.
3. Don't stop before the designated time is up.

Decide *before* you start how long you want to spend meditating. In the beginning, 5–8 minutes is about right. Later you may want to lengthen your sessions to 20 or even 30 minutes. It's helpful to set a timer so you aren't constantly distracted by looking at a clock. Start with one minute if you like, but don't quit before the time is up.

● *When you're comfortable and ready to begin, focus your attention on your breathing.*

● *Keeping your mouth closed, silently count "one" on the next inhalation and "two" on the exhalation, "three" on the next inhalation and "four" on the exhalation . . . and so on up to "ten." When you reach "ten," start over with "one" again on the next inhale.*

What to do if your brain tries to distract you with interesting thoughts, creative thoughts, bothersome thoughts, romantic thoughts, or whatever? As soon as you realize you've been sidetracked, go back to "one" and start counting again.

What to do if your body tries to distract you with twitches, itches, and "demands" to move? Go back to "one" and start counting again.

What to do if the world tries to distract you—if friends stop by, people knock on your door, your little brother barges in, or the next-door neighbor starts mowing the lawn? Go back to "one" and start counting again.

Try to set a regular time for your meditation—a time when you can be reasonably sure of not being interrupted. Choose a place that's off the beaten path (like your room, as long as you don't share it with 17 siblings). You may want to make a "Do Not Disturb" sign and hang it on your door. If you think that the people around you will understand, you may want to tell them what you're doing. It can be upsetting to see a young person sitting absolutely still, staring at a blank wall, if you don't know what he or she is doing and why.

Meditation is one of the greatest relaxers around. It slows down many of your body processes, including your heart rate and your breathing. It empties your mind of all sorts of extraneous thoughts. It settles and calms you from head to toe. People who meditate daily also claim that it gives them enormous amounts of energy, both physical and mental.

Earl Hipp is a speaker, trainer, consultant, and president of Human Resource Development, Inc. He is the author of Fighting Invisible Tigers: A Stress Management Guide for Teens *(Minneapolis: Free Spirit Publishing, 1995).*

Taking Charge of
Your Education

Sixty-eight percent of our survey respondents wanted to know how to get teachers to be more flexible (e.g., letting students test out of material they already know, skip some repetitive assignments, and/or pursue alternatives to traditional assignments). Thirty-nine percent were interested in learning how to be more productive in school, and 42 percent wanted to know why some gifted kids do poorly in school.

"HOW CAN I EXCEL MORE THAN MY SCHOOL WILL ALLOW?" MERIDITH, 13

Almost everyone wants school to be a positive experience—challenging, meaningful, interesting, enjoyable. The gifted students we've spoken with over the years report that the most important factors in a successful school experience are:

1. Teachers who:

- teach to students' individual learning levels, styles, and speeds
- are flexible
- challenge and motivate students
- encourage excellence but don't expect perfection
- don't pressure students or push too hard
- don't pretend to know everything
- respect their students' intelligence
- allow students to skip or test out of material they already know
- treat everyone like human beings
- have a good sense of humor
- help all students develop their talents and potential
- are willing to give specific help when it's needed (and requested)
- realize that gifted kids (like all young people) have lives outside of school.

2. Schools that:

- provide advanced courses, honors classes, and other opportunities beyond the standard curriculum,
- offer out-of-school options such as mentorships and community service projects, and
- provide opportunities for teachers and counselors to learn about the special needs of gifted students.

"I WANT TEACHERS TO UNDERSTAND US, TO BE FLEXIBLE, INTELLIGENT, AND TO NOT BE TRENDY BY FOCUSING ON GROUP WORK (BLEAH!)." ERIK, 14

"I'D LIKE TEACHERS TO UNDERSTAND THAT I'M NOT GIFTED IN ALL AREAS, AND THAT SOMETIMES I NEED HELP." GIRL, 14

But it's not entirely up to the teachers and the schools. It's also up to the students—including you. The successful students we interviewed shared these characteristics:

- They believed that they were responsible for their own performance. They didn't blame others when they did poorly (as in "I've got a lousy teacher for biology this year"), nor did they credit others for their achievements (as in "I got an A because the teacher likes me").
- They thought school was important but not all-important. They gave themselves time and space to enjoy other more social aspects of growing up.
- They understood and accepted that school isn't always 100 percent fulfilling—that it can be boring, maddening, and frustrating, too.

- *They perceived themselves as competent and capable.*
- *They didn't see themselves as failures if they achieved less than perfection, nor did they place too much emphasis on mistakes.*

More Labels

We all know people who "do school well"—students who are good assignment-finishers, test-takers, rule-obeyers, and fitters-into-the-status-quo. We all know kids whose performance lags behind their capabilities. And we all know students who take on enormous workloads and commitments, yet seem to do everything well.

Educators have labels for all three groups: "achievers," "underachievers," and "overachievers," respectively. Although there's some crossover among the categories—for example, the student who excels in science but struggles with (or could care less about) literature—students are usually pigeonholed into one of these categories. Each comes with its own set of assumptions and prognoses, which may or may not be accurate, justified, or fair. A label can work for you (especially for achievers), against you (underachievers, take note), or have little or no effect (if overachievers succeed at something, that's to be expected; if they fail, at least they tried).

Whichever label is applied to you, remember this: You are in charge of maintaining or changing the direction your efforts are taking you. Your teachers and parents may think they can predict your performance, but it's within your power to prove them right—or wrong.

Who Is School For?

The answer, of course, is that school is supposed to be for *everyone.* Ideally, we should all enter school at around age 5 and emerge at age 17 or 18 with a set of skills needed to survive as productive adults. By the time we graduate from high school, we should know how to read well, write competently, speak clearly and persuasively, listen carefully, solve problems, use math in our everyday lives, learn and remember new material, do research, have some grasp of the world beyond our immediate surroundings, and behave like responsible citizens.

> **"TEACHERS CAN'T HELP GIFTED STUDENTS UNTIL THEY RECOGNIZE THEM."** — BRIAN, 18

To that end, we are guided through a series of courses in English, math, science, history, social studies, family living, and myriad other topics, some of our own choosing. The core list of courses really hasn't changed much since your parents (and their parents) went to school, and perhaps that's as it should be. There are certain basics—reading, writing, arithmetic—we do need to know. Recently, there has also been an emphasis on "cultural literacy"—a body of "core knowledge" that all members of a society should hold in common.

Most schools do a decent job of teaching *average* kids *average* stuff. One reason for the emphasis on "average" is the need for cost-effectiveness. Schools have to get the most for their money because they simply don't have the funds to do everything. Except for those relatively few private schools with large endowments and wealthy supporters, they never have and never will. As a result, there isn't much room for creativity or so-called "extras." Students who need special assistance—a category that includes gifted kids as well as slow learners and students with disabilities—often get lost in the shuffle.

It doesn't help that gifted kids are sometimes assumed to "have it all" and not need individualized attention. The overworked teacher faced with a fourth grader who can't yet read at the first grade level and another who already reads at the eighth grade level will concentrate (understandably) on the slow reader. Apply this scenario to math, science, history, etc., and it's no wonder so many gifted students claim that school is boring, irrelevant, and unchallenging.

By the time you reach your senior year, you will have spent over 12,000 hours in school. You don't have to be a math whiz to figure out that this can translate into endless weeks, months, even years of daydreaming, thumb-twiddling, fingernail-biting, hair-twisting, toe-tapping, napping, and other coping strategies.

What you want is an education that fits the way your mind works. Nothing militant, nothing extraordinary; you just want to:

- *learn at your own speed*
- *opt out of work you already know and understand*
- *study things that interest you and go beyond the basics*

> **"IT'S FRUSTRATING TO KNOW THAT I'M NOT LEARNING A WHOLE LOT—ESPECIALLY CONSIDERING HOW MUCH TIME I SPEND IN SCHOOL. IT MAKES ME MAD."** ERIC, 13

> **"TO ME, THE READING WE DO IS SIMILAR TO WHAT WE DID IN FIRST GRADE! TEACHERS COULD HELP US BY CHALLENGING US—BY DOING THINGS THAT INTEREST US."** ELIZABETH ANN, 11

> **"HOMEWORK IS SUPPOSED TO BE PRACTICE TO MASTER A SKILL. IF YOU'VE ALREADY MASTERED A SKILL, WHY PRACTICE IT?"** ERIC, 14

"In pursuit of an educational program to suit the bright and not-so-bright we have watered down a rigid training for the elite until we now have an educational diet in many of our public high schools that nourishes neither the classes nor the masses."
Agnes Meyer

- work with abstract concepts that require more than simple thinking—such as creative, reflective, and analytical ideas
- work with peers who share your interests and abilities
- participate in options that connect your learning to the "real world."

When you don't have opportunities to stretch your mind in at least some of these ways, you get bored. And when you get bored, you may act out or drop out—by quitting school before graduation (for example, to work full-time at a job that seems more meaningful to you), or by mentally withdrawing into yourself and giving up on school.

Your Rights as a Student

Do you have the right to a challenging and appropriate education? Unequivocally, yes. Will your right always be recognized and respected? Unfortunately, no. But understanding that you do have

"It's kind of depressing to find out now, in my junior year, that it's okay for me to ask for things in school. It just never occurred to me that I could. I'd always assumed that I didn't have the right to ask for anything to be different, and that adults always knew what was best for me." Alicia, 17

rights as a student— and knowing what they are—is the first step toward getting what you want and need from school.

Many students we've heard from over the years feel powerless to do anything about their school situation. These feelings can prevent you from taking action.

What exactly are your rights relative to your education? Ideally, you should be able to place them on a continuum showing that the more you know and master, the more rights (and responsibilities) you have.

Infant ⟶ **Student** ⟶ **Adult**
Few educational rights   Some educational rights   Many educational rights
No responsibilities   Some responsibilities   Many responsibilities

But we don't live in an ideal world. Some adults still adhere to the antiquated belief that "children should be seen and not heard." Not all, but enough to make some kids' lives miserable. The good news is that such authoritarian attitudes have become less popular in recent years. From time immemorial, parents (and teachers) have ruled with an iron hand; today many families and schools are working to establish a more democratic balance, and many adults are recognizing that young people aren't pawns to be

"Everything we learn doesn't have to be relevant. But if some of our school learning isn't meaningful, we may get turned off enough so that we don't want to learn anything anywhere. We may simply drop out."
William Glasser

141

controlled and taught conformity. Still, old habits die hard. When you advocate for change in your school program, you're probably going to create headaches for some teachers. Keep in mind that your needs aren't "frills" but necessities for you. *It is your right to request and receive a quality education suited to your learning abilities and needs.*

In 1980, author Marilyn Ferguson helped pave the way for change with her groundbreaking book, *The Aquarian Conspiracy.* When she compared old assumptions about education with new assumptions about learning based on scientific discoveries and changes being made by individuals in society, this is what she found:*

Assumptions of the Old Paradigm of Education	**Assumptions of the New Paradigm of Learning**
Emphasis on *content;* acquiring a body of "right" information, once and for all.	Emphasis on learning how to learn; how to ask good questions, pay attention to the right things, be open to and evaluate new concepts, access information. What is now "known" may change. Importance of *context.*
Learning as a *product,* a destination.	Learning as a *process,* a journey.
Hierarchical and authoritarian structure. Rewards conformity, discourages dissent.	Egalitarian. Candor and dissent permitted. Students and teachers see each other as people, not roles. Encourages autonomy.
Relatively rigid structure; prescribed curriculum.	Relatively flexible structure. Belief that there are many ways to teach a given subject.
Lockstep progress, emphasis on the "appropriate" ages for certain activities, age segregation. Compartmentalized.	Flexibility and integration of age groupings. Individuals not automatically limited to certain subject matter by age.
Priority on performance.	Priority on self-image as the generator of performance.
Emphasis on external world. Inner experience often considered inappropriate in school setting.	Inner experience seen as context for learning. Use of imagery, storytelling, dream journals, "centering" exercises, and exploration of feelings encouraged.

---

* From *The Aquarian Conspiracy* by Marilyn Ferguson (Los Angeles: Jeremy P. Tarcher, Inc., 1987), p. 289–291. Copyright © by Marilyn Ferguson. Reprinted by permission of the publisher, Jeremy P. Tarcher, Inc.

Assumptions of the Old Paradigm of Education, *cont.*	Assumptions of the New Paradigm of Learning, *cont.*
Guessing and divergent thinking discouraged.	Guessing and divergent thinking encouraged as part of the creative process.
Emphasis on analytical, linear, left-brain thinking.	Strives for whole-brain education. Augments left-brain rationality with holistic, nonlinear, and intuitive strategies. Confluence and fusion of the two processes emphasized.
Labeling (remedial, gifted, minimally brain dysfunctional, etc.) contributes to self-fulfilling prophecy.	Labeling used only in minor prescriptive role and not as fixed evaluation that dogs the individual's educational career.
Concern with norms.	Concern with the individual's performance in terms of potential. Interest in testing outer limits, transcending perceived limitations.
Primary reliance on theoretical, abstract "book knowledge."	Theoretical and abstract knowledge heavily complemented by experiment and experience, both in and out of classroom. Field trips, apprenticeships, demonstrations, visiting experts.
Classrooms designed for efficiency, convenience.	Concern for the environment of learning: lighting, colors, air, physical comfort, needs for privacy and interaction, quiet and exuberant activities.
Bureaucratically determined, resistant to community input.	Encourages community input, even community control.
Education seen as a social necessity for a certain period of time, to inculcate minimal skills and train for a specific role.	Education seen as lifelong process, one only tangentially related to schools.
Increasing reliance on technology (audiovisual equipment, computers, tapes, texts), dehumanization.	Appropriate technology, human relationships between teachers and learners of primary importance.
Teacher imparts knowledge; one-way street.	Teacher is learner, too, learning from students.

In summary, Ferguson writes:

> "The old assumptions generate questions about how to achieve norms, obedience, and correct answers. The new assumptions lead to questions about how to motivate for lifelong learning, how to strengthen self-discipline, how to awaken curiosity, and how to encourage creative risk in people of all ages."

Despite the fact these ideas first appeared in 1980, they have improved with age. Many educational associations (e.g., the National Council for Teachers of Mathematics) are now looking for ways to make these goals real in school.

How many of the "new" assumptions are in place at your school? All of them? Some of them? One? None? Keep in mind that traditional ways of thinking don't change overnight—and sometimes not even in a decade or more. If you try to transform your school single-handedly, you'll be heading straight for trouble. However, you *can* take care of yourself by:

- *being assertive,*
- *pursuing available alternatives, and*
- *ensuring that your personal integrity isn't jeopardized.*

Going this route establishes you as an example worth following and may inspire others to reassess their own beliefs.

Asserting Your Rights

It's possible that you're satisfied with your school experience. If so, skip or skim this section. But if you're not altogether happy with school, you're not alone. The majority of the gifted students we've talked to think that school could be considerably more satisfying. Here are a few of the most common complaints we've heard:

> "A lot of homework, classroom activities, and rules don't have any point or don't make any sense."

> "A teacher shouldn't expect us to know everything. Otherwise, why are we going to school?"

> "I spend too much time waiting for the next new thing to be presented. I always seem to learn things more quickly than most of the other kids in my classes."

> "I'm forced to memorize instead of being taught how to think and how to learn."

Whatever your particular gripe might be, *you can do something about it.* You might begin by finding out where your school stands in terms of student rights, especially as they pertain to your specific situation in your community. Questions like the following can get you started thinking:

- *What can I expect from school as it relates to my interests and abilities?*
- *If I'm interested in a subject that isn't offered by my school, or if my abilities exceed what the standard curriculum has to offer, whose responsibility is it to find an alternative for me? Do I have the right to an alternative?*
- *Do I have the right to have some say in planning at least part of my curriculum?*
- *Do I have the right to work at my own pace rather than follow arbitrary timelines?*
- *Have my teachers received any special training in working with high-ability students? Have they learned alternative ways to challenge students? Has the school made a commitment to teaching thinking skills?*
- *Do I have the right to be recognized, even rewarded, for scholastic achievements? (Gifted athletes are recognized and rewarded; why not gifted artists, scholars, debaters, chemists, computer experts, journalists, etc.?)*

What other questions do you have about your rights vis-à-vis the quality of your education? To clarify your thinking, you might want to make a list.

Three Steps Toward Change

If you're in a special program for the gifted and talented—if your school offers challenges and opportunities commensurate with your abilities and interests—then you may be more acutely aware of shortcomings in your school's regular curriculum. Gifted program or not, if you're dissatisfied with a particular assignment, class, or other aspect of school and you don't ask for something different, no one else is going to ask for you.

"WITHOUT THE GIFTED PROGRAM I WOULD HAVE NO REASON TO GO TO SCHOOL." GIRL, 12

When trying to effect changes in your educational program, you might follow these three steps:

1. Be informed. Know your rights.
2. Identify your needs, interests, and ideas.
3. Prioritize your needs and interests. Choose the top two or three and plan your strategy around them.

Step 1: Be informed. Know your rights.

If you have a supportive teacher or guidance counselor, start by asking what he or she knows about students' rights in your school. Find out if anything on this topic has been formalized in writing, and if it has, request a copy.

> "It has always seemed strange to me that in our endless discussions about education so little stress is ever laid on the pleasure of becoming an educated person, the enormous interest it adds to life."
> Edith Hamilton

> "We know what happens to people who stay in the middle of the road; they get run over."
> Aneurin Bevan

States, school districts, and some individual schools have formulated philosophy, mission, or policy statements that describe their goals and objectives for education. Some are specific to the needs of gifted and talented students. You have a right to see such documents, if they exist at your school, but don't expect someone to just hand them to you. Ask!

Here are two examples of statements that focus on gifted students:

**"Ignorance is
not bliss."
American Library
Association**

From the California State Board of Education Policy Statement: "This State Board of Education policy statement reaffirms the importance of ensuring that every student is challenged to reach his or her potential, and charges local educational agencies to re-examine policies and procedures to make sure that all students, including gifted and advanced learners, are provided with rigorous educational opportunities commensurate with their accomplishments and needs....We should realize each student's potential, including students with outstanding gifts or talent potential. Just as underachieving students need supportive intervention, so the most advanced students should receive careful attention and program planning to ensure that they are provided opportunities to stretch and extend their knowledge and skills. No limits should ever be set on how much, or how fast students may learn."

From the Florida Statutes Pertaining to Exceptional Students: "The term 'exceptional students' includes students who are gifted....The school board [shall] provide for an appropriate program of special instruction, facilities, and services for exceptional students....the superintendent, principals, and teachers shall utilize the regular school facilities and adapt them to the needs of exceptional students to the maximum extent appropriate.... [Specialization requirements for teachers of the gifted include] fifteen (15) semester hours in gifted education.... Districts shall be responsible for developing educational plans for students who are gifted."

When and if you locate and learn the goals and objectives that pertain to your school, chances are you'll discover that your rights are already represented in whole or in part. Your school district probably recognizes your right to an education that meets your needs—at least on paper. The Big Question is: What, if anything, is being done in real life?

As you read your school's goals statements, highlight the catch phrases. You can use them later to substantiate your case for alternative education proposals. Here are some sample phrases pulled from several school districts' goal statements:

> *academic recognition . . . challenged to reach highest intellectual potential . . . changing society . . . commensurate with potential/ability . . . creative development . . . differentiated learning experiences . . . enrichment . . . equal opportunity . . . expanded opportunities . . . individual independence . . . meeting student needs and interests . . . prevention strategies . . . relevant curriculum . . . scholastic pursuits . . . social pursuits . . . standards for excellence . . . student exploration . . . superior ability . . . underserved populations.*

Once you're informed about the situation in your school— once you know what's already in place for you to work with— you're ready to move on.

Step 2: Identify your needs, interests, and ideas.

The following questions are meant to help you plan and articulate the questions you'll ask your teachers and administrators. Think about which individuals you'll need to approach. TIP: Choose the ones who have the power to make changes—for example, an influential teacher, your principal, the curriculum coordinator, or the superintendent.

1. In what ways are your educational needs already being met? (Whenever you're trying to implement changes that require enlisting the cooperation of others, it's smart to start with the positives. School usually isn't all bad.)
2. In what ways are your educational needs not being met? (Be specific.)
3. What changes do you think need to be made for school to be more meaningful, relevant, exciting, engaging, and challenging for you? (Again, be specific. Example: If you're tired of having to "learn" material you already know, you might suggest that you take a test to prove what you know, then use class time for a project or activity of your choosing.)

When gifted students in Arkansas were asked to brainstorm ways to get more out of school, they came up with these ideas:

go into greater depth . . . skip a grade level . . . be able to ask more questions without being ridiculed . . . have a positive outlook . . . participate in extracurricular activities . . . work ahead . . . be able to talk more with teachers . . . have more time to read . . . develop our emotional selves . . . meditate . . . learn to think more creatively . . . have time to draw . . . be able to change teachers when we don't "click" with someone . . . take extra classes . . . take college-level classes . . . have greater variety in class offerings, such as more foreign languages . . . be able to ask teachers for alternatives to regular assignments, such as writing papers . . . have more time to talk with other students about things that interest us . . . do independent studies . . . take Advanced Placement courses . . . have more time to sleep . . . be able to play music, listen to music, write music . . . help others.

Remember: *It's up to you to ask for changes.* If you wait for your school to metamorphose on its own, you may wait a lonnnnnnnnnnnnng time.

> "There are risks and costs to a program of action. But they are far less than the long-range risks and costs of comfortable inaction."
> John F. Kennedy

Step 3: Prioritize your needs and interests. Choose the top two or three and plan your strategy around them.

It isn't easy to take responsibility for your own education. But for many gifted people, not doing anything is even more tortuous. Sooner or later, they end up making choices that are unsatisfying, unhealthy, and/or unproductive.

> "IT HAS FINALLY DAWNED ON ME THAT IF THE SYSTEM WON'T CHANGE, IT'S UP TO ME TO MAKE MY CLASSES MORE INTERESTING. NOW, AS A RESULT OF LEARNING TO DO THINGS DIFFERENTLY, I CAN HONESTLY SAY SCHOOL IS REALLY LOOKING UP! ALL THE ACTION FEELS GOOD—I'M HAVING FUN. I'VE REALIZED I HAVE MORE OPPORTUNITIES AND CHOICES AVAILABLE TO ME THAN MOST KIDS. ALL I HAVE TO DO IS GO GET THEM." JANICE, 15

Once you have decided on a specific issue you want to start addressing in school, *put it in writing.* Some students find a proposal format helpful. A proposal shows teachers that you're serious, you've spent time and effort formulating your plan, and you aren't expecting them to do all of the work.

Make your proposal as clear, concise, and comprehensive as you can. Not only will this impress your teachers; it will also give you room to negotiate. You might use the following outline to start organizing and formalizing your thoughts.

Proposal

I.   Goal (what you want to change about school)
II. Steps (what you plan to do to reach your goal)
III. Resources (the people and things you need to reach your goal)

IV. Roadblocks (the people and things that might get in your way and impede your progress toward your goal)

V. Rewards (what you expect to get out of reaching your goal).

Let's say that your American Literature class has been studying T.S. Eliot's poem, "The Love Song of J. Alfred Prufrock." Your teacher has assigned a written report on the poem, but you'd like to try something different. See pages 150–51 for an example of how your proposal might look.

Creative Problem Solving

As an alternative to the Three Steps Toward Change described above, you might want to try a technique called Creative Problem Solving, or CPS for short. Developed by Dr. Alex Osborn, an advertising executive, and Dr. Sidney Parnes, a professor of creative studies, this famous five-step process has helped many students (and adults) to maximize their creative thinking and resolve difficult challenges. Here's how it works.

Step 1: Determine the facts.

By determining the facts related to your problem, you can start to see the whole picture. (Rarely is a problem just one problem. Usually it's several problems linked together.) Start by listing what you want to change or accomplish, using as many specifics as you can. Ask yourself these questions about the problem: Who? What? When? Where? How? Example:

● *Who seems to be preventing you from learning something new in English class?*

● *What happens to make that class seem irrelevant and/or dreary to you?*

● *When does it happen?*

● *Where does it happen?*

● *How does it happen?*

Step 2: Analyze the problem.

Here's where you begin to focus in on specific aspects of the problem. Ask yourself this question: Why? Examples:

● *Why am I having a problem in English class?*

● *Why do I feel like falling asleep at 10:26 A.M. every day?*

● *Why haven't I done anything to change the situation?*

● ●

PROPOSAL FOR AMERICAN LIT "PRUFROCK" ASSIGNMENT

Prepared by: _____   Prepared for: _____
                        name   teacher's name

Today's date: _____

I. Goal

To be able to use my artistic abilities in other subjects than art class. *Specifically:* Instead of writing a report on T.S. Eliot's poem, "The Love Song of J. Alfred Prufrock," for my American Lit class, I'd like to do a photo essay about it, using digital photographs so I can edit and manipulate them on the computer.

II. Steps

A. Get to know the poem. Read it and listen to recordings of it being read.
B. Read about the poem. Learn more about its history and find out what critics have said about it. See if anyone has ever tried to illustrate it.
C. Make a list of the kinds of pictures I want to take, based on my research. Show to American Lit teacher for discussion and approval.
D. Find out about borrowing the digital camera from the computer department.
E. Schedule time with the office to use the stage in the auditorium. (I think that's where I want to take the pictures.)
F. Take the pictures.
G. Download the pictures from the camera to a computer.
H. Schedule time to edit the pictures in Photoshop, add quotes from the poems, and create a digital slide show.
I. Arrange to present my slide show to the teacher and/or the class. (Maybe put it on CD-ROM?)

III. Resources

A. Books and articles about Eliot. Recordings of the poem being read aloud. (Check school library, local library, interlibrary loan, university library, Internet. Try to find a recording of Eliot reading it?).
B. Articles and critical essays about the poem. (Check periodicals indexes, microfiches, CD-ROMs, Internet. Find out when the poem was first published, then look for reviews from around that time.)
C. A cassette recorder for dictating notes to myself. (Ask Mom if I can borrow hers.)
D. A digital camera. (Ask computer department.)
E. Models. (Members of the Drama Club? Or students in American Lit?)
F. Props and costumes. (Ask Drama Club, English department.)
G. Computer time and hard drive space. (Remember that graphics take up a lot of space!).
H. CD-ROM burner and blank CD? (Not essential but would be nice.)

● ●

IV. Roadblocks

A. No one has ever done this type of project before (at least, not that I know about). The teacher may be reluctant to let me do something different from the rest of the class. *Possible solution:* Arrange a conference with the teacher to talk about the poem. I'll be doing as much research as anyone else, just using it differently. Prove that I know about the poem and can discuss it intelligently. *Also:* See if other students in the class want to work on the photo essay with me as a shared project? Then I won't be the only nonconformist! *Plus:* The School Philosophy Statement allows for "creative development," "differentiated learning experiences," "student exploration," "individual independence," "artistic pursuits," and "challenge to reach potential." I believe that my project fits all of these.

B. I may not be able to use the stage during school play time. *Possible solution:* Set up a studio in a garage or basement.

C. I may not be able to borrow the digital camera. *Possible solution:* See about renting one from Kinko's.

D. Drama Club members may not want to be models. *Possible solution:* Ask my friends or, as a last resort, my family!

E. Drama Club and English department may not let me use costumes and props. *Possible solution:* Rent clothes from the Old-Time Costume Emporium; rent props from Prop-Finders? (Or see if they'll let me borrow them for free if I give them credit in my presentation?)

V. Rewards

A. Credit for doing the assignment.

B. A chance to show my photography somewhere outside the art department.

C. More experience working with digital photography and Photoshop.

D. More experience working with live models, props, costumes.

E. Getting to know and work with students in the Drama Club.

F. Becoming a better photographer.

G. Helping other students understand the poem better. ("A picture is worth a thousand words.")

H. A great learning experience

SIGNED:

_____   _____
Student   Teacher

_____   _____
Date   Date

Step 3: Brainstorm potential solutions.

List as many solutions to the problem as possible. You probably already know the basic rules of brainstorming, but in case they're not fresh in your mind, here they are:

- *Come up with as many ideas as you can. In brainstorming, quantity breeds quality.*
- *Defer judgment of ideas. Criticism is taboo.*
- *Be wild, zany, and free. Accept every idea.*
- *Combine or improve on ideas. Piggyback, substitute, magnify, minify, eliminate, reverse, turn inside out, etc.*
- *Don't give up when there's a lull in production. This usually signifies a break between obvious and new ideas.*

Step 4: Evaluate potential solutions.

Look closely at your brainstormed list. Evaluate each idea according to your values and needs. Weigh each against the factors that will make the solution possible or impossible. Things to consider might include:

- *How much time will it involve?*
- *How much effort will it take?*
- *How much will it cost?*
- *What will I be risking?*
- *Who will I be helping? Who will I be hurting?*
- *Who can I approach as possible allies—people who will help me?*
- *How many people will I need?*
- *Is it legal?*
- *Is it ethical?*

Step 5: Select and carry out a solution.

Choose the solution that seems best to you and put it into action. If you have followed the five steps of CPS, you should now have a viable approach mapped out and ready to go.

CPS Tips

1. If a compelling solution comes to mind before you finish all five steps, stop and try it. You don't have to wait until you complete the process.

2. If you get stuck or encounter new problems, start over again to gain a fresh perspective.

3. You can do CPS alone or in a group. If you're in a group, remember that the brainstormed ideas belong to the group, not to individuals within the group. In Step 4, be sure to evaluate the ideas, not the people who offered them.

4. Don't expect to master CPS immediately. Practice will enable you to improve your technique.

5. Have fun! CPS really is *creative* problem solving. Enjoy the experience of focusing on a problem, figuring it out, brainstorming a variety of possible solutions, and trying one (or more) that seems promising. Learn from your failures and savor your successes.

Improving Your Attitude

To become an effective change agent for your own education, there's another important tool you'll want to use: a good attitude. Teachers and administrators aren't going to bend over backwards to accommodate you if you act like Genghis Khan.

First and foremost, you should communicate an attitude of cooperation, not condescension. Present yourself as an ally, not an aggressor. Most teachers want to help their students; that's one reason they've chosen the teaching profession. Acknowledge that, respect it, make it easier for them to work with you, and the rewards will be substantial. There's nothing better than having your teachers on your side, and it's not that difficult to enlist their aid. All it takes is a soupçon of diplomacy and the willingness to recognize that teachers are people, too. Consider the following—and notice the difference in each approach to the same problem:

Condescension

"This class is boring. I'm not learning anything."

"This A is meaningless to me."

"I'm sick of always being expected to get the highest grades in the class."

"You always say, 'If I give you special treatment, then everyone else will want it, too.' What a cop-out!"

Cooperation

"I learned most of this last year. Can I prove that I know it by taking a test or completing a special project?"

"I'd appreciate knowing what it was about my project that made you think it deserved an A. Can you give me some specifics?"

"I wish you would ease up on the pressure a bit. This is a tough class for me. I can't be Number One at everything all the time."

"I've come up with some ideas for completing my course requirements in a different way than usual. Can I talk to you about them?"

As a condescending aggressor, you create a situation in which someone will win and someone will lose. The battle lines are drawn and there's no going back. As a cooperative ally, you invite the other person to work with you to recognize, understand, and solve a problem. Rather than attacking or accusing, you state very clearly and directly, "Here's what's going on, here's how I feel about it, and this is what I suggest as an alternative. I'd like to know what you think, too."

A seventh grader from Texas told us this story: A teacher was alienating his students by constantly stressing the negative. "No matter what we did, it wasn't good enough," the student explained. "Even if the whole class did well on a test, he'd pick on the one idea we missed. He was really making us hate his class!" Then one day she walked up to him and said, "When you tell me that everything I do is wrong, it makes me feel dumb. You make me feel like I'll *never* be successful." How did her teacher respond? "He said he had no idea what a negative effect he was having. He thought his approach would make us want to work harder. He actually thanked me for being so honest!" Did the student take a risk? Yes. Did it pay off? You decide. Would she do it again? In her words: "If I thought my gripe was legitimate, yes,

> "YOU GET A BETTER RESPONSE FROM TEACHERS IF YOU TALK WITH THEM BEFORE OR AFTER SCHOOL. TRYING TO GET HELP IN BETWEEN CLASSES IS USELESS—THERE JUST ISN'T TIME. ASKING A TEACHER TO HELP YOU IN SOME WAY (ESPECIALLY IF WHAT YOU'RE DOING REQUIRES THAT THEY MAKE AN EXCEPTION TO THE RULE) IS BEST DONE WHEN OTHER PEOPLE AREN'T AROUND. BY TALKING TO THE TEACHER PRIVATELY, YOU DON'T PUT THEM IN AN AWKWARD POSITION IN FRONT OF OTHER KIDS." TIM, 14

I would. Also, what did I have to lose? The class couldn't have gotten any worse, so the only way to go was up!"

On a related note, a teacher we know once observed: "Teaching school can get boring, and sometimes I feel as though I have to be a superstar to get my students turned on. If a student approaches me in a non-threatening and helpful way, I appreciate hearing ideas about how things can be made more interesting. It takes some of the burden off me. I'm human. I don't react very well to a verbal attack about how boring school is—especially when the person hasn't got any ideas of his own."

Granted, you won't always achieve your objective, no matter what approach you choose. Unfortunately, some teachers believe that they must play the aggressor with their students. But you're much more likely to be heard if you put aside the verbal boxing gloves and come out smiling.

Ten Tips for Talking to Teachers

Are you having a problem with a class or an assignment? Can you see room for improvement in how a subject is taught? Do you have a better idea for a special project or term paper? Don't just tell your friends. Talk to the teacher!

Many students have told us that they don't know how to go about doing this. The following suggestions are meant to make it easier for everyone—students and teachers.

1. Make an appointment to meet and talk. This shows the teacher that you're serious and you have some understanding of his or her busy schedule. Tell the teacher about how much time you'll need, be flexible, and don't be late.

2. If you know other students who feel the way you do, consider approaching the teacher together. There's strength in numbers. If a teacher hears the same thing from four or five people, he or she is more likely to do something about it.

continued on next page

Ten Tips for Talking to Teachers *continued fron previous page*

3.   Think through what you want to say before you go into your meeting with the teacher. Write down your questions or concerns. Make a list of the items you want to cover. You may even want to copy your list for the teacher so both of you can consult it during your meeting. (Or consider giving it to the teacher ahead of time.)

4.   Choose your words carefully. Example: Instead of saying, "I hate doing reports; they're boring and a waste of time," try, "Is there some other way I could satisfy this requirement? Could I do a video instead?" Strike the word "boring" from your vocabulary. It's a buzzword for teachers.

5.   Don't expect the teacher to do all of the work or propose all of the answers. Be prepared to make suggestions, offer solutions, even recommend resources. The teacher will appreciate that you took the initiative.

6.   Be diplomatic, tactful, and respectful. Teachers have feelings, too. And they're more likely to be responsive if you remember that the purpose of your meeting is conversation, not confrontation.

7.   Focus on what you need, not on what you think the teacher is doing wrong. The more the teacher learns about you, the more he or she will be able to help. The more defensive the teacher feels, the less he or she will want to help.

8.   Don't forget to listen. Strange but true, many students need practice in this essential skill. The purpose of your meeting isn't just to hear yourself talk.

9.   Bring your sense of humor. Not necessarily the joke-telling sense of humor, but the one that lets you laugh at yourself and your own misunderstandings and mistakes.

10. If your meeting isn't successful, get help from another adult. "Successful" doesn't necessarily mean that you emerged victorious. Even if the teacher denies your request, your meeting can still be judged successful. If you had a real conversation—if you communicated openly, listened carefully, and respected each other's point of view—then congratulate yourself on a great meeting. If the air crackled with tension, the meeting fell apart, and you felt disrespected (or acted disrespectful), then it's time to bring in another adult. Suggestions: a guidance counselor, the gifted program coordinator, or another teacher you know and trust who seems likely to support you and advocate for you. Once you've found help, approach your teacher and try again.

What to Say When Teachers Say No

You know your rights, you've come up with a proposal that seems reasonable to you, and you've talked to your teacher clearly and politely. . . to no avail. Sometimes the best-laid plans go awry in the face of that formidable opponent known as The Implacable Teacher. Don't give up just yet! Depending on what your teacher says (and your own energy level), there are a few more rebuttals you can attempt to the following "standard refusals."

If your teacher says . . .	You might respond . . .
"I can't make an exception for you."	"That's okay with me, since I think there are a number of students who might benefit from being allowed to *[fill in here with whatever it is you're suggesting—e.g., testing out of material you already know, doing an alternative to the traditional assignment as long as it fulfills your class requirements, etc.].*"
"It's always been done this way."	"I know. And I'm sure there are probably some very good reasons for that. But how about letting me try this one time, and if it doesn't work, I'll agree to go back to the way it's been done in the past? Anyway, what's the worst that could happen—and would it really be so awful?"
"It would cause chaos in my classroom."	"I'd be willing to help see that chaos doesn't prevail. I could form a small committee of students who really care and who would help set some guidelines that would keep order in the classroom. We'd agree that if things got out of control, we'd lose the opportunity to *[fill in with the idea at hand].*"
"You're a straight-A student. Why not be satisfied with that? After all, what more could you ask for?"	"I know I get straight A's, but the thing is, I feel I could be learning so much *more.* If it was possible to get a higher grade than an A, just think of the possibilities! You know the old cliché—'The sky's the limit.' I'd like to aim higher, and I really need your help and support."

What if nothing works? If every response you make falls flat? Then it's time to stop trying, to accept that there are some things you simply can't change. Throughout your life, you'll encounter people who have "role power" over you—meaning the power to tell you what to do *just because* they're in charge. It's not reasonable, it's not fair, but sometimes that's the way it is. Take a deep breath, thank the teacher for his or her time, and be glad that this situation is only temporary. It may seem as if the school year will last forever, but it won't.

Exploring Your Options

Ask yourself these questions:

- *Is the work in most of your classes too easy for you?*
- *Is one specific subject too easy?*
- *Do you have a special interest that isn't taught by any teachers? (Astronomy? Paleontology? Chinese? Computer networking?)*
- *Have you taken most of the courses required for graduation and you're only a sophomore?*
- *Are you planning to go to college? Do you want a head start?*
- *Do you find that you need more uninterrupted work time for projects that interest you?*
- *Do you wish that there were more gifted students in your classes?*
- *Are you generally satisfied with your regular classes, but you wish they could be expanded to include higher level thinking?*
- *Do you want to work independently more often?*
- *Is there someone in your community you'd like to spend time with and learn from?*

If you answered yes to one or more of these questions, you can work to change your school so it provides what you want and need. Or maybe it already does and you just don't know it yet. Many schools today offer a variety of possibilities for gifted students—special programs and other alternatives that can make school meaningful and enjoyable. Following are general descriptions of some we know about. Find out which ones are available at your school and how you can take advantage of them.

Acceleration

Acceleration allows you to jump to a higher level of classwork than your age would ordinarily dictate. You might skip a particular class or an entire grade. While acceleration is reasonably commonplace, many adults have historically been against it. They worry that if

> "If we value independence . . . then we may wish to set up conditions of learning which make for uniqueness, for self-direction, and for self-initiated learning."
> Carl Rogers

> "You have to get everything you can from whatever environment you're thrown into."
> Toni Morrison

you start associating regularly with kids who are older than you, you'll somehow "suffer emotionally." Yet there isn't a single study that shows that acceleration has, in fact, caused any significant problems for anybody. On the contrary, many studies show that when you're allowed to learn at your own pace, you feel better about yourself, you're more motivated and creative, and you're generally more socially well-adjusted and comfortable.

Enrichment

School enrichment programs* are designed to replace or extend the regular school curriculum. The goal of enrichment should be to help you work on higher level skills, such as divergent and evaluative thinking, problem-solving, and creativity. Some of the ways these skills can be taught are through debates and discussions, research or simulations.

Independent Study

Independent study enables you to work at your own pace in a program designed to accommodate and address your special interest. A mentor or teacher serves as your guide, but mostly you're on your own—sink or swim. Independent study programs usually require you to:

- *develop a plan stating the object of your study,*
- *list your goals and objectives,*
- *plan activities to achieve your goals, and*
- *complete a final project.*

Study plans often take the form of a contract.

In one high school independent study program called the Autonomous Learning Project (ALP), students contract for projects throughout the school year and meet regularly in small groups. In the words of two ALP students:

> **Charles, 17:** "The main thing this program has taught me is how to kick myself in the rear. In a normal classroom, the teacher hangs over you ready to cut your head off if you don't do the assignments. In ALP, you get a project and it's up to you to get it done. I think it's important to learn to be responsible for yourself."

---

* In some schools, these may be called "honors programs" or "gifted programs" instead of "enrichment programs." Terminology for special programs for highly able students can vary from district to district and state to state. Find out what they are called in your school. If several types of programs are offered, find out what each one really means. You may discover that the simplest, most direct questions are the most effective—as in: "Is there a gifted program at our school? What is it called? What does it involve? And what does it take to get into it?"

Are Enrichment Programs Right for You?

If you're in a special program for gifted and talented students, you may find that it takes up a lot of your time. Too much, in fact. Especially if you're involved in other things—like sports, school clubs or organizations, and the pursuit of a healthy social life. And what if you also have an after-school job? Chores to do around the house? Plus the occasional, bothersome need to eat and sleep?

You might find yourself asking, "Is it worth it to stay in the gifted program?" There's nothing wrong with that question, and the answer is something only you can decide. A good way to approach this decision is to list all of the activities you're involved in (and have some control over), then rank them according to how important they are to you.

Jerry, 15, came up with this list:

- Track team
- Part-time job
- Stock market club
- Gifted program
- Scouts
- Computer games
- Goofing off

When he was through ranking the items, his list looked like this:

1. Part-time job
2. Track team
3. Scouts
4. Computer games
5. Gifted program
6. Stock market club
7. Goofing off

Jerry needed his part-time job to earn money for college—plus he liked it and the people he worked with. He'd been on the track team for years and was hoping that his talents in that area might help him to earn a college scholarship. He'd been in scouts since elementary school and was on his way to Eagle, so he wasn't about to give that up. And his great joy in life—aside from track and scouting—was playing computer games. That put the gifted program at number 5, relatively low on his list.

After you've made your list and assigned each item a number, put it away for a week to ten days and don't look at it. Then create a new list with new rankings, take out your first list, and compare the two. Activities low on both lists may be ripe for re-evaluating and perhaps eliminating.

Your decisions don't have to be etched in stone. You may decide that working on the school paper is too demanding now, and then choose to go back to it next term or next year. You may want to take a temporary leave of absence from the karate club, with the option of returning in a month or two. And you may determine that the honors program in English isn't worth the effort, but the honors program in math is.

Circumstances change, people change, priorities and interests change. You may need to reassess and realign your options at a later date, depending on who you are by then and what's important to you.

Don't feel as if you have to apologize for your choices. Whatever activities you decide to curtail—be it the stock market club or the gifted program—there will probably be people (teachers, coaches, advisors, parents) who may try to convince you to change your mind, especially if they have made a personal investment in your performance. Hear them out respectfully, weigh their arguments carefully, but remember that the final decision is yours.

Greg, 15: "For me, the best part of this program is being able to do your own thing. I do about three major studies each year—all things I wouldn't have the opportunity to study in regular classes. It really challenges you to accomplish more."

Advanced Placement

Advanced Placement (AP) classes are college-level courses taught in many high schools by qualified high school teachers. They are ideal for students who are looking for greater academic challenges and more opportunities for individual progress. Each course often takes a full year to complete, but since there's usually greater emphasis on scholarship than on rote memorization, the work is more rewarding. Here's what AP students have said about the program:

> "I was just learning facts and more facts. [The AP teacher] taught us the tools and techniques of scholarship so you could see what facts you need to know and how to get them."

> "I liked working with kids of my ability or even more ability. Maybe it's because it makes me work harder."

AP classes may take the form of honors classes, strong regular classes, or independent studies. A warning: Honors courses and AP courses are very different in some respects. If you're in your school's honors program, you'll probably get top-notch content taught by some of your school's best teachers, but at the end of the quarter, you'll take a regular exam that will be credited only on your high school transcript. If you successfully complete an AP course and the subsequent rigorous exam (offered in May or June), you'll earn college credit. Some students start college with a full semester or more of credits, thanks to the AP program. The tests aren't free—each one costs about $75—but most states will pay the fees if your family can't afford them. Ask your school counselor. (Even if you do have to pay the fees yourself, they are a lot less than the cost of college credits for those courses.)

But even good ideas have flaws, and AP is no exception. For example, some high schools offer AP courses but don't inform students about the optional end-of-the-course exams. From our perspective, that's bizarre; you deserve the chance to show what you know. Also, some teachers claim to teach AP courses but don't follow the AP curriculum guidelines. This can result in a major disappointment at test time, when you discover that what you've been taught bears little resemblance to what's on the exam. Finally, there are some colleges and universities that don't allow you to use AP credits toward graduation. They permit you to take higher level courses but grant no college credit for passing AP exams. This policy doesn't show much respect for you as a student, and it doesn't save you a penny of college tuition. Before applying to the college of your choice, be sure to ask about its AP policies.

Another AP-related hurdle concerns high school size. If your school is too small to offer the AP program (or offers it on a limited scale—one or two courses), you may feel as if you'll miss out on this unique opportunity. In fact, you may still be able to take the AP exams for subjects in which you are especially proficient. The College Level Examination Program (CLEP) is administered by the same company that handles the AP curriculum, and it's open to you if your school doesn't offer AP courses in your areas of expertise. Many colleges accept high scores on AP exams offered through CLEP just as if you had taken the AP courses.

AP isn't perfect, but it can open up a world of options for high school students on the academic fast track. For more about AP, see pages 179–80.

Weighted Grades and Transcripts

Many students are given the option of taking high school courses at the honors level. Although these aren't AP courses, their content and requirements may be just as demanding. Since you'll be asked to expend more effort in these classes, you ought to get more out of them, such as extra credit—literally. When you take harder courses, you risk earning lower grades than if you take courses from the regular curriculum, so it's not unreasonable to expect something in return.

Ask your principal or guidance counselor what rewards exist for students who take honors level courses. Often an honors grade will be weighted—that is, a B or B+ in Honors English will be noted on your transcript as being equivalent to an A in the non-honors track. At the very least, a notation should be made on your transcript indicating which courses you took at the honors level.

One 15-year-old student took up the issue of weighted grades at her high school. She researched the topic and found, among other things, that a statute in another state required all honors courses to be weighted. Armed with this precedent and the support of several teachers and the PTA, she approached her local school board with a weighted grades proposal. The board accepted her recommendation.

A word of caution: Some people are opposed to weighted grades, arguing that "bright students shouldn't need extra incentive to take harder courses." If you hear someone voice this line of unreasoning, remain calm. Try asking the person, "Would you work overtime every day without pay just because you're a valued employee?" This may help to get your point across. Then again, it may not.

Early College Entrance

Early college entrance is a time-tested strategy that's available to many gifted high school students. It usually works in one of two ways:

1. Early admission. You do well enough in your freshman through junior years to apply early to a college of your choice. If you show strong promise (high grades and ACT/SAT scores), many colleges will consider accepting you as a full-time student at the end of your junior year. Check with the colleges you're interested in to see if they allow for the early admission option.

2. Dual enrollment. This option allows you to take college courses at a local university while you're attending high school. It works best when you live near a college campus and transportation between the two schools isn't a problem. Even if the nearest college is 100 miles away, you may be able to take summer courses to augment your academic credentials.

Akash attended college while still in high school, and here's what he says about his experience:

> "When I told people that I was planning on taking a few college classes in my senior year of high school, the most common questions they asked me were, 'Won't you miss all of your friends?' and 'Do you think you can handle it?' Many people share these misconceptions about high school students taking college courses. In fact, I think it has been one of the most enriching and beneficial experiences of my life. I didn't lose any of my old friends; instead, I made several new ones. Not only were the college courses more challenging, they were also fun. I learned more than I ever could have at high school, and I received college credit at the same time. I highly recommend that any motivated student give college a try while in high school."

Which option is right for you? If you asked your parents, teachers, and counselors, they would probably vote for dual enrollment over early admission. Adults believe that it's important for high school students to participate in high school social events—proms, pep rallies, yearbook committees, clubs, and the like—and they have a point. It's easier to make up for lost time in academics than in dating and other forms of social development. On the other hand, some high school students could care less about football, dances, and homecoming floats. We feel that each decision about early college entrance should be made on an individual basis. When it comes to planning academic futures, there's no such thing as "one size fits all."

Can High School Students Succeed in College Classes?

In one Midwestern state, the answer is a resounding YES. Beginning in 1985, high school juniors and seniors in Minnesota had the opportunity to participate in the Postsecondary Enrollment Options Program and take college-level courses at state expense. From 1985–1995, tens of thousands of students signed up for the program and took courses at state universities, private colleges, vocational schools, and industrialization centers while still in high school. From 1995–1996, a team of researchers studied the program and prepared a report for the State of Minnesota Legislative Audit Commission. The report focused on students who participated in the program during the 1994–1995 school year. Some findings:

● In 1994–95, 6,671 Minnesota public school juniors and seniors took courses at 87 postsecondary schools.

● Most of the courses they took were in core academic areas— social sciences (27 percent), language arts (23 percent), math (8 percent), science (7 percent), and world languages (4 percent).

● Students reported that the courses proceeded at a faster pace, were more in-depth, and required more homework time than regular high school courses, yet they still earned higher grades than regularly admitted postsecondary students (except at technical colleges, where did they somewhat worse).

● At the University of Minnesota, 76 percent of the grades earned by 11th and 12th graders were A's or B's.

● 73 percent of participating students reported being "very satisfied" with their program experience; 95 percent of their parents said they would "definitely" or "probably" encourage their children to participate again.

In addition, students and their parents saved a lot of money in post-secondary tuition, fees, books, and materials that they would have paid for if the students had enrolled in the courses without the program. At the time of the report, actual figures weren't yet available for the 1994–95 school year, so the researchers cited figures for the 1993–94 school year: a total of $10.9 *million* in savings for students and their parents.

Back-to-Back Classes

How many times have you started an exciting new project only to be interrupted by the bell? Pairing classes—scheduling them one right after another—is an inventive way to create an extra-long class period. It gives teachers and students more opportunities to do things that require more time and effort than a 45-minute class can provide. Back-to-back classes (sometimes called "double-block scheduling") also make it easier for teachers to use a variety of learning and teaching styles like independent study, debate, drama, field trips, or extended discussions, or to combine one content area with another (for example, language arts and social studies) for more in-depth learning.

Resource Rooms

Resource rooms can be havens for gifted students—places where they can make new friends of similar intellect, work on fascinating projects, and use special equipment. Usually, the teachers who work in these special resource rooms are sensitive to the needs of gifted and talented students and aren't threatened by students who quite often know more than they do about certain things. If you want to work in an atmosphere where you're free to use your talents and abilities without criticism from others, a resource room could be the answer. (Note: Because of scheduling programs, resource rooms are seldom found in high schools.)

Mentorships

In a mentorship, a student is paired with an adult (or sometimes another student) who is an expert in a particular study or profession the student would like to pursue. Mentors can come from either the academic or business community. Usually students and mentors agree to work together closely for a set period of time; meetings are arranged during or after school hours, as determined by the participants. Accelerated and enriched learning are the natural consequences of mentorships—which also provide good career exploration opportunities. For more about mentorships, see pages 99–100.

Field Trips and Cultural Events

Everyone benefits from field trips and cultural events, especially gifted and talented students. Why? Because they perceive things more deeply, they're more inquisitive, and they want to know how things work. Trips to the zoo, the symphony, a museum, a baker, a bank, or a sewage plant will all broaden your horizons. Where would you like to visit?

Seminars and Mini-Courses

These classes, now becoming quite commonplace, are for students, gifted or not, with similar interests and abilities. There's nothing new about recognizing that people with common interests support one another and make learning more enjoyable. Classes may be offered during or after school or on weekends. Usually they're taught by teachers or members of the community.

Summer School

Summer school programs vary greatly from school to school and district to district. When budgets are tight, some schools eliminate summer school altogether. But when schools can, they may offer a variety of classes designed to challenge and motivate gifted and talented students.

In one state, seven school districts pooled their resources to offer summer school programs for bright students. The program provides more than 35 courses each summer. When asked about the program, one 10th grader said, "The hardest part for me was making a decision about which class to take—there's such a variety." One parent wrote, "A true test [of the school's success] was that our son was willing to get up and go that early on a summer morning."

The Smörgasbord Approach

There's no rule that says you must try enrichment classes *or* AP *or* early admission *or* dual enrollment. If you can't make up your mind about which option is best for you, then perhaps you can decide not to decide. Don't do anything, or do a little bit of everything, trying bits and pieces of each program you find appealing. For example, you might register for two AP classes and, at the same time, contact colleges about transferring the credits you earn. Couple this request with a query about their summer enrollment policies for qualified high school students, and you may be on your way to designing an academic program that's ideal for you.

Which Options Are Available to You?

If you don't know or you're not sure, ask! If the program involves a specific academic area, go to the teacher who teaches that subject or a department head. You might also check with your school counselor. (Strange but true, most gifted kids don't consult with counselors. Yet counselors are there to help you as much as any other student.) If you can't get answers from either of these sources, go straight to your school principal. Make an appointment to see him or her, and come prepared with questions about what your school offers to bright, motivated students.

If your school has requirements for participation in a program that you want to join, find out what they are. If you don't qualify, see what you can do to change your status. If the requirements seem unreasonable or unfair to you, list your reasons for feeling that way and share them with the person in charge. Request admission on probation if necessary. If, after a reasonable period of time, it becomes clear that the class or program isn't for you, be prepared to withdraw and move on to something else. What's important is to keep trying. Remember, it's *your* education and *your* future.

GIFTED PEOPLE SPEAK OUT

Jerry Simmons

My experience with the independent studies program in my school district began when I was fed up with dealing with boring teachers who made no attempt to teach at a level high enough for me to learn. All attempts at trying to change the system were met with resistance, so I searched high and low for a way out. After considering several options, I decided the San Jose Unified School District's Independent Studies Program would meet my needs. It's one of the district's best-kept secrets, but luckily my father is a teacher in the program and was able to give me information about it.

Once I got through all the red tape involved in transferring to a new school, I found a learning system that met my needs perfectly. I was always an independent person, and I enjoy reading, writing, and learning. I am also highly motivated and often ended up directing that motivation to non-school activities in an effort to learn new things and grow.

The San Jose independent studies program is designed for students who can't handle being taught in regular classes for one reason or another. Some were always getting into fights, some were dropouts wanting to get their diplomas, some had to work full-time to support their families, some were young pregnant girls, some came because of religious reasons. The reasons are many, but basically they were all people who couldn't or wouldn't go to a regular school.

All independent studies programs are different. Some have no restrictions on who can get in; others are designed specifically for gifted and talented or other groups of students. My school district is so large that they have the program in one location separate from the middle and high schools. In some districts, the program is based at each of the middle or high schools.

All of these programs have a set of benefits and drawbacks for students. Probably the biggest single benefit is that the program can be tailored to meet your needs. I wanted to complete as many of my senior-year courses as possible because I expected to pass a proficiency exam (a test that serves as the equivalent of a high-school diploma) and transfer to college at the end of my junior year. My teacher let me take those classes early so that I wouldn't miss any of the academic courses I would have taken if I had stayed in high school another year. It was perfect for me because I needed very little guidance to get my work done, and staying in high school another year would have meant hundreds of days wasted on "busy" work.

The drawback that comes with this sort of program is that, depending on the structure of the program and abilities of the teacher, you might not be able to take as many different courses as you could in a regular school. Some classes that require a lot of equipment (most science classes) and training (foreign languages or high level math) for the teacher aren't always available to independent studies students. In my case, I had one teacher who was teaching me all of my subjects. She was very knowledgeable in the areas I wanted to study, so I lucked out. Had I needed to be taught fourth-year French, trigonometry, or drafting, I wouldn't have been so lucky. Be sure to check into what classes are offered by the program in your area before making a change.

To be a part of any independent studies program, you must be motivated. I hadn't always shown my motivation in school, but I wanted to get out and stay out of regular high school so badly that I made a commitment to work as hard as possible to do well in the program. Anyone thinking about getting involved in this sort of program must have commitment to make it to the meetings and set aside time for study each day.

In my district, students are expected to come in once a week. Each student meets individually with a teacher, who goes over all the assignments made the previous week and makes assignments for the following week. Those students who aren't motivated enough to come to their appointments or don't complete their assignments are dropped from the program. This system works very well for motivated students who complete their assignments.

The major drawback to an independent studies program is that when working alone, the students have little contact with their friends and don't have a normal school social life. This was certainly a problem for me because I was very involved in student government and enjoyed the social aspects of high school. Also, I missed the regular routine that school provided me. While in the program, I could eat, sleep, and study whenever I wanted to, as long as I completed my assignments on time. That was a big adjustment from my highly structured regular high school, where student life is run by bells. I overcame this problem by making the extra effort to reach out to my peers at church and through non-school clubs and by trying to establish routines at home.

In weighing all the positives and negatives, independent study was definitely for me. It allowed me to explore necessary subjects early, to be challenged academically, and to grow as a person by devoting large blocks of my time to worthwhile non-school activities. I wish more of my schooling could have been done in independent study.

If this type of program sounds like something you're interested in, ask at school if your school or district has an independent studies program and find out whether it will meet your needs better than school does now. All programs are different, and the one offered to you may have positive or negative points that my district's program didn't have. Above all, the best advice I can give is to remember that it's your education and you must plot a course that's right for you. Just because most students go through the regular system doesn't mean that it's the best option for you. Check it out!

Jerry Simmons wrote this article while attending West Valley Community College in Saratoga, California.

Step-by-Step to Systemic Change

You've done your research, followed all available leads, asked the right people the right questions . . . and emerged empty-handed. Your school offers *no* courses, programs, or alternatives that will meet your learning needs. Nothing, nada, zip, zero. Now what?

"Learning is
discovering
that something
is possible."
Fritz Perls

Don't give up. Your situation may be desperate, but it's not hopeless. What you're looking for is a challenge, right? Congratulations: you've found one!

Throughout life, we all face obstacles in carrying out our plans. It's inevitable. But how we *perceive* those obstacles often determines whether we surmount them. Some people retreat from a difficult situation because they perceive it as too much to handle. Whether it really is too much becomes academic; they give up before finding out. Other people view problems as opportunities. Instead of reciting the reasons why something *can't* be done, they start looking for ways in which it *can* be done. Then they do it.

You can give up on school and resign yourself to spending the next several years in unrelieved tedium. Or you can follow these steps and perhaps bring about the kind of systemic change that will make school more meaningful for everyone, not only you.

1. Prepare for Change

Set Goals

Without exception, the major movers and shakers in any school (or business, or community) are those who set goals. Decide what your goals are, then articulate them. Write them down, review them, revise them. For more about goal setting, see pages 84–89.

Question Authority

Change rarely happens unless someone is willing to step forward, question authority, and challenge the system. Administrators make mistakes; teachers make mistakes. (So do you, but we've already covered that on pages 79–81.) Contrary to what they may want you to believe, adults don't have all of the answers or even the best answers.

Mike, a high school senior, has been very successful at implementing changes at his school. Here's what he has to say:

> "I think a lack of assertiveness can prevent kids from asking for changes in school. There are those who simply put their fate in the hands of others and trust that everything will come out right. They just don't push. . . . Another thing I see is kids who aren't willing to accept that the school could make a mistake. They believe the school always knows best. I even know some kids who are afraid to change things for fear they'll hurt the teacher's feelings by dropping out of their class and taking something else. In that situation, kids just live a lie. Everybody loses."

Take Risks

Any time there's something to gain, there's also something to lose. Perhaps your favorite teacher will resent you for "rocking the boat." Or the principal will feel threatened by you and become defensive. Or your friends will question why you're upsetting the status quo. Or your parents will caution you against challenging the system. Stand firm!

2. Commit Yourself and Make a Plan

Be prepared to commit your heart, body, and soul to your dreams and goals. Otherwise you may not be strong enough to do what needs to be done.

Be prepared to devote considerable time, energy, and thought to making a plan. Otherwise you won't know where to begin or how to proceed. Remember that most people don't plan to fail; they simply fail to plan.

Example: You're dissatisfied with the regular biology class and would like to propose a new one especially for gifted students. Your plan should include detailed answers to the following questions:

- *How will the gifted biology class be different from the regular biology class?*
- *When and where will it meet?*
- *How many other students might want to take the new class?*
- *What will be the qualifications for getting into the class?*
- *Who will teach it?*
- *Will it cost the school money? Save the school money?*
- *What are some problems that might come up along the way?*
- *Why will this class be valuable?*
- *What will this class replace?*

These are the kinds of questions that administrators will ask. If you can't answer all or most of them, go back to the drawing board until you can. Then put it down on paper in a clear, comprehensible, and organized way.

3. Find Supporters

In the hierarchy of any school system, there are individuals who have the power to make change. They might include the principal, a department head, the superintendent of schools, an influential teacher, or all of the above. It's up to you to identify the people who can actually implement the change you desire.

Taking
Charge of
Your
Education

"Life is either a daring adventure, or nothing."
Helen Keller

"You can't hit a home run unless you step up to the plate. You can't catch fish unless you put your line in the water. You can't reach your goals if you don't try."
Kathy Seligman

"We must remind ourselves . . . that no change takes place without working hard and without getting our hands dirty."
Joseph Zinker

Start by bringing your plan to a person who may be directly involved. For example, if you want to start an accelerated biology class, go to someone in the biology department. Present your plan, give the person time to read it and think it over, then find out if he or she supports it. Finally, ask: "Can you help me put this plan into action?" If the answer is no, move on to someone else.

You may need all the help you can get to find and influence the people in power, so be ready to broaden your scope. What about a parent? The local PTA? Your school board? A counselor? The student council? Other gifted students? A gifted education advocacy group? Who else do you know, who else can you call?

You might have to do some things you don't feel comfortable doing, such as attending PTA or school board meetings. Sweaty palms are a small price to pay for a chance at success.

While some adults are insensitive, sarcastic, boring, or disrespectful of kids, most are not. Surround yourself with as many considerate, caring, broad-minded adults as you can find.

4. Stop Procrastinating

If you know that a change is essential to your education, if you've decided what you want to try, if you've made a plan and found supporters, what are you waiting for?

5. Remember That You're Not Alone

Sometimes it may feel as if you're the only person who has ever had problems with school. As if no one else could possibly understand. As if you're all alone on a mountain top, looking out at the landscape and wondering what the heck is going on.

In fact, you have a lot in common with many other creative, intelligent, talented people. Check with your parents, neighbors, and other adults in your community. Write letters to people you admire, explain your situation, and ask them to tell you about their experiences. You'll likely find that some of them had a tough time in school, and some of them had to figure out their own ways of dealing with the pressures, frustrations, and occasional inanities involved in getting a decent education. You may discover that many of them felt like loners, too. In fact, they would probably agree with these Three Great Truths of Getting an Education:

Caution

Try not to be discouraged if the first people you approach don't like your plan and/or don't offer to support it. They may have their own agendas. Perhaps they don't believe in separate classes for gifted students, or they are the ones who would have to teach the class, and they don't want the extra work. Perhaps they may think that your plan is unrealistic or foolish. Thank them for their time and consideration, then move on.

1. Teachers *can* help, if you give them a chance.

2. No situation is perfect, and some educators and students are overtly antagonistic toward gifted kids.

3. If you expect learning to happen to you—like an accident or a suntan—you'll end up learning only what others want you to learn.

Ultimately, you're the one who has to decide whether to learn only what you must, or to take advantage of all the opportunities and options available to you. But you can take comfort in knowing that others have been there before you, confronting the same challenges, obstacles, quandaries—and possibilities—that you're facing today.

College Bound: A Prescription for Success

Chances are you'll want to go to college someday, and it's never too soon to start planning. By "planning," we don't mean spending the rest of your pre-college years with your nose buried in a book, or hiring private tutors to supplement your schooling, or signing up for study courses that are "guaranteed" to improve your SAT scores. We perceive "planning" as a series of purposeful decisions that can improve your chances of being accepted by the college of your choice. Following are some suggestions to keep in mind as you face those decisions.

"IT'S HARD FOR ME TO LOOK INTO MY HIGH SCHOOL AND COLLEGE FUTURE." BOY, 12

If You're in Grades 7–9 . . .

Accept the Challenge

Middle school offers more options for course selection than you've ever had before. Based on your performance in elementary school, you may be channeled into particular courses. If you've been a

Taking
Charge of
Your
Education

strong student, you'll be guided into the more challenging classes; if not, you'll be steered toward the basic (easier) courses.

If this type of academic "tracking" or "ability grouping" of students takes place in your school, we advise you to do whatever you can to get into the more challenging classes. Many of the courses you may want to take in the future are based on completing "prerequisites" now. Taking lower-level courses in middle school makes it harder to get into upper-level courses in high school. It's kind of like trying to catch a train after it's already left the station; you have to do a lot of running to catch up to a place you should have been anyway.

We don't suggest that you do this in every subject, but math and English/language arts/reading would be our first choices. These courses offer the basic building blocks you need to succeed in other courses; also, schools are more likely to offer different levels for these subjects, less likely for social studies or health.

Note: Some middle schools and junior high schools are doing away with ability grouped classes altogether. If this is the case in your school, you (and your parents) still have the right to ask how your high abilities will be challenged.

Take a Study Skills Course

Many gifted students seem to be able to earn A's all through elementary school without ever opening a book. They only need to hear something once or twice in order to absorb it. This is a good "talent" to have, but as you enter middle school, you may find it inexorably waning.

This has little to do with your natural abilities and a lot to do with knowing how to learn. Note taking, reading for comprehension, time management, and studying textbooks effectively are skills, not gifts. They must be learned and practiced.

Also during elementary school, you probably had one or two subject area teachers per day. It didn't take long for you to figure out what they expected from you. In middle school, you might have five or more teachers each day, and they may or may not communicate with each other. Suddenly you're juggling several teachers' styles and expectations, plus you have five tests scheduled for the same day or three major projects due on the first Tuesday in February. . . . Help!

No one enjoys this academic pressure, but many students can handle it because they learned long ago how to allocate their time, break large assignments into smaller pieces, quickly locate the most important information in textbooks, focus on their work, and so on—all study skills. Meanwhile, you're wondering why your so-called "photographic memory" has faded away.

Fortunately, many schools offer courses in study skills. Often they cover a lot of ground, from homework shortcuts ("Do the most boring or hardest assignments first") to tips for pleasing teachers ("Use a word processor for your written work and proof-read it before turning it in"). A study skills course can prepare you for everything from test-taking to scheduling your homework around your favorite TV programs.

Find Out More

To learn more about study skills (especially if your school doesn't offer a study skills course), read:

Ellis, David B. *Becoming a Master Student.* Boston, MA: Houghton Mifflin Company, 1994. Written for college freshmen, this book is also valuable for junior high and high school students who need help learning how to learn.

Fry, Ron. *Last Minute Study Tips.* Franklin Lakes, NJ: Career Press, 1996. Cramming isn't ideal, but for times when you don't have a choice (because of other commitments or procrastination), these accelerated study techniques can help.

Schumm, Jeanne Shay, and Marguerite Radencich. *School Power: Strategies for Succeeding in School.* Minneapolis: Free Spirit Publishing, 1992.

Learn About Your Learning Style

Some people learn best by listening (to lectures, tapes, etc.); others learn best by seeing (reading books, the board, charts, graphs, etc.); still others learn best by touching and moving (building models, using hands-on materials and manipulatives, solving puzzles, etc.). Some are explorers who consider a question or problem from many different angles before arriving at an answer; others are "efficiency experts" who prefer to make decisions quickly. Some are practical and down-to-earth; others are dreamers. Some are highly organized; others seem to prefer a perpetual state of chaos. Some are risk-takers; others play it safe. Some learn best in groups; others are loners. We could go on forever describing different ways people learn and think, because the fact is that we all learn and think in different ways.

The unique and highly individualized way in which you learn is called your *learning style*. The more you know about your learning style, the more you can take advantage of your learning strengths. You'll perceive yourself more accurately, relate more effectively to others, and be a better learner at school, on your own, and throughout your life.

Over the past several years, many researchers have studied learning styles, and many educators are aware of the importance of understanding learning styles and teaching in ways that match their students' styles. It's possible that your teachers have some knowledge of learning styles and have incorporated this into their lessons. Ask your teachers to share with you what they know about learning styles, or ask if they can point you toward a class on learning styles. As you pursue this growing field of knowledge, keep in mind this advice from expert Kathleen Butler:*

> "There is no one best style or style of learning. When you understand your own style, however, you are better prepared to make wiser decisions and choices, to be self-directed in your own learning, and to work more appreciatively with others. Because your teachers and assignments will not favor just your style all the time, the more you know, the more you will be able to adjust your style without losing your own sense of worth; the more you understand, the more you will be able to communicate your needs most effectively without making excuses.... When all is said and done, it matters most that you appreciate that you have your own unique style and your own ways of being intelligent, and that you make the most of your own strengths."

* Kathleen Butler, *Learning Styles: Personal Exploration and Practical Applications: An Inquiry Guide for Students*. Columbia, CT: The Learner's Dimension, 1995, pp. 4, 58.

Find Out More

To learn more about learning styles, read:

Butler, Kathleen A. *Learning Styles: Personal Exploration and Practical Applications: An Inquiry Guide for Students*. Columbia, CT: The Learner's Dimension, 1995. This hands-on workbook helps you to explore your special abilities and qualities as a person, learner, and thinker. Exercises, checklists, and questionnaires encourage you to find new ways of looking at yourself, consider different approaches for understanding how you naturally learn and think, and make the most of your learning abilities. Case studies invite you to consider your own strengths and reflect on how you use your style. For more information, write to: The Learner's Dimension, P.O. Box 6, Columbia, CT 06237. Or call (203) 228-3786. Also available: *The Teacher's Guide for Learning Styles*.

Be a Joiner

Every school has a social pecking order in which some activities (such as basketball, football, student council) are considered more acceptable than others (math club, bowling league, Basket Weavers Cooperative). What happens when your talents and interests lie in distinctly unpopular areas? Do you join the Future Paleontologists of America or hold back for fear of becoming a social leper? Sad but true, many kids won't consider a team or club that could brand them as a bookworm or a nerd. Others become "closet joiners," meeting at times and places far removed from the judgmental gaze of their classmates.

We suggest that you try to balance the dual and often conflicting demands of social acceptability and personal satisfaction. Join the clubs and teams that genuinely interest you *and* get involved in one or two that have been given the stamp of approval at your school. This strategy should give you the best of both worlds. It will also demonstrate that while you may be idiosyncratic in some respects, in others you're a regular person.

If you attend a school where every student is respected for being an individual (a likely story), or if your interests naturally fall within the "worthy" range, this is a non-issue for you. If you believe that playing the social acceptance game is demeaning or immoral, then please don't play it. You need to be true to yourself. But it may help to remember that part of life is a game whose rules are set by many people in addition to you. When you play by their rules occasionally, you are neither betraying your individuality nor succumbing to mob pressure. You're astute enough to recognize that you're not alone in the universe. Besides, in learning this skill now, you won't have to relearn it when you enter the worlds of business, politics, and/or marriage, all of which require compromise for ultimate success.

If You're In Grades 10–12 . . .

Get a Head Start on College

Seventy percent of our survey respondents wanted to be able to earn college credit while they were in high school. There are two ways to do this:

1. by taking college courses at the same time you're completing your high school graduation requirements (dual enrollment), and
2. by earning qualifying scores on Advanced Placement (AP) exams.

Dual enrollment is described on pages 163–64. Here's more of the AP story, continued from pages 161–62.

Jeff Flynn went directly from high school graduation to his sophomore year in college. He saved a year's worth of high tuition, a lot of boredom in courses he already understood (yes, that happens in college, too), and a year of time in his eight-year preparation for a Ph.D. in engineering. His story is not unique. Each year, thousands of students qualify for college credit through the AP program while still in high school.

AP courses—ranging from English to chemistry, biology to studio art—are offered at more than 11,000 U.S. high schools. In 1994, more than 700,000 AP exams were taken by students in grades 9 through 12. AP exams are graded on a scale of 1 ("no recommendation") to 5 ("extremely well qualified"), and most colleges accept scores from 3–5. If you took AP History, scored a 4 on the exam, and submitted this score when you applied to one of the 3,000 colleges that honors AP credits, you would have "tested out" of a four-credit college course and saved somewhere between $400 and $2,000. Multiply these savings of time and money across several subjects, and you'll be doing the Jeff Flynn Shuffle—completing college sooner, cheaper, and in a very interesting way.

To request a free copy of the "Guide to the Advanced Placement Program," write or call: Advanced Placement Program, Educational Testing Service, P.O. Box 6671, Princeton, NJ 08541-6671;

(609) 771-7300. Mention item #201154. Or ask your school counselor if he or she has a copy you can borrow. You can also contact the Advanced Placement Program through the World Wide Web at:

http://www.collegeboard.org/ap/html/students/indx001.html

This will take you to a page on the Web with links to answers to FAQs (Frequently Asked Questions) about AP, study skills and test-taking strategies for specific AP exams, information about exam dates and costs, and much more.

Explore the Liberal Arts

You may choose to take a high school course load that is strictly academic, squeezing in that one fine arts requirement credit only grudgingly during your last semester of senior year. If so, too bad for you. You've just limited yourself in unnecessary and unfortunate ways.

For too long, high school courses in music, art, film, and the social sciences (e.g., psychology, sociology, economics, political science) have been considered the "fluff" rather than the "stuff" of learning. But as more colleges discover the benefits of an education that is well-rounded and well-grounded in the arts and sciences, they are actively seeking students who have done more than ace every trigonometry test. They want students who know that Manet and Monet are two different artists, that baroque is a style of both architecture and music, and that Steinbeck, Hesse, Cather, and Baraka are all worth reading. So don't belittle or avoid courses in the liberal arts. If you take them seriously, they can help you in specific ways. Examples:

- *You'll be able to write erudite college admissions essays, with references to the impact of art and literature on your life and the lives of other educated people.*
- *Teachers will love the literary and artistic allusions that pepper your writing.*
- *You'll see the connections among specific periods in history and the art, music, design, and literature of each era. That makes both history and the arts more interesting.*
- *You'll be a bigger hit at parties and with parents. It's embarrassing to have to admit that the last really great book you read was* How to Bonsai Your Pet.

While you're at it, learn about belief systems different from your own by taking a course in comparative religions. Shaping more of our world's political and economic structure than any other force, religions hold the key to understanding the world that did, does, or might exist. Don't worry about being manipulated or "converted"; these courses merely compare, contrast, and explain what different countries and cultures believe.

Choosing a College

Sixty-three percent of our survey respondents wanted information about options for after high school; 71 percent wanted to know what the first year of college would be like. And 70 percent wanted help selecting a career or field of study.

● **"WHAT COLLEGES ARE BEST FOR GIFTED STUDENTS?**
● **HOW DO YOU FIND OUT ABOUT COLLEGES AND**
● **UNIVERSITIES?"** MALCOLM, 14

A recent reader of the original *Gifted Kids Survival Guide* wanted to know, "Are all colleges great for gifted students? Is there an easy way to tell which college is the right one?" For answers, we turned to Rob and Akash, high school seniors who have both been accepted at the colleges of their choice. Here's what they had to say:

● **"HOW DOES ONE DEAL WITH LEAVING PARENTS AND**
● **FRIENDS TO GO TO COLLEGE?"** JENNIFER, 12

> "No. It is not safe to say that all colleges are great for gifted students, although there are many that are. *U.S. News and World Report* publishes an annual list of the top universities and colleges in the United States. This is a great resource when looking for the right college. The list offers an overall ranking system, as well as rankings for special areas of interest. Generally, if the school is ranked in the top 40 it will have some programs geared specifically towards gifted students. One good way to find out about lesser-known universities and colleges is to call or to write to them and ask about special honors programs and opportunities for students who excel. Many state universities have excellent programs that are ideally suited to gifted students, yet this information may not be widely known....Another great resource is *Best Colleges,* published by Princeton Review.* They have interviewed students at the top universities and colleges, and the book offers a good feel for how the schools view gifted students."

With over 4,000 four-year colleges in the U.S. alone, you're certain to find more than one that meets your requirements for a satisfying college experience. Meanwhile, you can start compiling literature about possible college choices. (If you take the PSAT during high school, the literature will compile itself in your mailbox.) As you initiate your search, you're bound to have questions like the following.

---

* As of this writing, the current edition is *The Student Access Guide to the Best 309 Colleges, 1997 Edition* by Tom Meltzer, Zachary Knower, John Katzman, and Edward T. Custard. 675 pages, paperback, $18. Check your school library, community library, or counseling office to see if they have a copy, or order one by calling 1-800-793-2665.

Nine Nagging Questions About College

#1 Should I attend a large college, a small one, or something in between?

Colleges range in size from 12 students (an environmental college in Arizona) to 50,000 (Ohio State University). At smaller colleges (2,000 or less), you can expect more one-on-one contact with professors who know your name. Also, class sizes tend to be in the range you're probably used to in high school.

At a large university, your Introduction to Psychology class will most likely consist of hundreds of students in a large lecture hall. This mass of humanity will be moderated somewhat by weekly "tutorials," "study sessions," or "labs," all of which translate into smaller groups of 15–30 students and a TA (Teaching Assistant) who answers questions and explains any concepts that the professor in the large group neglected to address. Even at the largest universities, courses tend to get smaller as you take classes in your major area of study, eventually approaching somewhere between 20–35 students.

Initially, a large university can be as intimidating to a kid from a small town as a small college is to a kid from a big city. So don't rule out any college due to size alone. You'll be surprised how adaptable you can be when you're finally away from home. Also, even on a campus of 20,000 students, you "become a number" only if you choose to be. A college of any size will offer many opportunities for your face and name to be known to others.

#2 How far away from home should I plan to go?

If you were raised on a farm in southern Alabama, you might think that the University of Colorado in Boulder is the most exciting and exotic place on earth. The mountains and stars are so close you can almost touch them. And if you go to Boulder and like it (hint: Pearl Street is the best!), then you'll be content to come home once or twice a year. On the other hand, if you have a tough time adjusting to life without your family, even Boulder can lose its charm quickly.

Here's one way to predict how you'd handle being far from home: Consider how you've reacted during recent times when you were away from your family and friends for two weeks or more. Was it something you'd do again, or were you counting the minutes until you returned to more familiar surroundings? If your college is more than 300 miles away, you'll be hard-pressed to visit home except during extended holidays. This may sound fine now, but it could be tough when you're just another homesick freshman.

The good news is that most colleges are used to handling homesickness and related problems. Everyone from your dorm's RA (Resident Assistant) to the counselors in the Admissions or Student Services Office will lend an ear if you're willing to talk. You will have to take the initiative in asking for help, however.

Distance may make the heart grow fonder, but you'll be contending with enough new experiences—dorm life, individual freedom, campus parties, studying, exploring your surroundings, making new friends—that you really won't need the additional burden of trying to estimate how many days, hours, and minutes remain before you can go home again. You know yourself better than anyone else does, so be honest about the mileage factor: How far is too far for you?

#3 How much academic pressure will I experience?

Almost any guide to colleges will include a section detailing whether the college is *noncompetitive* (all you need to get in is a high school diploma and a tuition deposit) or *highly selective* (admission is limited to no more than 20 percent of the applicants). Between these two extremes are *less competitive, competitive,* and *selective*—broad-based indicators of how much pushing and shoving goes on (figuratively speaking) to gain admission.

While getting in is probably three-fourths of the battle, especially at highly selective schools, staying in is another challenge. Suddenly you're competing with a more diverse student body than you've ever experienced before. You also may be competing with a much smarter group of students than you're accustomed to.

When it comes to pressure, you have three choices:

1. *If you want to be a big fish in a small pond,* attend a college with relatively low academic requirements. Your abilities and talents will rise to the top fairly quickly without much effort on your part.
2. *If you want to be a medium fish in a medium pond,* seek a college that fits your academic style and past performance. Most other freshmen will also have come from the top quarter of their high school graduating classes, excelling in ways that are obvious yet commonplace in this competitive setting.
3. *If you want to be a small fish in an ocean,* accept only the best. Soon after you arrive, you'll assume that everyone there is smarter than you. Don't panic! At least half of the entering freshman will share the same fear.

As you consider a prospective college's academic qualities, keep these guidelines in mind:

- *Even noncompetitive schools have some strong programs, and even highly se-lective schools have some weaker ones. Don't just look at a university's repu-tation; look (closely) at the department that interests you (e.g., history, education, biology, English, computer science).*

- *Prestige doesn't matter when everyone has it. It may feel great to tell your high school friends, "I'm attending Highbrow University in September," but once you arrive at HBU, it's not news anymore. If you choose a school strictly on the basis of prestige, you may be in for a rude awakening.*

- *Honors Colleges can give you a first-class education for a discount fare. Many large state universities offer a "college-within-a-college" for their most academ-ically oriented students. For the same tuition you'd pay to attend mega-classes in lecture halls, you'll experience smaller classes, more personalized attention, dynamic professors, and a cohort of intelligent students who share your major and even your interests. Check out the Honors College route; it's like a gifted program at the university level, and the quality often rivals programs at more intense and expensive private schools.*

- *Remember the transfer factor. More than 50 percent of entering college fresh-men change their academic majors at least once during their college career, and up to 30 percent transfer from one university to another before attaining a Bachelor's degree. So if you make a decision as a high school senior that you later regret, you'll be able to switch directions without losing any of the academic credits you've earned (at least through the end of your sophomore year). Your credits, like you, will move to a new department or a new home.*

> "College ain't so much where you been as how you talk when you get back."
> **Ossie Davis**

#4 Can I reasonably expect to finish college in four years?

The four-year college experience is rapidly becoming a relic of earlier, simpler, and less costly times. Today it's not unusual—and at many large public universities, it's becoming the norm—for a college degree to take four and a half to five years to complete. There are several reasons for this, including:

- ***Cost.*** *Tuition has become so expensive that many students must work while attending college. This cuts down on the number of courses you can take each term. Remember, in college you can decide how many courses you'll take each term. There's no guidance counselor or homeroom teacher breathing down your neck. (Fifteen credit hours per term is typical.)*

- ***Internships and co-op programs.*** *If your major requires or allows these options, you may find yourself at work in a real business, hospital, etc., while earning college credit for your efforts. Usually, though, this reduces the number of courses you can take at one time. Still, it can be worth trading the time for the experience. Many college graduates end up working for the firms where they interned.*

- **Cutbacks.** *Over the last decade, colleges and universities have absorbed some major budget cuts. In response, many of them have eliminated courses that they would ordinarily offer. This may prevent you from taking a required course on schedule, throwing off your plan to graduate in four years.*

- **Life.** *You want to spend a year abroad, you get married, your parents split up, you want a break from the college routine; none of these will necessarily prevent you from getting a degree in four years, but each of them might. Life's exigencies sometimes waylay even the best-laid plans.*

If it's absolutely essential that you graduate within four years, make sure to ask your preferred colleges how many students finish within this time. If their answer is "less than 50 percent," ask for an honest explanation before you commit to that school. Also, remember those AP credits you earned in high school? They will help you to finish college within a timeline that is more comfortable and cheaper than the "five-year plan" now endured by so many undergraduates.

#5 How can I find out about scholarships and grants?

Each year, hundreds of thousands of dollars in scholarships and grants (which never have to be paid back) aren't awarded because no one bothers to apply for them. Imagine—free money and no takers!

Your high school counselor should have ample information on available scholarships based on *need* (when you and your family can't afford to pay college costs) or *merit* (money given to you because of your academic record regardless of your family's income). Also, there are literally millions of dollars available to highly able and motivated students from particular states, or those whose heritage is Hispanic, Italian, or whatever, or who happen to be female, or who plan to major in aerospace engineering or some other career of interest to a particular company or charity. Many books describe the scholarships and grants available to you. Some of the most popular titles include:

- *The A's & B's of Academic Scholarships,* published by Octameron Associates, 1900 Mt. Vernon Avenue, Alexandria, VA 22301-1302. Distributed by Dearborn Trade, toll-free telephone 1-800-621-9621.

- *The College Money Handbook: The Complete Guide to Expenses, Scholarships, Loans, Jobs, and Special Aid Programs at Four-Year Colleges,* published by Peterson's Guides, P.O. Box 2123, Princeton, NJ 08543; toll-free telephone 1-800-EDU-DATA (1-800-338-3282).

- *Dan Cassidy's Worldwide College Scholarship Directory,* published by The Career Press Inc., 3 Tice Road, P.O. Box 687, Franklin Lakes, NJ 07417-1322; toll-free telephone 1-800-227-3371.

- *Loans & Grants from Uncle Sam: Am I Eligible & for How Much?* published by Octameron Associates, 1900 Mt. Vernon Avenue, Alexandria, VA 22301-1302. Distributed by Dearborn Trade, toll-free telephone 1-800-621-9621.

- *Prentice Hall Guide to Scholarships & Fellowships for Math & Science Students: A Resource Guide for Students Pursuing Careers in Mathematics, Science, & Engineering,* published by Prentice Hall, toll-free telephone 1-800-922-0579.

With the help of your high school counselor and one or more books, you'll probably discover several colleges within your financial reach.

You can also search for financial aid information on the World Wide Web. For more information, see pages 188–89.

#6 Should I aim for a public or private college?

Public schools (state colleges and universities) are allocated money by their respective state governments. These "subsidies" lower the cost of tuition. Private schools don't have access to state dollars, so you pay a premium to attend these schools. As a very general comparison, tuition at a public university might range from $3,000–$6,000 per year, while a private school's tuition would more likely be from $7,000–$15,000 or more. Don't forget to add room and board costs, too—about $5,000 per year.

If your heart is set on a private school but your wallet is screaming poverty, don't despair. Most private colleges have quite a bit of money—more than public schools—to dole out in scholarships. So, when all is said and done, if you're a smart, achieving student, you may get enough financial aid from a private school to make it equivalent to (or cheaper than) the public alternative. TIP: Never rule out a private school because of cost alone. Most private colleges have both the wherewithal and the willingness to help capable students.

#7 Are campus visits really necessary?

If your parents' employers asked them to transfer to a new city, one of the first things Mom and Dad would want to do is visit the place. Since you'll likely be spending four or more years at a college, it's wise to do the same. Although campus visits can get expensive, it's even more costly to invest in a school that looks great on paper but not in person.

On a typical campus visit (they're scheduled regularly and generally led by students), you learn about costs, programs, and student facilities—gyms, dorms, the library, etc. You also have a chance to get a feel for the campus. Is the student body diverse? Does it appear liberal or conservative? How close is the nearest off-campus sign of life? These kinds of questions can't be adequately addressed by a college catalog, yet they will be more vital to you in the long run than how late the library stays open on Friday nights.

Many colleges will allow you to sit in on a class or two during your visit. With enough advice notice, you'll even be able to stay overnight in a dorm and sample the cafeteria cuisine.

If visiting a campus isn't possible, ask the admissions office to send you a video. Recruiting top students has become a high-pressure, high-tech effort, and more colleges are using these and other public relations tools (including Web sites; see pages 188–89). Also ask if any recent graduates live in your area. Alumni can give you their personal views of the place from which your parents will be accepting collect calls for the next several years.

Two final pointers: Most airlines have reinstituted "student fares" for passengers age 22 and under, so you may be able to travel even on a tight budget. Lastly, avoid visiting a campus when classes are not in session. You won't get a true picture of what it's like to be a student there.

College Information on the World Wide Web

If you've spent any time at all on the Web, then you know how much information is literally at your fingertips. With a good browser and a fast modem, you can find almost anything— including college Web sites, financial aid information, reviews, maps, photographs, even video clips of campus tours. You can contact admissions officers, submit applications, sign up for newsletters and mailing lists, E-mail students and alumni, etc., etc., *ad infinitum*.

Web sites come and go, URLs change (URL = Uniform Resource Locator = Internet address), so we can't guarantee that the following list will always be current. But it should give you a good start when it comes to collecting mountains of college information from the 'net.

CollegeNet
http://www.collegenet.com/cnmain.html
A fun and comprehensive online source for information on enrollment, fees, and contacts for colleges, universities, and graduate programs.

Ecola's College Locator
http://www.ecola.com/college/
Fast access to many college and university Web sites.

Internet College Exchange (ICX)
http://www.usmall.com/
PC Magazine named this one of the "Top 100 Web Sites" in 1996, saying that " . . . the Internet College Exchange can help you develop a list of potential colleges, select the ideal school from that list, fill out an application, look into financial aid, and respond to your acceptance letter." Lists more than 5,000 colleges and universities in the U.S.

Peterson's Education Center
http://www.petersons.com/
Information on colleges, universities, financial aid, and more from the publishers of the respected Peterson's Guides.

Princeton Review
http://www.review.com/
Information on colleges, admissions, and testing; search *The Best 309 Colleges* by school name, region, or state.

You can also use a search engine to locate information. Here's an example of how we found Cornell University by starting our search on Yahoo, a popular search engine:

http://www.yahoo.com/
click on Education link, go to
http://www.yahoo.com/Education/
click on College Entrance link, go to
http://www.yahoo.com/Education/College_Entrance/
click on Admissions Offices, go to
http://www.yahoo.com/Education/College_Entrance/Admissions_Offices/
click on Cornell University, go to
http://www.cornell.edu/UAO/Undergrad_Admissions.html

We ended up on Cornell's home page, with links to undergraduate colleges and majors, requirements for incoming freshmen, admission timetable, application procedures and helpful hints, financial aid, tuition, fees, and expenses, a mailing list, and more.

#8 What should I do about essays and recommendations?

If essays are required on your college applications, start writing them far in advance of the deadline. You'll go crazy trying to prepare two different essays for five different colleges in the midst of studying for finals in your senior year of high school. If an essay is not required, write one anyway and attach it to your application.

Compose a general "here's-why-I-want-to-attend-your-school" statement, then explain how your talents and interests match what the college has to offer.

In the same vein, ask for recommendations early, before your teachers are flooded with other requests. Approach teachers and counselors who know you as an individual, not just as a student. This personal touch will help the writers create a more complete picture of who you are. If recommendations aren't mandatory, get one or two anyway; they can only help your admission chances, especially if your academic record is somewhat spotty or your standardized test scores are a bit weak.

#9 What's the story on campus housing?

If you've ever shared a bedroom with a sibling, you've had good practice for dorm life. Virtually all freshmen live on campus, and virtually all of them have one or more roommates. Unfortunately, you probably won't get matched with someone on the basis of whether you're an early riser or a night owl, a heavy metallist or a classical oboe fanatic, a neatnik or a slob. Most colleges consider only the basics: your gender (they may have co-ed dorms, but never co-ed rooms) and whether or not you smoke. After that, you're subject to the luck of the draw.

"No problem," you may think. "My best friend from high school is attending the same college, so I'll just room with

> **"TRANSITIONS AFTER HIGH SCHOOL CAN BE ROUGH, BUT ALSO CHARACTER-BUILDING."**
> **PAULITA, 18**

him/her." This could work out, or it could destroy your friendship; knowing someone well isn't the same as living together. A wiser alternative might be to live on the same floor as your friend—in the same "neighborhood," so to speak—while rooming with someone else. You'll preserve your friendship and mingle with new and interesting people. Is it risky to room with a stranger? Of course, but it's no riskier for you than it is for him or her.

Many colleges offer "specialty dorms" designated by academic major. These are good ways to meet people with interests similar to yours. You might also check out the availability of "honors dorms" where quiet hours are enforced. Neither type of dorm has a sign in front saying "Nerds Only," but they are more likely to attract students who are serious about their college education.

Find Out More

To learn more about colleges, look for the latest editions of:

The Big Book of Colleges. Published by the Princeton Review. Helps you to find colleges based on factors that are important to you—location, size, tuition, extracurriculars, selectivity, etc. Lists and describes 1,200 colleges in North America.

Peterson's Guide to Four-Year Colleges. Profiles all 2,000 accredited colleges and universities in the U.S. and Canada; includes narratives written by admissions directors.

Peterson's Competitive Colleges. Enables you to easily compare details on more than 375 leading colleges that admit top students.

GIFTED PEOPLE SPEAK OUT

Wendy D. Isdell, 21

College. It's a scary idea, especially from the outside. I remember how it stressed me out in high school, especially when I hit my senior year and it was Time To Apply. Where should I go? What would it be like? That stress, I think, is what deters some gifted students from going on to college. Here's some advice for them and for everyone else.

If you're wavering about college, go. Besides the obvious benefit of that twenty-thousand-dollar-a-year piece of paper (theoretically, a better-paying job), you get an entirely different, extremely important thing out of college. You get a chance to *live*—that is, to grow a little bit more, have a chance to enjoy yourself a little—before you hit that hard, cold job market. Believe me, it is well worth the money. (Especially if the money isn't yours!) And if you're like me and you have no idea what you want to do with your life, college gives you four—or six, or eight—more years to decide! Isn't that great? Oh, yeah, and you get an education, too.

If you decide you want to go, start planning *now*. It doesn't matter if you're six or sixteen. Visit a lot of colleges, explore, sniff around. You can take the packaged official tour if you want, but the only real way to learn about a college is to talk to the students. Don't be afraid. Go to where the club offices are located—those are the most active students on campus. (And usually the friendliest.) Talk to them about life on campus. Ask about crime, whether the tuition is too high, whether there are cockroaches. And above all else, *ask about the food.* You're going to be stuffing yourself with that junk for the next four—or six, or eight—years. Make sure it's good! Try it out yourself, and not on "Parents' Visitation Weekend," when they serve escargot with white wine sauce. Don't fall for that. Try the ordinary fare three times. If you're not sick of it by then, you've got a winner.

When you decide to apply, apply to more than one. I applied to four, and I wish I had applied to ten. Only one gave me any significant financial aid. I wish I had had more choices, because . . . well, I'm not eating escargot right now, let me leave it at that. In addition to praying for money from the college, apply to every independent scholarship you can find. Buy or borrow one of those books full of them. Check out the Internet. Ask in your school's guidance department and in your local church, if you have one. College is expensive! And try to talk your parents into sending you a monthly "spending money" check, or get a part-time job on-campus. You've got to have drinking money, right? Well, not until you're twenty-one. (I'm chuckling as I type that line, trying to count how many drunk freshmen I've seen staggering back to their rooms, not remembering where they put their keys, and banging on the door for their equally sodden roommates to let them in.)

Overall, college is fun. There's a lot of work, don't let me mislead you there, but there's a lot of other stuff to do, too. Well, usually; that depends on the college. But at the very least, you can hang out with your friends—an art that is refined by your second week there, unless you glue your door shut. And sometimes that's not such a bad idea, depending on the people who are out there. (Look out especially for groups of guys chucking beer cans into nine-inch trash cans across the hall. They're probably drunk, and their aim is bad. Close the door.) And ladies, let me give you a special bit of advice. Unless you're looking for that specific kind of relationship, say *no* to any non-freshman guy who approaches you in those first three weeks. They're not going to call you later, unless they're one of the few and far-between exceptions. And ladies, be safe. Walk in groups until you get a feel for the security of your campus. Stay with people you know.

Though I risk sounding trite, I have to conclude that college is "a very rewarding experience." You can learn a lot, both about your chosen area of study and about life. As long as you take it easy, don't overwork and overstress yourself that first semester, it should be okay. Just remember, as you sit down for that final exam, that "SSN" does not stand for "Student's Sorority Name." (Try your telephone number there; sometimes it works. . . . Okay, maybe not.)

Wendy D. Isdell is the author of four books for Free Spirit Publishing: A Gebra Named Al and A Chemy Called Al, both novels for young adults, and two teachers' guides. She is currently studying for her bachelor's degree at a private university, where she enjoys playing her guitar, hanging out with friends, talking to her plants, and producing her own television shows for the university station.

GIFTED PEOPLE SPEAK OUT

Chad Gervich

On the first day of my freshman year at Vanderbilt University, I showed up wearing denim overalls. Although overalls were the hottest thing to hit my hometown of Iowa Falls, Iowa, since hot pants and leisure suits, little did I know that they had gone out of style in the rest of the world about three years earlier. There I stood on the brink of adulthood, away from parents, teachers, curfews, ready to face new challenges, obstacles, responsibilities . . . and I looked like Opie Taylor (son of Sheriff Taylor, as in *The Andy Griffith Show,* for those of you who don't watch old sitcoms).

Not that it mattered. Away from the cliquishness of high school, friends were no longer chosen on the basis of wardrobe, appearance, or how fast their cars could go.

College's greatest attribute may be its tolerance level. Because most colleges boast a spectrum of students of all nationalities, income levels, religions, colors, sexual orientations, athletic abilities, races, interests, political affiliations, heights, widths, weights, depths, fragrances, textures, genders, and cultures, people look beyond these incidental traits when choosing friends. College has a niche for everyone. It is your responsibility, however, to find your own niche.

The most important two words in creating a successful college career are . . . *get involved.* No one ever made friends while sitting alone in a dorm room, and as exciting as

Molecular Biology 101 may be, the heart of the college experience lies not in classes, but in friends and activities.

Most colleges, at the beginning of every year, have some sort of Organizations Fair, where all the campus clubs, groups, and associations set up booths for interested students. Don't miss it—and sign up for everything. Even if you don't have time for 216 extracurricular activities, you'll get a lot of mail and your friends will think you're really popular. You'll find organizations for writers, readers, artists, artsy people, people named Art, athletes, scholars, athletes who date scholars, athletes with scholarships, scholars with ships, scholars with lips, lippy people, Mick Jagger fans, people who fan dance, line dancers, dance majors, military majors, military protesters, protesters who protest protesters, animal rights protesters, party animals, animal lovers, animal crackers, cracked-up people, people who crack up easily, easy people, sleazy people, people with fleas, people with trees, tree-huggers, people who like hugs, and virtually any other social organization imaginable. There's an outlet for everyone, and those who don't find anything join the Young Republicans.

Sign up for more extracurricular activities than you could ever possibly handle. The busier you stay, the less of a chance you give yourself to get bored or homesick. Ninety-nine percent of bored and homesick kids haven't allowed themselves the opportunity to make friends or find extracurricular activities. Although you may not ultimately commit to every group on campus, you'll make a ton of friends simply by meeting people. The more things you do, the more people you'll meet, and the more friends you'll make. And in the process of sampling all the organizations, you may stumble across something new and exciting.

As the year progresses, and you realize what organizations you would actually like to commit to, the problem arises of how to budget your time. Although classes are a nuisance, and The History of Dadaism in Southern Texas may not offer much practical information, without sufficient grades your more pleasurable activities may begin to fade away. Mom, Dad, and the deans usually don't care how much money you raised at the Junior Birdwatchers' Bake-a-thon, but they do care that your tuition checks buy you an education. It's important, therefore, to keep your grades at an optimal level.

The best way to find study time is to allow a few hours each day when you can sneak off and be alone. If you can get into a pattern of studying at the same time and place every day, studying becomes painless. Try and find a secret hideaway where you won't be bothered by the commotion of campus life . . . a special corner of the library, an old desk in the dorm basement, a table in a deserted classroom. Avoid places like the fifty-yard line or the floor of the chancellor's office.

You may want to divide your study time. A couple of hours in the morning, an hour in the afternoon, and some time after dinner makes studying seem less monotonous. Take a ten-minute break every hour to get a snack, write a letter, sing some Neil Sedaka songs, or do whatever you do to relax.

The more you organize your days, the less stressed you will become. Schedule in time for studying, exercising, classes, meetings, even for goofing off with your friends. As you grow more accustomed to your day's schedule, you will find free moments when you can be spontaneous, but your schedule acts as a guide.

If you're having trouble with your homework, get in to see your professor as soon as possible. Make an appointment with the professor's secretary or go in during office hours. Professors love helping students (with the amount of tuition we pay, they should), and most of them enjoy getting to know their students on a personal level (not *too* personal, however). Relationships with professors can develop into lifelong friendships; most of them have friends and contacts around the world, so they're great when it comes to pulling strings at graduate schools and job interviews, writing letters of recommendation and letters of parole, or lending a hand at any other life-determining crossroads.

Contrary to what your high school chemistry teacher tells you, college is not all that excruciating. While college is meant to challenge you, it also offers you the means to tackle those challenges. Open the door when Opportunity knocks, and don't be afraid to taste samples from the great collegiate smörgasbord. You only get one shot at college, and despite the view as you move into your freshman dorm, four years whip by amazingly fast.

College has a place for everyone; you simply must find yours . . . even if you're wearing overalls.

Chad Gervich graduated from Vanderbilt University and currently attends UCLA on a full graduate scholarship, where he majors in creative writing. In his spare time, Chad writes screenplays and dabbles in acting, most recently as the "Purple Grape Guy" in a Fruit-of-the-Loom commercial produced for the Nashville Network.

Do You Have What It Takes? Insiders' Tips from Admissions Officers*

Not long ago, Stanford University in California received 14,912 applications to its incoming freshman class. Of these, 3,200 were straight-A students, and most of the rest weren't far behind. Yet Stanford accepted only 2,626 applications. To some students who thought they had taken all the right classes and jumped through all the right hoops to gain admission to this prestigious university, the rejection letter they received was more than disappointing— it was devastating.

So what's a kid supposed to do to get into a top-ranking college? Although there are no guarantees, there are ways to make yourself stand out from the crowd. Following are some valuable tips gathered from admissions officers at Stanford, Bowdoin College, Brown University, Massachusetts Institute of Technology (MIT), Haverford College, the University of Virginia, and Penn State:

- Essays are very important. Not only do they highlight your writing talents; they also reveal your personality.

- Many colleges compute their own GPA's, counting only "academically solid" courses and dropping grades for subjects like Drivers' Education and gym. (Stanford even drops all ninth grade marks, assuming that long-ago year has little bearing on your collegiate ability.)

- Demanding course loads are more impressive than high grades. As one admissions counselor observed, "We'd rather see a student take AP and honors courses and get B's than regular academic courses and get A's."

---

* The information in this section is based on "Do you have what it takes? How the top colleges choose their students," *Washington Post*, Education Review Section, November 19, 1989, pp. 1, 12, 16.

- Don't get lazy during your senior year of high school. First semester grades in particular remain important. Some students have even lost their tentative admission status (which colleges do compute) because of a lackluster senior year.

- The combination of high SAT/ACT scores and low course grades is a red flag to admissions officers. In the words of one, colleges generally avoid "the kind of person . . . whose teacher says he or she is gifted but not using it."

- Diversity is important—ethnic, geographic, socioeconomic. Brown University's Dean of Admissions said that an applicant from Montana has a better chance of being accepted (other qualities being equal) than one from northern New Jersey.

- Preference is generally given to children or relatives of alumni. Check your family's academic credentials to see who went where.

- Teacher recommendations work in your favor only if they are specific.

- Real talent—athletic, artistic, musical, or otherwise—is always noticed. But don't try to round out your résumé by suddenly signing up for every school activity. As one admissions official says, "You could play third trumpet for four years and by sticking it out, you'd still be showing loyalty, commitment, and dependability."

- Volunteer work is looked upon very favorably, especially leadership roles: "Somebody who works in a soup kitchen is going to look good, but someone who got funding for a new center is going to be special," explains one admissions director.

In summary, while there's no magic formula for getting into the most prestigious colleges, it's obvious that it takes more than high grades alone. The good news is: 90 percent of all applicants are admitted to at least one of their top two college choices.

> "I learned three
> important things
> in college—to
> use a library, to
> memorize
> quickly and
> visually, and to
> drop asleep at
> any time given a
> horizontal
> surface and
> fifteen minutes."
> Agnes de Mille

> "If you feel that
> you have both
> feet planted on
> level ground,
> then the
> university has
> failed you."
> Robert Goheen,
> speech,
> Princeton
> University

The Envelope, Please

You've just been admitted to all of your top three college choices. Congratulations! Now what?

Once again, it's comparison time. After you've considered the factors most relevant to you—cost, distance, reputation, size, etc.—eliminate the *one* college that ends up at the bottom. This will be hard initially, but it will ultimately make your decision easier. Next, reread from cover to cover the catalogs from your remaining two options, keeping a running checklist of pluses and minuses. If the decision is still too close to call, visit the campuses again. If this isn't possible, call the admissions officials you've been dealing with to date and ask them to give you their best pitches one more time. Finally, after talking over your choices with other people whose opinions you value and respect, select the college that your *heart,* not your head, tells you is the best place for you.

College is so much more than classes and tests. During your four (or more) years there, you'll mature in ways you never thought possible, discover new interests and passions, encounter challenges you never knew existed, make new friends, establish contacts you'll draw on for years into the future, and perhaps even meet your life partner. All other things being equal, let emotion, intuition, gut feeling, your "sixth sense," or whatever you want to call it be your guide. And remember, there's always the transfer factor.

GIFTED PEOPLE SPEAK OUT
Michael M. Hughes, M.D.

I was born in the relatively small southern town of Anderson, South Carolina. There were 176 students in my class when I graduated from high school in 1975.

I was lucky to have been in the homeroom class of Mr. Richard Palmer, a mathematics teacher. Mr. Palmer, by words and deeds, showed me that no matter what the odds are, a person who put his or her mind to it and really tried hard and put forth the effort could do anything. He made math fun and he worked two jobs, as both a teacher and as a design engineer. He would, at times, bring his work into the classroom to show us the worth and usefulness of what we were learning. In doing so, he made the connection between the world of school and the world beyond it.

Looking back, it seems pretty amazing that of the 32 students in Mr. Palmer's homeroom, nine of us are now M.D.s, two more are D.V.M.s (Doctors of Veterinary Medicine), and at least one is a pharmacist. If that isn't some sort of record, it should be.

Above all, though, it was my parents who were the most important in instilling a "can-do" attitude in me. My dad only finished eighth grade and my mom completed two years of business college. I was the first person in my family to go to a four-year college. My dad built himself a successful contracting business based on the principles of hard work, integrity, and dealing fairly with people. He taught me to work and to be proud of what I accomplished, no matter what the task. He taught me that to dig a ditch correctly was just as important as to save a life in the Cath Lab.

At my parents' urging, I went to college at Clemson University. I had wanted to work with my dad in his business, but just before graduating from Clemson, my parents and I made a deal: I agreed to apply to medical school at one place, the Medical University of South Carolina. If I got accepted, I would go there and do as my dad had always asked me to do—my best. Well, I got accepted and later graduated twelfth in my class of 161. Subsequently, I went on to complete my training at Wake Forest University, Akron General Medical Center, and the Cleveland Clinic.

At this point in my life, I am very interested in trying to give back to those who helped me along. I realize that it was several influential teachers who really got me started believing in myself, and I'd like you to know that it's important to find even one such soul as you go through school.

I also would like to say that if anyone had seen me or my classmates in the situation we grew up in, no one could have predicted that twelve of us would graduate from professional colleges. Please remember that appearances are deceiving. What you make of yourself depends as much on your attitude as it does your abilities. Of note, I don't even know my IQ, but I know what I can do.

Michael M. Hughes, M.D., is the Director of Interventional Cardiology at Akron General Hospital.

A Semi-Serious Glossary of Terms

Academic Advisor: A full-time professor, hopefully in your major, with whom you are supposed to meet regularly to ensure that you're on the right path toward graduation. It's up to you to make appointments with your advisor. Don't be surprised if he or she knows less about your program than you do; just be sure to get any special requests or "course waivers" in writing. *Related term:* Professor Who?

Bursar: Just like on a cruise ship, the bursar is the person who collects your money. He or she also sends threatening letters promising to cancel your registration if you don't pay the library fines or parking tickets you've been collecting as souvenirs. Warning! The bursar can hold up your graduation or refuse to send out a course transcript if you still owe even one cent to your soon-to-be alma mater. Also, unpaid fines appear on your next tuition bill, so there's no escape. *Related term:* Bloodsucking leech.

Core Curriculum/Liberal Education Requirements: A cluster of courses you are required to take no matter what you choose as an academic major. Employed by the majority of colleges, these courses read like a menu at a Chinese restaurant: two courses from column A (math), three from column B (English), etc. They can take you as little as a semester or as long as two years to complete. *Advice:* Take them early on in your college career.

Early Decision: If you are absolutely, positively sure you will attend a specific college if you get accepted there, early decision allows you to hear far in advance—as early as November or December of your senior high school year—of your acceptance. But there's a hitch: You can apply it to only one college and must withdraw all other applications if you do get admitted to your first choice. A good option for you if you're positive about your first college choice, early decision can relieve springtime anxiety in your senior year of high school.

Freshman 15: A reference to the minimum amount of weight, in pounds, that you'll gain during your freshman year while enjoying unlimited seconds of cafeteria food. *Sad fact:* You may claim to hate the food, but your waistline will show otherwise.

Going Greek: Having nothing to do with nationalities, dating, or ethnic festivals, "Going Greek" means opting to join a fraternity (like Delta Sigma Phi) or a sorority (like Chi Omega). *Related terms:* Rush (when Greeks have parties to look you over before they decide whether or not to accept you into their house); Hell Week (an artifact of another era that requires you to perform embarrassing acts to prove that you'll do anything to join the club); Pledge (a peon, like you, who gets accepted to join the house during Rush).

Parents' Weekend: Especially popular among parents of freshmen, this fall weekend usually coincides with a home football game with a weak competitor (it looks good to win when your folks are around) and your first serious bout with homesickness. The newness of college has worn off, mid-term exams are upon you, and it's great to see your mommy and/or daddy, who usually arrive with fresh sheets and food. *Happy fact:* Cafeteria food is better than usual this weekend.

Sectional: A sub-group of a large, lecture-style course, meeting weekly with a TA (Teaching Assistant), GA (Graduate Assistant), or TF (Teaching Fellow), all of whom are overworked and underpaid graduate students. Sectionals help to personalize and explain what's going on in your overpopulated American Government course. *Related terms:* Tutorials, labs, study groups.

Alternatives to College (ATC)

Your parents, teachers, counselors, and others will likely assume that someone with your kind of mind is clearly college bound. They may insist that a college or university degree is essential to your success. Especially if your parents were the first in their families to attend college, they will take it for granted that you'll go, too. But what if you have made different plans for your future? Not attending college is a perfectly valid choice for some people, including gifted students. Following are several suggestions that can help make your decision more palatable to others.

1. Have some idea of what you will do, not just what you won't do.

Merely saying, "College isn't for me right now," won't get you very far with parents and teachers unless you also have a solid notion of what you'll do instead—think of it as an Alternative to College (ATC). The Armed Forces, a trade school, full-time employment, or a part-time job in some far-off place (usually a ski resort, a beach, or a big city) where you'll try to figure out how you want to spend your next few years are ATCs with differing degrees of acceptability, depending on your parents' lifestyles, belief systems, and tolerance for ambiguity. Whatever you choose, and whatever your reasons, express them calmly and fully. There's no guarantee of acceptance, but you'll be better off with a well-defined ATC than a loosely sketched plan.

> "College is always on the road to somewhere else."
> Tom Robbins

2. Find an advocate.

Somewhere there's someone who will support your ATC. When you find this person—an uncle from Dubuque, a counselor at your school, an adult sibling who believes in you—explain your position, share your ideas, ask for suggestions on how to broach this topic with your parents, and use his or her shoulder to lean on if you need a comforting word. Ideally, your advocate will offer to speak to your parents on your behalf.

3. Never say never.

Teenagers tend to talk in absolutes—as in "I'll never . . ." or "I'll always. . . ." The problem with absolutes is that they eventually require retractions. As you mature, you start to see the world in more colors than black and white. Also, when teenagers say "never," they may not mean "forever," but that's usually how the word is interpreted by most adults, who respond by attacking the shortsightedness of this type of thinking.

To avoid misunderstandings, try not to make proclamations like "I'll *never* go to college! There's no point!" First of all, those are fighting words; second, they are naive. You can't possibly know how your dreams and goals will change in a year or a decade down the road. Instead of saying never, try something along these lines: "Right now, college is not my top priority. I'd rather do [fill in the blank] because [fill in the blank]. Who knows if I'll feel this same way next year or in ten years, but it's what I'm feeling now. Please respect that." You're being honest, you're not claiming omniscience, you're leaving the door open for the future, and you're showing sensitivity to the people whose dreams you may have deflated.

4. Explain that your decision to pursue an ATC is your choice, not someone else's fault.

When relatives and teachers hear of your non-college plans, their first response (spoken or not) may be, "Where did we go wrong?" Allay their anxiety by explaining that you've devoted a lot of time and thought to your decision, and it's not a snap judgment. Relieve them of the "fault burden" by reminding them that the strength it took for you to make this choice is a direct result of the way you were raised or taught—to be an independent thinker. Thank them for giving you the inner wherewithal to pursue the course that's right for you.

5. Be excited about your ATC.

Enthusiasm is infectious, so be sure to praise the benefits of your ATC in glowing terms. By learning as much about it as you can— what you'll be doing, where you'll live, how you'll earn money, how you'll stay safe—you will gain the respect (and grudging support) of even the most committed naysayers. You'll know that you have succeeded when one doubter says, "Well, this might not be the worst decision after all." Most adults yearn for the time when they had fewer responsibilities and more options, just like you do now. Use their nostalgia to your advantage. Since you'll be an adult for the rest of your life, you might as well squeeze as much out of your waning adolescence as you can.

6. Cover your bases.

When the PSAT, SAT, and/or ACT tests are offered, take them. When "Career and College Night" rolls through your high school cafeteria, go and hear what the presenters have to say. When you're able to sign up for AP and honors courses, do.

If you've already determined that you're not going to college, why bother? For at least three reasons:

- *Your impressions of what you can do and learn in college might not be accurate. Make sure that you know what you're turning down.*

- *Test-taking is easier when you're 17 and used to weekly exams.*

- *If you ever change your mind about college, you'll be glad that your transcript is strong. Challenging courses and solid test scores will prove that you once were college material, and it shouldn't be too difficult to show that you still are.*

> ## Find Out More
>
> **To learn more about alternatives to college, contact:**
>
> **Center for Interim Programs, P.O. Box 2347, Cambridge, MA 02238; telephone (617) 547-0980.**
>
> **David Denman's Time Out, 3030 Bridgeway, Sausalito, CA 94965; telephone (415) 332-1831.**

THE BENEFITS OF TAKING A BREAK

Amy Witenen and James Macgillivary both finished high school in 1994—Amy with a 3.7 GPA from a school in Michigan, and James ranking seventh in his class of 138 in a Canadian secondary school. Both seem like college material . . . and they are, but not just yet.

Amy and James both opted to take a year to explore other possibilities. They work together in Phoenix, Arizona, on an architecture and ecology project for a company called Arcosanti.

"I'm exploring things so I can decide what to study," says Amy. "I don't think of this as taking a year off. I think it's another way to get an education."

Gifted students often feel overwhelmed by the possibilities that await them in the world of work. Often, being good at and interested in so many things makes it difficult to decide on a college major. So some independent thinkers, like Amy and James, trek down a path less traveled, hoping to find a career direction while getting a taste of the real world of employment.

The Center for Interim Programs,* based in Cambridge, Massachusetts, helps people gain a foothold on their futures by matching students (for a $1,200 fee) to various short-term and long-term projects that pique their interest. (For example, the Arcosanti program lasts a minimum of five weeks). Since the majority of entering college freshmen don't know what they want to major in, and since many students change majors five or six times before graduation, an immersion program in an area of interest might be just the ticket to help you decide.

The Center's Director, Dr. Neil Bull, notes that they have worked with more than 3,000 students, all of whom eventually went on to college. Bull advises parents that "unless you're financially masochistic and enjoy writing checks for a child who doesn't really want to be in school," there is no sense in sending an 18-year-old off to a place he or she isn't ready to tackle seriously. For example, Wes Edwards of Ohio wanted something more immediately after high school—he had been a good student, intent on entering the "right" college, but he just didn't know where. Following a year of volunteer work on a schooner in the Caribbean, teaching at a nature school in Kentucky, and backpacking in the West, Wes entered the University of Montana at Missoula. As a freshman, he's made the Dean's List.

There are alternatives to college, and if you choose one that's right for you, you're not wasting time, you're buying time. College will wait until you're ready.

The information in this section is based on "Program Helps Youth Pin Down Educational Goals" by Fran Henry, Cleveland Plain Dealer, April 15, 1995.

---

* For information on how to contact the Center for Interim Programs, see page 203.

Relationships

To your parents, you may be the smart son or daughter they're always bragging about—or nagging. To your classmates, you may be the brain, the know-it-all, the one with the answers. Sometimes being gifted is a pain, especially when it affects your relationships with others. No matter how good you are at entertaining yourself, no matter how much time you spend inside your head solving problems, dreaming dreams, or thinking fascinating and creative thoughts, you need other people in your life, including age mates and adults. This chapter is about relationships—making new ones, reassessing some existing ones, and strengthening those that matter to you.

"SO OFTEN I FEEL THAT GIFTED KIDS ARE DEFINED BY THEIR SMARTNESS, BY TEACHERS, OTHER KIDS, PARENTS—NOBODY SHOULD BE DEFINED SOLELY BY THEIR INTELLECT." PAULITA, 18

Friends

Forty percent of our survey respondents wanted to know more about making friends; many wondered if age really mattered that much when it came to friendships. Some gifted teenagers who took our survey felt that their social lives were in great shape. (If you fall into that group, you may want to skip this section.)

"SOMETIMES I FEEL LIKE I JUST DON'T FIT IN."
JOSHUA, 12

**"WHY AREN'T GIFTED KIDS AS POPULAR AS THE
OTHER KIDS?" ALISON, 12**

No one can argue about the importance of having friends. They support us in good times and bad; they enhance our enjoyment of many things, from athletic events to parties, special projects, even studying. Especially as your parents and teachers start exerting less influence over your actions and beliefs—a normal and natural part of your development that begins at around age 12—your friends assume greater influence and play a more central role in your life.

"Intimate
relationships
cannot
substitute for a
life plan. But to
have any
meaning or
viability at all,
a life plan must
include intimate
relationships."
Harriet Lerner

Gifted or not, we all need friends; gifted or not, we all sometimes have problems making and keeping friends. But being gifted can put a unique spin on social relationships and occasionally complicate them. Following are some questions about friends and friendship that gifted students have shared with us in surveys, interviews, letters, and conversations.

Ten Common Questions about Friends and Friendship

#1 Some of my friends seem to resent me, or they're prejudiced against me because I'm gifted. Why is that?

Usually people have prejudices when they don't understand something or someone. They may feel inferior if they don't have enough good things going on in their own lives. So putting you down may make them feel better about themselves (at least for the moment). Just be yourself, and they may come around—or you may need to start hanging out with other people.

#2 Does everyone have trouble making friends, or is it just me?

Relax; it's not just you. Some people seem to make friends effortlessly—they're in the right place at the right time with the right social skills. Other people find it difficult to connect because of shyness, circumstances, or whatever. But everyone—whether adept or awkward—has to work at forming and sustaining meaningful friendships. (For tips on making friends, see page 209.)

#3 I don't have any trouble making friends, so why is there all this talk about gifted people being social misfits?

It's true that many gifted children and teens make friends easily, but for others it's not so easy. They might perceive themselves as "social misfits," which sabotages their self-confidence. Also, some people assume that because gifted kids are brighter and more intellectually advanced than their peers, they will automatically have problems relating to so-called "normal" kids. For whatever reason, many of our survey respondents said they wanted help in this area, so obviously there are some gifted students who have trouble making friends (or think they do).

#4 Does it matter if my friends are two, three, or even four years older or younger than I am?

No. Adults have friendships with people of all ages, so why shouldn't you? What matters is to cultivate friends you can count on and relate to. Sharing the same birth year isn't as important as sharing interests, goals, and values. (For more about breaking age barriers, see pages 212–14.)

#5 Is it normal to have just a few close friends?

Yes. Gifted children and teens tend to be more adult-like in their relationships, favoring a few intense relationships over several more casual ones. What's important is to have at least one or two friends that you can rely on. When it comes to relationships, quality matters more than quantity.

#6 Do I have to conform to be accepted?

It's not a bad thing to go along with the crowd—as long as the crowd is right for you. It's only when you compromise your own values, beliefs, and goals that conformity becomes a problem and can even be dangerous. On the other hand, if you always insist on doing things your way, be prepared for a lonely life. (For more about popularity, see pages 215–16.)

#7 I've just met someone I'd like to be friends with, and he asked me what "gifted" means. What can I say that won't alienate him or sound arrogant?

You might begin by asking him what he thinks it means. If he really wants to know, this could lead to an interesting discussion about your individual points of view. Remember, there are no right or wrong answers about giftedness; even the experts can't agree on a single definition (see pages 8–9). By now you probably have your own ideas about giftedness. Share as much or as little as you want.

#8 How can I cope with "leech" friends—people who rely on me for homework and test answers?

First, ask yourself, "Are they really my friends?" People who like you only for what they can get from you don't qualify as "friends." So that's something you'll have to decide. Second, if you feel like helping (with homework, not with test answers), and if you have the time, then go ahead and do it. Otherwise simply explain that you have your own work to do and you're not available this time around. Maybe the "leeches" will take the hint—or maybe not. (For more about "friends" you can do without, see pages 216–18.)

#9 How should I respond when my friends tease me about being smart?

There's no single foolproof way to cope with teasing. If the teaser is someone you respect and care about, be honest and tell her how the teasing makes you feel. Ask her to stop being critical of you and explain that the teasing isn't helping your friendship. If the teaser is someone you don't respect or care about, ignore her and walk away. At first this may seem hard to do, and it may hurt, but if the teaser doesn't get a response from you, eventually she'll move on. (For more about teasing and how to handle it, see pages 218–22.)

#10 Do gifted students date less often than others?

We're not aware of any formal studies that document an answer to this question. However, some of our survey respondents have told us—based on their own experience and that of their friends—that gifted kids are slower to date than others, and they might not date as often. Some feel that it's hard to be popular and intelligent at the same time; girls in particular believe that being smart intimidates boys and makes them less "dateable." Dating is stressful for everyone, regardless of gender or age. If you're ready to date but it's not happening, you may wonder if there's something wrong with you. Instead of worrying or blaming yourself, you might need to go beyond your regular circle of friends (at your school, place of worship, or wherever) and find other people with whom you share common interests.

12 Tips for Making and Keeping Friends

1. **_Reach out._** Don't always wait for someone else to make the first move. A simple "hi" and a smile go a long way. It may sound corny, but you'll be amazed at the response you'll receive when you extend a friendly greeting.

2. **_Get involved._** Join clubs that interest you; take special classes inside or outside of school. Seek out neighborhood and community organizations and other opportunities to give service to others.

3. **_Let people know that you're interested in them._** Don't just talk about yourself; ask questions about them and their interests. Make this a habit and you'll have mastered the art of conversation. It's amazing how many people haven't yet grasped this basic social skill.

4. **_Be a good listener._** This means looking at people while they're talking to you and genuinely paying attention to what they're saying. (A long litany of "uh-huhs" is a dead giveaway that your mind is somewhere else.)

5. **_Risk telling people about yourself._** When it feels right, let your interests and talents be known. For example, if you love science fiction and you'd like to know others who feel the same way, spread the word. If you're an expert on the history of science fiction, you might want to share your knowledge. **BUT . . .**

6. **_Don't be a show-off._** Not everyone you meet will share your interests and abilities. (On the other hand, you shouldn't have to hide them—which you won't, once you find people who like and appreciate you.)

7. **_Be honest._** Tell the truth about yourself and your convictions. When asked for your opinion, be sincere. Friends appreciate forthrightness in each other. **BUT . . .**

8. **_When necessary, temper your honesty with diplomacy._** The truth doesn't have to hurt. It's better to say "Gee, your new haircut is interesting" than to exclaim "You actually paid money for THAT?" There are times when frankness is inappropriate and unnecessary.

9. **_Don't just use your friends as sounding boards for your problems and complaints._** Include them in the good times, too.

10. **_Do your share of the work._** That's right, work. Any relationship takes effort. Don't always depend on your friends to make the plans and carry the weight.

11. **_Be accepting._** Not all of your friends have to think and act like you do. (Wouldn't it be boring if they did?)

12. **_Learn to recognize the so-called friends you can do without._** Some gifted kids get so lonely that they put up with anyone—including friends who aren't really friends at all. Follow tips 1–11 and this shouldn't happen to you.

GIFTED PEOPLE SPEAK OUT

Bryan A. Mantz

The transition from elementary school to junior high school was very difficult for me. I was a straight-A student coming from an elementary school in Charleston, West Virginia. Many of the students in my class regarded me as a "nerd," and they conveyed this fact to the students coming into the junior high from other schools in Charleston. Thus, I had it bad from the start. I was picked on by many of the older students, and I had difficulty making new friends. The first three months of junior high were hellish for me, and I was often depressed.

Then I met Tim. He was a seventh grader who had come from another elementary school. He was also a straight-A student but, unlike me, people liked and respected him. He had a quick wit and a great sense of humor. He made friends very easily.

I met Tim one day as I arrived at school. My bus came early, so I had quite a bit of time before classes began. I began looking around the lobby to see if I could find someone to talk to. That's when I spotted him. He was sitting on a chair talking to another boy whose name was, as I later discovered, Dan. I went over to them and said hello. Then I pulled up a chair and joined in the conversation. At first we mainly discussed school matters, but soon we moved on to different subjects and discovered that we all had much in common.

This was the first step towards a deep friendship that developed between Tim, Dan, and me. Each day when I went to school, I would go over to them and talk. I was very happy to finally have friends that I could truly communicate my inner feelings to. As time progressed, the three of us did many other things together. We went bowling and stayed over at each others' houses. I will never forget the time we all went to King's Island Amusement Park in Ohio for one day. That was one of the most enjoyable days I had ever had. (I finally gathered enough courage to go on the roller-coasters.)

My eighth-grade year was filled with more fun and excitement with my friends. Another new boy joined our group; his name was Steve, and he was a math whiz with a terrible sense of humor. (He told the worst jokes!) The four of us became great friends.

My ninth-grade year was awesome! We were finally at the top and loved every minute of it. Dan had a girlfriend, and Steve won all-county recognition for his trombone playing as well as for his math ability. Tim began pursuing a seventh grader, and I was playing football. Yet still we gathered together every weekend to do something, whatever it might be.

A boy named Greg joined our group. At first he was very shy, but he soon loosened up and we became close friends.

The transition from junior high school to senior high school was a big step for all of us, though not as big as when we had gone from elementary school to junior high. I soon realized that my courses were much harder than they had been before, as evidenced by the amount of homework I had each night. Sometimes I had three or four tests to study for in a single evening. But I got used to this quickly and made decent grades.

It was during this time that our group expanded. Chris, Mark, and Matt started hanging around with us, too. There were even some girls who would occasionally socialize with us.

This was a time in my life when I really started to think seriously about my future. I realized that my friends would not be around forever. I would have to make new friends and establish new social relationships. A wave of uncertainty hit me as I wondered if I would ever have companions as close as the seven I associated with.

In the end, everything worked out fine. I went to boarding school for my fourth and fifth years of high school and made many new friends. By then I understood that friendships were started by two or more people willing to make a commitment to each other. I tried hard not to alienate people and to show them that I really wanted to get to know them better. In the process, I became a better friend and a better person.

But I still remember what it was like to make the transition from elementary school to junior high, and from junior high to high school. And I know that having friends makes a big difference.

Bryan A. Mantz wrote this article while attending Episcopal High School in Alexandria, Virginia.

Finding Friends Who Are Right for You

Many of the gifted students we've talked with over the years feel more strongly about world problems than their peers. They worry about hunger, pollution, international relations, the economy, poverty, overpopulation, human rights, the spread of AIDS, and other global issues.

"SOME OF THE PEOPLE I KNOW CARE MORE ABOUT THEIR HAIR THAN WORLD HUNGER. THEY JUST AREN'T CONCERNED ABOUT ANYTHING OUTSIDE THEIR OWN LITTLE WORLD." GIRL, 13

It's important to find friends who think as you do, because life gets lonely when you only have yourself to talk to. And it's easy to start thinking that there's something wrong with you if there isn't someone around who can relate on the same level.

Gifted students need to spend at least part of each day with others of similar interests and abilities. One way to accomplish this is by taking gifted, accelerated, or honors classes. Students who do this have told us that these classes are places where they can really be themselves. They don't have to worry about using certain vocabulary for fear that other students will accuse them of showing

"I MADE MOST OF MY FRIENDS IN THE ADVANCED CLASSES AT SCHOOL. THEIR GOALS AND INTERESTS WERE COMPATIBLE WITH MINE AND THAT'S WHAT MADE ME FEEL SO COMFORTABLE AROUND THEM." BOY, 16

off; they don't have to concern themselves with whether the rest of the class understands what they are saying because it sounds "too complicated or philosophical." They can brainstorm freely, ask sophisticated questions, and contribute to discussions without being

"IT'S A GREAT ADVANTAGE TO BE GIFTED. SOMETIMES YOU FEEL LIKE YOU'RE REALLY ALONE, BUT YOU'RE NOT. IT'S GREAT TO BE YOUR OWN PERSON, AND YOU SHOULDN'T TRY TO BE LIKE EVERYONE ELSE JUST SO PEOPLE WILL LIKE YOU. IT'S VERY IMPORTANT NOT TO LET YOUR TALENTS SLIP THROUGH YOUR FINGERS BY TRYING TO FIT IN WITH EVERYONE. RATHER, YOU SHOULD FIND FRIENDS WHO COMPLEMENT YOUR ABILITIES." RENE, 15

belittled or teased. Some gifted students have said that their gifted class was *the* most important time of the day or the week for them.

But what if your school doesn't offer these classes? Where else can you go to find people who are like you? Fortunately, you have several options to choose from.

Breaking Age Barriers

For a 10-year-old whose mind grasps the theory of relativity, or the 15-year-old whose goal is to discover a cure for cancer, friendship—*true* friendship that involves sharing, understanding, and mutual respect—may seem rare or even unattainable. For this reason (among others), some gifted students often seek relationships with adults or older students.

Some gifted students form close friendships with parents, teachers, and neighbors—adults whose interests are in keeping with theirs. The adults don't accuse them of "showing off" their intellectual abilities; they don't chide them because they are "different." Adult friends can be wiser, more objective, and less judgmental than peers.

> **"I HAVE A LOT OF TROUBLE RELATING TO KIDS MY AGE. IT'S AS THOUGH WE'RE ON A TOTALLY DIFFERENT WAVELENGTH. I PREFER ADULT COMPANY OVER KID COMPANY BECAUSE I CAN CONTRIBUTE TO THEIR CONVERSATIONS WITHOUT BEING THOUGHT OF AS STRANGE FOR KNOWING WHAT'S GOING ON."** BILLY, 14

Other gifted students have found that the people they most enjoy are several years older or younger than they are. In fact, either is common for bright, creative young people. Here are a couple of reasons why:

* *If you prefer older friends—for example, you're 13 and they're 16—it may be because they are more at your level mentally and socially than people your age. You may have "outgrown" your 13-year-old classmates several years ago.*
* *If you prefer younger friends—for example, you're 12 and they're 10—it may be because you appreciate their open-minded acceptance of you. They don't seem as interested in competing with you or pointing out that you're not as smart as you think you are. You feel safe in their company, plus they're more playful and fun to be around than people your age.*

When you're an adult, you'll probably have friends, colleagues, and coworkers who are old enough to be your grandparents or young enough to be your children. About the only time in life when friendships are determined primarily by age is from kindergarten through 12th grade. After that, years matter less and other things matter more—compatibility, common interests, mutual respect, and the countless other factors that bring people together. As one woman in her early 30s says:

> "My friends run the gamut when it comes to age—from their early 20s all the way up to 60. One is 15 years younger than I am, and another is older than my mom. I was in college before I discovered that I could have friends of all ages, and I wish I'd figured it out a lot sooner."

Oddly, the social worlds of children and teenagers operate under a set of more stringent and complex rules than the adult world. For example, it's no big deal for a 30-year-old person to be dating someone who's 25, but a five-year disparity is significant if you're 15 and the person you're dating is 20.

"Eggheads, unite! You have nothing to lose but your yolks."
Adlai Stevenson

Most people don't understand that there's a big difference between *age mates* and *peers*. Just because you happen to have been born in the same year as 90 percent of your classmates doesn't mean that you must look only to them for social gratification and acceptance. If you prefer alliances with older or younger people, then that's who you should seek out. There may be a few raised eyebrows or expressions of concern by those who care about you, so you'll need to be mature enough to accept these comments. Even better, talk these concerns over with the people you enjoy spending time with. They will probably understand perfectly why some people have questions about your relationship.

How can you meet people who are likely to be your peers? It's difficult to do this at school, where grade levels still function as social hurdles. It may be easier if you're in an open or nontraditional school, where students from different grades are grouped in homerooms and take classes together. (Actually, this isn't such a modern notion after all; it happened in the one-room schools our grandparents and great-grandparents attended.)

You may have better luck if you look outside of school for opportunities to meet and make friends. Examples:

- *Take a class through a university extension or adult education program that attracts people of all ages. Or see what's available at your local community college or neighborhood recreation center.*

- *If your interests lie in the arts, volunteer to work at a museum or usher at a concert hall or theater. Find out about special projects or activities that use volunteers, then get involved.*

- *Join a hobby club or other special interest group. If you're into computers, try a local users' group. If you play a musical instrument, look into a community orchestra or band, or start a small ensemble of your own. If you're passionate about Victorian novels, beat poetry, or the plays of Tennessee Williams, check out a book discussion group, or start one of your own.*

CAUTION

If you prefer the company of older peers, their chronological ages may have made them eligible for certain privileges that are still taboo for you—for example, drinking, driving, or overnight stays. The surest way to lose the right to hang out with older peers is to abuse the rules that your parents (or society) have established for you. Enjoy your friends, whatever their ages, but remember the legal limits of your youth.

Also: There are some so-called adults who take advantage of younger people. We're not suggesting that you live your life being constantly suspicious and on your guard, but don't be naive, either. If you feel uncomfortable around someone, trust your instincts. When something doesn't feel right, it usually *isn't* right.

So be careful out there, okay?

Friendship vs. Popularity

There's a big difference between having friends and being popular. It may be hard to recognize at times when you seem to be the only person not surrounded by a crowd of admirers and acquaintances, but the distinction is real and significant. As one Canadian college student explained:

> "It is only in the last year and a half that I've discovered the delights of belonging in a group of real friends. We are an odd, sometimes ridiculous crew who are accepted as such by others. . . . Many kids who have social problems in high school discover that things get better by the second or third year of university—maybe earlier, depending on how quickly they learn the rules. It's no fun to go through bad social times, but I know now that I wouldn't trade popularity and 'ordinariness' for the solid friendships and ability to function on my own that I have now."

A woman in her 40s looks back at her high school years and remembers:

> "It wasn't until my senior year that I fell into a group of friends. Up until then, I'd been a loner. I was the 'class brain,' the one with the funny glasses and hair and weird clothes who never fit in, never went out, never got asked on dates. Then my English teacher pushed me to join the newspaper staff, and guess what? Everyone there was brainy, wore glasses, and had funny hair and unfashionable clothes. Even better, they all went out together, and suddenly I was included in group parties and picnics and social events. None of us were popular in school, but we were all popular with each other. Each of us was a social misfit outside the newspaper office, but inside, we ruled!"

Things *will* get better if you're willing to be patient and make the effort. You might try these "survival tips" gleaned from the experiences of people who have been there:

- *Be content with one or two solid friendships; they're worth more than you realize.*
- *Don't expect everyone to like you. (Do you like everyone you meet?)*
- *Seek out activities and groups that form around a common interest. Don't let your relationships be determined by age alone.*
- *Talk to your parents—sometimes to get advice and sometimes just to sound off. Problems seem less daunting and more manageable if you share them.*
- *Be yourself. It's too tiring to maintain a facade for someone else's sake; besides, you're bound to be found out sooner or later. Friendships work best when they're based on honesty, sincerity, and WYSIWYG (what you see is what you get).*

Friendship vs. Popularity and Other Fine-Line Distinctions

Friendship vs. Popularity

Friendship implies acceptance of you at all times, while **popularity** means that you're accepted only when it's convenient or fashionable.

Loneliness vs. Being Alone

Loneliness hurts, while **being alone** feels good because it gives you the chance to experience solitude and freedom.

Age vs. Maturity

Age is a number that happens to you, while **maturity** is an attitude and a set of behaviors you develop to face facts, set goals, and dream dreams.

Knowledge vs. Wisdom

Knowledge is a storehouse of facts, while **wisdom** is the ability to take your knowledge, draw on your experience, and work to improve your life and the lives of others.

"Friends" You Can Do Without

Even though we try to choose our friends carefully, everyone comes with positive traits and not-so-positive traits. Sometimes the latter include expecting you to "help" with homework assignments and/or tests. When this happens, it's natural to feel uncomfortable, conflicted, pressured, or used.

"MY REAL FRIENDS DON'T ASK ME FOR HELP, BUT OTHER KIDS DO." TRACY, 15

"OTHER STUDENTS DON'T ASK ME FOR HELP ON TESTS SO MUCH AS ON ASSIGNMENTS WHEN THEY'RE TOO LAZY TO DO THE WORK THEMSELVES." JON, 14

"Helping" with Homework

Examine your motives for being a homework assistant. Many gifted students feel good about being able to help others. They experience a sense of pride when their classmates (especially popular ones) ask them questions. If that's how you feel, then go ahead and help.

But sometimes "helping" becomes a hassle. And you'll ask yourself, "Should I or shouldn't I?" One way to approach an answer that's right for you is by considering the possible consequences of helping others with their homework. Examples:

1. Helping can get out of hand. When it does, you may not have time for your own work. What to do? Say no politely but firmly. As in "Sorry, but I just can't. I've got a pre-calc test tomorrow and a paper on Friday, plus a biology lab to finish up."
2. Some people will try to take advantage of your help. You're the best judge of when that happens. If it appears that you're doing more of their work than they are, something's amiss.
3. Helping can get you in trouble if it violates classroom rules.

"Helping" with Tests

It's hardly worth talking about. You know what's right, and you know what you stand to lose if you're caught. You'll have to make up your own mind on this issue. If you choose not to cheat, just ignore the request. You don't need to explain why. The person whispering across the row or over your shoulder will know why.

A friend who asks you to do something dishonest is not a friend.

How to Handle Teasing

You've heard the names gifted students are called. Once armed with labels (especially ones that hurt), children and teenagers will use them at every opportunity. But don't think that gifted students are the only ones who suffer. Every teenager experiences some type of teasing for being "different." If you're tall, short, heavy, thin, white, black, or brown, if you chew your food with your mouth open or closed, if you wear your shirt tucked in or out, if you live in a trailer or a Park Avenue penthouse, if your ears are too big or too small, if your hair is straight or curly, if your clothes are from The Gap or the Salvation Army, you can be sure that you'll hear about it. You name it, somebody's got a label for it, and labels are seldom flattering or affirming.

"**I GET TIRED OF BEING CALLED A BRAIN ALL THE TIME.**" AMY, 13

"**PEOPLE MY AGE JUST DON'T UNDERSTAND ME, AND THEY TEASE ME A LOT. I WISH THEY WOULD ACCEPT ME FOR WHO I AM.**" ALICE, 15

"**I DON'T JUST GET TEASED BECAUSE DO WELL IN SCHOOL—I GET BULLIED.**" TOM, 13

"**SOME PEOPLE CALL ME A FREAK BECAUSE I'M GIFTED. IT'S SCARY.**" DIANE, 17

If someone makes fun of adults, and if the adults are reasonably well-adjusted, they'll likely shrug it off for what it's worth: an opinion right or wrong from someone they either respect or don't, on a subject or situation that may or may not matter to them. Adults generally have the life experience necessary to evaluate situations fairly quickly. Most teenagers haven't yet accumulated this experience, and they aren't as adept at dodging painful remarks.

We all need to feel as if we belong somewhere. As a gifted person, you want to be part of the crowd, accepted and admired. You don't necessarily want to be different. Teasing sets you apart so you feel even *more* different and disconnected. Eventually, you may start to question whether being gifted is such a great thing after all. And you may begin to wish that you *weren't* gifted.

In order to handle teasing, it's important to recognize that the problem comes from the outside *and* the inside. First, you need to understand that as a gifted person, it's absolutely okay for you to:

- study a lot
- enjoy reading
- learn and know about many things
- get high grades
- worry about world problems
- be inquisitive

- seek out and savor challenges
- pursue demanding goals
- have a wide variety of interests
- solve complex problems
- have an advanced vocabulary
- achieve great things.

And it's absolutely okay for you to:

- go to parties
- goof off
- date
- dance
- play video games
- watch TV
- talk on the phone
- read comic books

- swim, skate, bike, sail, surf, rock climb, play street hockey, and/or shoot hoops
- listen to loud music
- sleep late
- take part in other activities that have nothing to do with school, learning, books, and grades.

If you enjoy some, most, or a few things from both lists, you're not so different after all. If you feel that you're especially susceptible or vulnerable to teasing, maybe you need to take a closer look at yourself. Nothing attracts a teaser more than someone who lacks self-confidence and self-esteem. Many teasers are also bullies, and they seek out victims who can't or won't fight back. For tips and insights, see Sol Gordon's "Ten Cardinal Mistakes of Self-Esteem" on pages 81–83.

Why Teasing Works

Effective teasing depends on three things:

1. who's doing the teasing,
2. the reason why they're teasing, and
3. whether you accept or reject the teasing.

1. Who's doing the teasing?

Suppose someone calls you a "junior genius." It makes a difference whether the teaser is 1) your mother or father, 2) someone you barely know, 3) a close friend, 4) a teacher, 5) your grandmother, or 6) the class bully who has been making your life miserable since kindergarten. The person behind the words can determine whether you feel 1) embarrassed, 2) annoyed, 3) amused, 4) elated, 5) proud, or 6) homicidal.

Now suppose someone calls you a "boring bookworm." Obviously it matters whether the teaser is someone you care about,

> "As the internal-combustion engine runs on gasoline, so the person runs on self-esteem: if he is full of it, he is good for a long run; if he is partly filled, he will soon need to be refueled; and if he is empty, he will come to a stop."
> Thomas Szasz

feel close to, trust, and respect. You'll need to tell the person how you feel about the teasing. Chances are that he or she didn't mean to hurt you and was just trying to be funny. Or perhaps you took the teasing too seriously. Either way, real friends can usually reach an agreement about acceptable vs. unacceptable teasing.

2. Why are they teasing?

There are several reasons why people you know (including your friends) might tease you:

- *They may be jealous of you and your accomplishments.*
- *They may not know a better way to tell you that they're proud of you and happy to be your friend. Strange as it seems, teasing can sometimes mean "I like and admire you."*
- *Some teenagers regard genuine compliments as "sappy" or "mushy" or "lame." Teasing is more acceptable. (Think about football players who pound each other on the back and/or knock each other down, and this starts to make sense.)*
- *Consciously or unconsciously, they may feel inferior to you because they don't have enough good things going on in their own lives. Teasing is a way to bring you down a notch.*
- *They may not like you, period.*
- *They may feel defensive around you. Check your own behaviors—what you do and what you say. Observations like "If you weren't so stupid, you'd know the answer" are not going to win any diplomacy awards.*

Of course, you may never learn the reason behind the teasing, but you can still appreciate the importance of the question. Depending on how well you know the teaser, you may want to try the direct approach. Asking "Why did you just call me that?" or "Why would you say such a thing?" might elicit a shrug and an "I don't know," but it might also cause the teaser to think twice before teasing you in the future.

3. Should you accept or reject the teasing?

That's entirely up to you. No one can *make* you feel bad or sad or weird. Depending on the source of the teasing, it may be worth

"WHEN OTHER KIDS SAY, 'OH, YOU'RE SUCH A BRAIN,' I JUST TRY TO IGNORE IT." BRIAN, 14

pondering whether the teasing was warranted. Is it possible that you've been studying so hard that your friends feel neglected? Has your third blue ribbon in the annual art fair given you a fat head? Are you a little too full of yourself, too focused on your own interests? The teasing could be a mini wake-up call.

On the other hand, it could be an attempt to hurt you or "get back at you" simply because you're gifted and talented, qualities that threaten and intimidate some people. The point is, whether you accept or reject the teasing is a choice only you can make.

What You Can Do

If you automatically accept the teasing that comes your way, you relinquish control of your own feelings—not a good idea if you plan to stay mentally healthy. Instead, consider the source, try to figure out the reason, and choose to believe it or not. You *always* have a choice.

An example: You get a C on a very tough biology test. Your friend finds out and immediately starts giving you a hard time. As in: "What? The genius got a C? How the mighty have fallen!" You can either think like this:

A. I got a C on the test, and
B. my friend is making fun of me for not getting an A, therefore
C. "You're right. I'm an idiot. I can't believe I let everyone down—myself, my parents, the biology teacher, even you."

Or you can think like this:

A. I got a C on the test, and
B. my friend is making fun of me for not getting an A, therefore

(Choose one):

C. "You're right, I didn't get the grade I was hoping for. But I can afford to blow a test once in a while."
C. "Oh well, nobody's perfect."
C. "You don't think I'm a genius anymore? I can live with that."
C. "I certainly did bomb that test. So what?"
C. "Actually, I deserved an A on that test, and I'm going to find out why I didn't get one."

> "I have endured a great deal of ridicule without much malice; and have received a great deal of kindness, not quite free from ridicule. I am used to it."
> Abraham Lincoln

c. "Where is it written that I must get A's at all times?"

c. "Yes, I got a C. I guess they'll be arresting me along with all the other C students."

c. "Yes, I got a C, which is exactly what I deserved, since I didn't study."

c. "Thank you for your support. Can we change the subject now?"

c. _____

(your response here)

Find Out More

To learn more about friendship, popularity, and ways to know and accept yourself, read:

McFarland, Rhoda. *Coping Through Self-Esteem.* New York: Rosen Publishing Group, 1993.

Powell, John. *Why Am I Afraid to Tell You Who I Am?* Allen, TX: Thomas More, 1995.

Online Relationships: How to Be "Net Smart"

Young people the world over are traveling the Internet, downloading shareware, checking out Web sites and newsgroups, setting up their own home pages, playing games, hanging out on message boards, chatting online—and making friends. When it comes to relationships, the Internet is a great equalizer. Age, appearance, social status, gender, geographic location, income, grades, IQ, test scores, learning strengths, learning differences—all are meaningless if you can express yourself reasonably well in writing. We know teenagers who correspond with E-mail friends at colleges and universities (and elementary schools), who have "visited" Iceland and Japan, and who

"IT'S EASIER NOT KNOWING WHAT THE KIDS I TALK TO LOOK LIKE. I'M MORE RELAXED." DOUG, 13*

---

* Quoted in Carin M. Rubenstein, "Internet Dangers," *Parents Magazine,* March, 1996, p. 148.

aren't shy about sending messages to their senators, the White House, CNN, rock stars, magazine editors, and *Dilbert* creator Scott Adams (who loves getting E-mail and often bases his cartoon strips on ideas from fans). These students are true global citizens, and we applaud them.

Of course, we've all seen news reports and articles about the dark side of cyberspace—about adults who prey on children and teens, about how easy it is to access inappropriate "adult-oriented" materials, about how young people are vulnerable to crime, exploitation, and harassment. We wish the media would give equal time to the *positive* aspects of exploring and using the Internet. Until they do, parents (such as yours) may worry about letting their kids (such as you) travel the information highway. Some are equipping their children's computers with software (such as Surfwatch or CyberSitter) that blocks access to X-rated areas. Others are just saying no to kids' requests to surf the 'net.

We believe that children and teens should be allowed to go online. The benefits are real and substantial: incredible amounts of information, a vast array of services, unlimited learning opportunities, and fascinating new discoveries every time you sign on. And while we acknowledge that the dangers are also real, we believe that most, if not all, can be avoided with a combination of savvy and common sense.

In the words of Lawrence J. Magid,* a syndicated columnist for the *Los Angeles Times* and author of *Cruising Online: Larry Magid's Guide to the New Digital Highway:*

> "When I took my family to New York last year, we caught a Broadway play and visited museums and walked about town—and we encountered, inevitably, adult theaters and bookstores and other places that were not appropriate for kids to enter. My kids know that such places are off-limits. They also know it's a good idea to beware of high-crime areas in a place like New York. And they know the safe way to behave around strangers and in public. It's all part of being 'street smart.'
>
> "In the same way, kids who hang around the Internet and on-line services need to be 'net smart.' The rules, in many ways, are similar to those in the real world. Be careful how you behave around strangers and stay away from potentially dangerous areas."

You're already smart, so becoming "net smart" shouldn't be much of a stretch for you. Use your head, follow your instincts, and avoid dark alleys. Keep in mind that people online aren't always who

---

* Lawrence J. Magid, "How to Help Children Become 'Net Smart,' " *Los Angeles Times,* September 27, 1995.

they seem to be, not everything you read online can be accepted as fact, and any offer that sounds too good to be true probably is.

If your parents are reluctant to turn you loose on the Internet, you'll need to prove to them that you're responsible, sensible, trustworthy, and unlikely to get into trouble. One way to do this is by agreeing up front on some basic ground rules. The following guidelines would be a good starting point for a family contract on Internet use:*

- *Never give out personal information (such as your home address, telephone number, parents' work address/telephone number, or the name and location of your school) in a chat room or on a bulletin board.*
- *Never give out personal information in an E-mail message unless you and your parents are certain of the recipient's identity.*
- *Never agree to a face-to-face meeting with another computer user without first checking with your parents. If they agree to the meeting, make sure it's in a public place, and bring your mother or father along.*
- *Never send a person your picture (or anything else) without first checking with your parents.*
- *Don't respond to messages that are rude, obnoxious, insulting, demeaning, suggestive, obscene, belligerent, threatening, or otherwise make you feel uncomfortable. If you receive such messages while logged on to a service such as America Online, Genie, Delphi, Prodigy, or CompuServe, contact the service immediately and report what is happening.*
- *If you feel that you're being harassed during an online session, sign off. If you start getting offensive E-mail, change your E-mail address. If a bulletin board or message board gets raunchy or weird, stop visiting it. If a newsgroup gets abusive or strange, stop reading it. (Remember that your computer is similar to your TV in at least one important way:* **You can turn it off.***)*
- *Don't download files sent to you by strangers. (This is good anti-virus protection as well as a way to avoid graphic surprises.)*
- *Agree on the time (or times) of day when you will go online and how long you will spend there. ("How long" is especially important if you subscribe to an online service that charges by the minute or the hour.)*

If you *really* want to prove to your parents that the Internet is basically okay, share it with them. Invite them to sit in with you when you go online. Show them some of your favorite sites. Let them read a recent E-mail from someone you've been corresponding with. If they don't know how to go online, teach them. And don't make the Internet your whole life. Parents are understandably apprehensive when children and teens sign on late at night and/or spend endless hours glued to the computer. Limit your own online time and your parents won't have to do it for you. A

---

* Some of these guidelines are adapted from "Child Safety on the Information Highway," a booklet from the National Center for Missing and Exploited Children. For a free copy of the complete booklet, call 1-800-843-5678. Or download a copy from author Larry Magid's home page: http://www.omix.com/magid/child.safety.html

teenager we know recommends the use of an alarm clock or other sign-off reminder because "time flies when you're on the Internet."

Depending on how brave you are (and how tolerant and broad-minded your parents are), you might even take Mom and Dad into a chat session with you. Because chat sessions are live, you can't always predict what messages and comments people will post. The language can get lewd, discussions can rapidly decay, and there's always the chance that someone will drop in just long enough to say something odious. You might take this opportunity to remind your parents that you can't control what other people say online, but you can control what you say. Then keep it clean.

Finally, you need to decide for yourself that you won't attempt to access "inappropriate materials"—a euphemism that covers everything from pornography to live sex chats, bomb-building instructions to bulletin boards run by hate groups. You probably have a good idea of other areas that would drive your parents wild if they knew you were visiting them. No matter how curious you are, no matter how tempting certain "off limits" sites might be, it's probably not worth the risk to go there. If you don't have anything to hide, your parents won't have anything to find. What you *want* is the freedom to explore the best the Internet has to offer; what you *don't* want is for your privileges to be revoked or suspended. Once you earn your parents' trust concerning the Internet, treat it as the more-precious-than-gold, liberty-granting, world-at-your-fingertips commodity that it is.

> **"PARENTS NEED TO GET INVOLVED IN HOW THEIR KIDS USE THE INTERNET. THEY SHOULD TAKE RESPONSIBILITY FOR MONITORING WHERE THEIR KIDS GO AND WHAT THEY SEE AND DO. THIS SHOULDN'T BE A GOVERNMENT THING; IT SHOULD BE A PARENT THING. . . . WHAT'S IMPORTANT IS FOR PARENTS AND KIDS TO BUILD A TRUST RELATIONSHIP."** JONAH, 17

GIFTED PEOPLE SPEAK OUT

Reanna Alder, 15

The reasons I use the Internet are:

Information

I am convinced that you can find anything on the Internet. (Some people even find true love). Think of any obscure interest—something you've been curious about. I guarantee there will be something about it on the Internet. Really.

Now, depending on HOW obscure it is, it may take a while to find, but someone will have a Web page devoted to it, an article about it, a link to it, or an address to write to for the information.

The Internet definitely helps me learn: It allows me to pursue many interests to whatever extent I want, and satisfies many curiosities. Like when I want to find the lyrics to a song, or when I wanted to learn about women cartoonists, I was able to quickly find the information. I think I also learn a lot about different kinds of people and communication. The Internet will never, ever replace real life, but it has a place in our society, and I doubt it will go away.

Nothing on the Internet is worth being intimidated by. The technical aspects and the etiquette are not as complicated as they sound. If you are interested, come and check it out. It won't bite.

People

I appreciate the people I meet on the net as useful sources of information, but I'm not really into the long-term pen pal thing. Obviously lots of people do get really close, and enjoy long-term friendships and pen pals on the net, but so far this has not been my experience. For example, I met this girl who is into making comics, which is something I've just gotten interested in, so we wrote a bunch of messages back and forth, comparing notes, characters, problems and so on, and eventually it faded out. We both gained something from each other, and we moved on. That suits me just fine. If you get really into long-term pen pals and stuff, you'll probably enjoy the speed of E-mail. Either way, it is fun.

How to make contact on the Internet

It takes work to find friends on the Internet. You have to put something of yourself out—advertise yourself—otherwise you might as well be invisible. Here are some ways to "put something out." A combination of a few of these would probably work best.

1. Poke around the Web and write letters to the people whose Home Pages you enjoy. Give something back. I would advise that you not say things along the lines of "Hi, I liked your page, can we be pen pals?" Just like you don't ask someone to marry you on the first date. I definitely prefer getting a neat message with something about the person, a reaction to my page, something totally weird, with just a simple "write me back." Low commitment, I guess.

2. Make your own Web page. This could be the most or the least rewarding way to make friends, depending on how much you enjoy it and how much effort you put into it. You can get piles of mail from a home page, or one letter a year, depending on how many people see it and how many of them like what they see.

3. Participate in live chats. It's generally a pretty good way to screen out people you're not interested in. You'll probably meet a lot of nice people, and maybe really "click" with a couple of them.

4. Participate in newsgroup discussions. Newsgroups are similar to chats, in that if you hang around in one for a while, you'll get to know the locals. Newsgroups have the added bonus that the people you talk to will share your interest.

5. Learn to "stand out from the crowd." There are literally millions of people on the Web, and a lot of them sound exactly alike. Ask yourself, "What kind of message would I enjoy getting?" Either because it's silly, sweet, humorous, ironic . . . whatever. Learn to write those kinds of messages. Be yourself. It takes a while to get good at, but it's definitely worth it. Also remember to give the person you're writing to things to respond to, either questions or opinions about things. Give your messages value by putting yourself into them. The more interesting the messages you write are, the better the messages you get back will be.

A Few Safety Tips

Learn to be safe on the Internet: Don't give out your address, phone number, or photo to anyone until you have . . .

● *had a chance to talk to your parents about it and get their input, and*

● *decided if it's really necessary.*

Think before you type, especially in a live chat. Treat others as you'd have them treat you. Wander around and be a silent observer for a while; learn the rules of the game before you jump in.

Reanna Alder, 15, lives in Vancouver, British Columbia, Canada. She is self-educated, meaning she learns without school, mostly without curriculum, and with large doses of people, experience, books, an Internet account, and life. Don't hold her to what she writes. You can send her E-mail at reanna@wimsey.com or visit her home page:

http://www.wimsey.com/~reanna

Parents

Forty-four percent of our survey respondents said they could use some help getting along with their parents. This came as no surprise, since most young people need assistance in this department at least part of the time. However, some of the conflicts and challenges you face with respect to your parents may be related to your giftedness, and those are the issues we'll address here.

> **"MANY GIFTED KIDS ARE NOT UNDERSTOOD IN SCHOOL, AND THEY NEED PARENTAL SUPPORT. THEY NEED SOMEONE ON THEIR SIDE."** GIRL, 14

> **"I DON'T NEED A BIG DEAL, BUT A LITTLE ENCOURAGEMENT HELPS A LOT."** JOE, 12

Parents and the Quest for Perfection

If you're like many gifted students, it may seem as if your parents are on a quest for perfection—*yours*. This can manifest itself in a variety of ways. Examples:

- *They expect you to study every night.*
- *They try to control the kinds of courses you take.*
- *They expect you to get perfect grades.*
- *They expect you to behave perfectly.*

The next time your parents start pushing perfection your way, try to understand where they're coming from. When you know something about their motivation, you're in a better position to negotiate change in your favor. (Please note that we're not saying it's *right* for them to think and feel as they do, only that they do it.)

"MY BIGGEST HASSLE IN LIFE RIGHT NOW IS THAT I ALWAYS HAVE TO BE TOTALLY RESPONSIBLE. TO PLEASE MY PARENTS, I HAVE TO STAY HOME AND WORK INSTEAD OF BEING WITH FRIENDS. I DON'T SEE WHY THEY CAN'T UNDERSTAND THAT I CAN BE RESPONSIBLE AND SPEND SOME TIME WITH MY FRIENDS, TOO."
JAN, 15

"THEY'RE ALWAYS SAYING THINGS LIKE, 'YOU'RE GIFTED. WHY CAN'T YOU GET STRAIGHT A'S IN THAT GEOMETRY CLASS YOU'RE TAKING?'" GIRL, 12

"IT'S LIKE I'M NOT A GOOD PERSON IF I MESS UP."
CHUCK, 14

What Gifted Students Want from Their Parents

According to our survey, these are the top ten things gifted students wish their parents would do (or not do):

1. Be supportive and encouraging; be there for us; be on our side.
2. Don't expect too much of us; don't expect perfection.
3. Don't pressure us, be too demanding, or push too hard.
4. Help us with our schoolwork/homework.
5. Help us to develop our talents.
6. Be understanding.
7. Don't expect straight A's.
8. Allow us some independence; give us space; trust us, because chances are we know what we're doing.
9. Talk to us; listen to us.
10. Let us try alternative education/special programs.

Six Reasons Why Parents Are the Way They Are

1. Some parents believe that if they set their expectations high, their children will naturally rise to meet them. Most children

> **"MY PARENTS EXPECT TOO MUCH OF ME. THEY CONSTANTLY TELL ME TO DO MY HOMEWORK WHEN I'M ALREADY GETTING STRAIGHT A'S. IT DOESN'T MAKE SENSE TO ME." MIKE, 16**

> **"I WISH MY PARENTS WOULD STOP SAYING, 'I KNOW YOU'RE SMARTER THAN THIS, SO WHY THE BAD GRADES?' " GIRL, 11**

want to please their parents (especially when the children are very young and Mom and Dad are All Powerful), so this technique often "works." Your parents expect great things of you, you do great things, and this proves that they're doing a wonderful job as parents.

2. Parents often see themselves reflected in their children. In other words, if you get A's, awards, commendations, etc., then *they* (vicariously) get A's, awards, commendations, etc. If someone praises your behavior, then *they* feel praised.

Think about what happens when Parent X goes up to Parent Y and says, "I can't help but notice that your son Agamemnon is *so* polite and well-mannered." In response, Parent Y doesn't say, "I'll pass your comments on to Ag." Parent Y says, "Thank you!" Most parents are more than happy to take the credit for their children's positive achievements and good manners, and they're not entirely wrong to do so. It's quite possible that your success has some connection with how you were raised and the values your parents taught you.

On the other hand, if you don't get A's, awards, and commendations, or if someone criticizes your behavior, your parents will more than likely take the blame. They will assume that your "failure" brands them as lousy parents.

3. Sometimes parents make demands on their children in an effort to fulfill their own hopes and dreams. For example, if your

> **"MY PARENTS STRESS LAW, BUSINESS, OR MEDICINE AND LOOK UPON THE ARTS AS A WASTE OF TIME. I HAVE A TERRIBLE TIME PUTTING TOGETHER WHAT I WANT TO DO AND WHAT MY PARENTS WANT ME TO DO." ESTHER, 17**

parents wanted to go to college but never could, they may insist that you attend college—whether you want to or not. Or they may think that a particular occupation or profession (usually Mom's or Dad's, or one Mom or Dad once aspired to) is right for you and will urge you in that direction. They forget that it's *your* life.

4. Perhaps one (or both) of your parents is also gifted. Gifted people tend to impose high standards on themselves—and live up to them. So your parent(s) may be thinking, "If I can do it, so can my son/daughter" (meaning you).

5. Parents suffer frequent memory lapses. They often forget what it's like to be a teenager—and what it means to be a teenager. They sometimes forget that *you're* a teenager. Especially if you occasionally prefer adult company over the company of people your age, have friends who are several years older than you, engage in conversations with your parents and other adults about world issues and other weighty matters, and/or are generally a responsible sort of person, then in their eyes you're practically an adult. After all, you spend time with adults, talk like an adult, think like an adult, and even act like an adult. So it's no wonder that they perceive you as an adult (although they don't always treat you like one—more about that later). On the other hand, when you don't behave like an adult (which is bound to happen sooner or later), this is what you'll hear:

> "With your intelligence, I would have expected you to . . .
> . . . act more maturely." OR
> . . . be more responsible." OR
> . . . stop this silliness." OR
> . . . act your age."

6. Parents are worriers. They can't help it. They worry about your future (will you go to college? will you get a job and be able to support yourself? will you get married? will you be okay? will you still love them?). As they read the newspapers and watch the news, they worry about the present, because often it's a dangerous world out there. They worry about peer pressure, bad influences, advertising, pornography on the Internet, trashy TV, drugs and alcohol, random violence, etc., *ad infinitum.* They think that if they set high expectations for you, you'll be so busy meeting them that you won't have time to get into trouble.

What You Can Do

Now that you know some reasons why parents are the way they are, what can you do about it? FIRST, you can make a vow to avoid the Seven Statements Guaranteed to Drive Parents Crazy. Here are the basics, although you probably have your own variations:

1. "You *always* want me to be perfect." (Usually said in a whiny voice.)
2. "But that's not *fair.*" (Pout, pout.)
3. "But none of my *other* friends has to. . . ." (To which the sensible parent will reply, "But I'm not their parent. I'm *your* parent." Or, more succinctly, "So what?")
4. "If I can't do it/have it today, can I do it/have it next week (next month, next year, next . . .)?" (To which the annoyed parent will reply, "You can't do it/have it EVER. Period. Now go away.")

"Family is just an accident. . . . They don't mean to get on your nerves. They don't even mean to be your family, they just are."
Marsha Norman

"Are anybody's parents typical?"
Madeleine L'Engle

"Oh, to be only half as wonderful as my child thought I was when he was small, and only half as stupid as my teenager now thinks I am."
Rebecca Richards

5. "You're just trying to get me to be like you." (Ouch! The ultimate insult.)

6. "You *never* understand anything." (In other words, Mom and Dad, you're stupid.)

7. "Just because *you* grew up in the Stone Age. . . ." (Most parents don't like to be reminded that they are slowly but inexorably growing old. Especially not today's parents, the majority of whom are Baby Boomers in deep denial of their advancing years.)

SECOND, you can take positive steps to cope with and perhaps even change your parents' great expectations. Examples:

Talk to them.

According to gifted teenagers we've spoken with, surveyed, and interviewed over the years, the most effective way to get your parents to set more realistic expectations for you is to talk to them. (For more about talking to parents, see pages 233–36.)

Trust yourself.

Don't let your parents' expectations control you. After all, you're the one who ultimately has to live with your choices. Obviously, this doesn't mean that you should ignore your parents' counsel; they do have more life experience than you, probably tempered with real wisdom, and we all have to abide by some rules. But whenever possible, try to make your own decisions and take responsibility for the consequences.

Pick and choose the times when you'll do your best.

Contrary to popular opinion (and parental pressure), you don't have to put 100 percent effort into everything you do. Sometimes it's impossible; sometimes it's impractical. When your parents encourage you to do your best and it doesn't seem feasible for whatever reason, talk it over with them. Evaluate and explain why you may not want to strive for perfection in this particular instance.

> "When I was a boy of fourteen, my father was so ignorant I could hardly stand to have the old man around. But when I got to be twenty-one, I was astonished at how much he had learned in seven years."
> Mark Twain

> "I FIND THAT THE BEST STUDENTS ARE THE ONES WHO PUT PRESSURE ON THEMSELVES TO BE THE BEST!"
> GIRL, 15

Encourage your parents to learn more about giftedness and what it means.

Gather information for them, if you must, and read it before you give it to them. If they aren't interested in knowing more, at least you'll have learned something new.

Seek support from other adults you trust and respect.

If there's absolutely no way you can get through to your parents, find another adult you can talk to who will give you the support you need. Not everyone is blessed with attentive, cooperative parents who are willing to listen to their children and take them seriously. Some of us have to look elsewhere for role models and advocates, and that's okay.

How to Talk to Parents: Strategies for Successful Conversations*

You've got a problem at home. Maybe you think your parents' expectations of you are unreasonable. Maybe you're tired of the way they keep comparing you to your brilliant older sister. Maybe you feel that their rules are too strict. Whatever the situation, don't just stew about it; do something about it. Open your mouth, move your lips, and vibrate your vocal chords. *Talk to your parents.*

For many young people, the hardest part of talking to their parents is getting started. They worry for days or weeks or months about what to say first. Meanwhile, the problem becomes more serious, and what could have been a conversation becomes a potential confrontation.

The best approach for you to take depends on the relationship you have with your parents. Based on your situation, here are some strategies to try.

Situation #1: You and your parents have a long history of talking to each other.

Maybe your parents have already talked to you (or tried to talk to you) about a lot of things including heavy-duty topics like sex,

---

* For this section and "Ten Tips for Talking to Parents" on page 235, we gratefully acknowledge the assistance of Dr. Tom Greenspon, a Minneapolis psychologist who specializes in working with bright, talented kids and adults.

drugs, and school performance. If this is the case, it should be fairly easy for you to sit down with one or both of them and say, "There's something I would like to talk with you about. I'd be willing to hear what you have to say; would you be willing to hear what I have to say?" You can probably expect a positive response.

Situation #2: You and your parents have limited experience in talking to each other.

Maybe you've never formed the habit of talking to them. And maybe they don't know where to start either. You might want to preface your conversation like this: "I've been thinking really hard about something, and I wonder if I could get your help with it." Note that you're not making demands. Instead, you're making a request. And that makes a big difference where parents are concerned.

Situation #3: You and your parents have almost no experience in talking to each other.

If your family has this kind of track record, and if you suspect that your parents may not be willing to talk to you about your problem, don't give up. Ask another trusted adult friend or acquaintance to act as an intermediary. This could be your school's gifted program coordinator, your classroom teacher, or the principal. It could be the school counselor, a neighbor, or a relative. It could be the youth leader at your place of worship. It could be *any* adult you feel comfortable talking to.

Go to him or her and say, "There's something I need to talk to my parents about, and I'm not sure that we can do it on our own. Would you be willing to participate if I can get my parents to come?"

If that person says yes, go to one or both of your parents and say, "There's something that's been bothering me. It's been on my mind a lot. I'm wondering if we could go to someone else and talk about it together."

They might not agree right away. They might even get angry because you took your problem to an "outsider." Try saying, "This is really hard for me, too, and I might feel better if the other person was there with us." Tell your parents that you don't want to fight; you just want to talk!

Situation #4: You and your parents never talk to each other.

Or you're convinced that you can't talk to them about this particular problem. Either way, talk to *somebody;* don't keep your problem locked up inside. Think about the adult professionals in your life:

the gifted coordinator, your teacher, the school counselor, the youth coordinator at your place of worship. What you need is someone who knows you and has experience helping kids. Tell the person that you want to talk, and chances are excellent that he or she will be willing to listen.

Ten Tips for Talking to Parents

1. Choose your time wisely. Don't try to start a serious conversation when your parents are obviously 1) cranky, 2) stressed out, 3) busy doing something else, or 4) sleeping.

2. Be respectful. Your parents will be much more willing to hear you out if they don't feel like they're being attacked or ridiculed.

3. Speak precisely and concisely. Say what you mean and don't take forever to say it.

4. When you approach your parents with a problem, come prepared with suggestions for solving it. Why should they do all the work? (Make sure that you present these as suggestions, not demands.)

5. Make a genuine effort to see their point of view. Put yourself in their shoes. Try to empathize with them. You're not the only person with an opinion, a brain, or feelings.

6. Watch your body language. Glaring, turning your back, slouching, shaking a fist, pointing a finger, sneering, gagging, and rolling your eyes are not recommended.

7. Keep your voice down, please. Nobody likes to be yelled at.

8. Avoid "you statements." "You don't understand me" or "You never let me do what I want" don't help to get your point across. Instead, use "I statements"—like "I guess I haven't done a very good job of explaining myself to you" or "I feel like you don't trust me to make decisions about what's most important to do in school."

9. Pay attention. You'll be more effective if you look at your parents (not at the wall or out the window) while they're speaking.

10. Be willing to compromise. Give a little and you might get a lot.

If you feel that you don't have anybody in the world you can talk to—if you're feeling isolated, alone, and even suicidal—then *pick up a telephone book and look up a hotline.* Start by checking under "Suicide Prevention" or "Crisis Intervention." Most cities and many towns have hotlines staffed 24 hours a day, 7 days a week with people who are ready and willing to listen. Most cities and many towns also have mental health centers that will provide initial services to young people free of charge. Look in the Yellow Pages under "Mental Health Services," or ask your school counselor to put you in touch with someone who can help you. (For more about teen suicide, see pages 267–78.)

No matter what your problem is or how bad it seems, *talking about it always helps.* The more people can talk together—especially family members—the more likely they will be able to solve their problems and improve their relationships with one another. Luckily, the vast majority of families are able to talk (and listen). And yours is probably among them. Give your parents a fair chance; start with them.

How to Get More Freedom

Frequently, gifted kids mature faster than their parents are willing to admit. The result? A painful gap between what children and teens *want* to do and what their parents will *let* them do. Here are

"BEING ON A SHORT LEASH IS DEPRESSING. IT MAKES ME FEEL DEPRIVED." ERIK, 14

some freedom issues that may become sore spots with you and your parents (if they aren't already):

- *how late you can stay up*
- *places you can go*
- *classes you can take*
- *friends you can spend time with/have over/hang out with*
- *after-school activities you can pursue*
- *how you can spend your money*
- *what you should do with your life.*

Undoubtedly you could add several items of your own to this list, but suffice it say that you don't want to wait until you're 18 before you're allowed to take advantage of life's opportunities. You want it all right now.

What do parents have to say about that? The ones we talked to admit that they often have difficulty knowing how much freedom to grant their children without being too permissive (or too restrictive). Examples:

> **Lee, the parent of a 16-year-old:** "My son would make a great lawyer someday. I think that the rules I set are reasonable, but he comes back with arguments against them—and they make sense! Often I find that I'm willing to compromise, but sometimes I feel as if he's the one making the rules, and I'm not comfortable with that."

> **Jim, the parent of an 18-year-old:** "When Mark was younger, his mom and I always trusted him because he'd never given us a good reason to not trust him. Things worked out well, and when we needed to discuss sensitive issues regarding sex and drugs, Mark seemed more willing to listen to us because we had always listened to him. Still ... it's tough knowing just how far to 'let go of the leash.' We always worried about whether we'd been too lenient with Mark, and maybe even given him the impression that we didn't really care about him. I guess most parents question this type of thing."

Without guidelines of some kind—without rules, expectations, and even restrictions—life is chaos. Too many guidelines feel like a prison sentence; too few and nobody gets what they want. The solution lies somewhere in between, and it's complicated by the fact that you're at that in-between stage when liberties are bestowed begrudgingly.

If you want your parents to grant you more freedom, you first have to establish a level of trust with them. They need to know that you can handle the rights you're asking for. In their minds, there's a logical connection between 1) how responsible you are and 2) how much freedom you should have. And they usually think that evidence of responsibility should come first. In other words, "Let me stay out past curfew on Friday and I'll clean my room on Saturday" probably won't work. But "I've cleaned my room every week for a month, and I'd like to stay out a half-hour past curfew on Friday" just might.

Take an honest look at your own performance in the responsibility realm. Do you usually do your homework without being reminded? Do you keep your room reasonably neat? Do you handle your money wisely? If you walk or drive to school (as opposed to taking the bus), do you arrive on time? Do you assume your fair share of the family chores? Think of other ways of proving yourself that are valued by your family. What's your record for the past week? The past month or year?

> "An atmosphere of trust, love, and humor can nourish extraordinary human capacity. One key is authenticity: parents acting as people, not as roles."
> Marilyn Ferguson

The Art of Negotiation

If you really are a responsible and trustworthy sort of person, then you should be in a stronger position to negotiate for more freedom. Start by setting up a meeting with your parents. Express your desire to assume even more responsibility (around the house, at school, within the family). Lay out your plan and try to arrive at a consensus—an agreement about what you want and what you can actually have. Here are some tips for negotiating with parents:

- **Pick a time for your meeting that is agreeable to everyone.** *Make an appointment if necessary as "insurance" that the meeting will happen. Plan to show up a few minutes early.*

- **Choose a comfortable and reasonably quiet place to meet.** *It's hard to talk when the TV is blaring, the phone is ringing, and your little brother is being a nuisance. If home is usually a busy, noisy place, consider meeting in a park, going for a walk, or finding a quiet table at a favorite restaurant.*

- **Make an agenda for your meeting.** *Write down some of the points you want to raise. Often, during discussions like these, we forget some of the things we want to say, or we get distracted by side issues. An agenda will help to jog your memory and keep you on track.*

- **Do your part to keep the meeting positive, upbeat, and civil.** *This should not be a gripe session. Be prepared to express and exchange points of view, negotiate, compromise, and plan for action; encourage your parents to participate and have their say. What does each person want? What is each person willing to do?*

- **If at first you don't succeed, don't be discouraged.** *Especially if this is your first attempt at opening the lines of communication with your parents, you may get a few wires crossed. If the meeting goes nowhere, suggest that you adjourn and reconvene in a week or so. Then be on your best behavior until you meet again.*

It may seem as if you have no freedom, no rights, and no fun; as if your parents don't trust you, won't give an inch, and are determined to control every aspect of your life. You may be mentally exaggerating your situation, or they may, in fact, be too strict and restrictive. In any case, it won't matter for much longer. Eventually you *will* be on your own, making your own decisions and managing your own life. Part of what your parents are trying to do is teach you the skills to succeed when you're out there without them. You might extend them a little credit for having good intentions.

Think About It, Talk About It

- In what areas of your life are you becoming more independent and self-sufficient?

- What are some freedoms you have now that you didn't have six months ago? A year ago?

- What decisions are you making on your own?

- What are some current areas of conflict between you and your parents? What steps are you taking to resolve or lessen the conflict?

- What do you think your parents are worrying about as you become more independent?

- If a real crisis arose in your life, would you feel free to talk about it with either or both of your parents? If so, why? If not, who could you talk with?

Enough About You—What About Them?

You may have noticed that much of this discussion has centered on *you*—what you need and want from your relationship with your parents. One of our main goals in writing this book is to empower you to shape your own life, and that includes having some say about your life at home. But the wise person knows that the world doesn't revolve around him or her, and that sometimes we need to see things from another person's perspective.

You may think that your parents are the most demanding, despotic, tyrannical people in the world; that they must have learned their parenting skills at the feet of Attila the Hun; that they are totally unfair in their treatment of you, not to mention uncaring and clueless. You have the right to your own opinion, and if that's what you want to believe, there's not much we can say to change your mind. But if you're willing to reconsider, read on.

First, you should know that raising a gifted child poses special challenges for parents. From the time you were an infant, you

"A smart child can ask more questions than a wise parent can answer."
Sally Walker

were probably a handful. Generally speaking, gifted children tend to have the following characteristics:

● *They are thirsty for knowledge, and they ask endless questions.*

It's likely that your parents weren't prepared for the barrage of whys, whens, what fors, whos, and how comes you inflicted on them. Either they had to admit they didn't know the answers, or they had to find the answers. (Think back on those many library visits when you were very young. While you curled up with a picture book in the beanbag chair in the children's room, your mom/dad searched the microfiche, trying to find out what penguins eat because you asked that question over breakfast.)

● *They are driven to explore their world, and they are extremely active—some to the point of being considered hyperactive. They seem to have endless energy, and they often sleep less than other children. They have a hard time settling down; they may be the first in their age group to give up naps.*

Just what all parents want and need: a child who won't go to bed, won't nap, and runs them ragged. You might ask your parents if they're still exhausted from when you were a toddler.

● *They have excellent memories, which they frequently put to good use by reminding their parents of things they may have forgotten (or wanted to forget).*

Another positive trait (groan). As in: "Hey, Mom, remember when you got that speeding ticket when I was three years old? Ha ha ha!" Or: "Two months ago last Tuesday, you promised to take me to a movie and you never did. Can we go today?" Or: "When I was in fifth grade, you said I could have my own computer when I started high school, so. . . ."

● *They develop sophisticated vocabularies at an early age.*

Perhaps you were a "motor mouth" who seldom stopped talking. Or maybe you learned early to use your excellent verbal ability to get what you wanted. Chances are you've been arguing with and/or pestering your parents since you first learned to talk. Some fun for them!

● *They often prefer the company of older children and adults.*

While the other kids ran off to play in the sandbox, you stayed close to your parents and their friends. Their conversation was simply more interesting to you. But what about the times when the grown-ups felt constrained by your presence?

● *They often have a mature sense of humor, and they especially enjoy puns and plays on words.*

One mother reported that her son appreciated and understood adult jokes from about age four. If you were predicting punch lines or making complicated puns as a young child, no wonder you sometimes unnerved your parents.

● *They are fast learners, and they enjoy learning new things in depth.*

Did you drive your parents crazy with your passions? Dinosaurs when you were five, rocks when you were five and a half, rockets when you were five and three-quarters, snakes when you were six? If your parents supported and encouraged your many and changing interests, thank them now.

Other characteristics of gifted children include:

● *they take on more than they can handle*
● *because they are acutely aware of the world and its problems, they often develop a variety of fears and concerns*
● *they are able to concentrate for long periods of time, shutting out the world (and messages like "Lunch time!")*
● *they have a special tolerance for confusion and junk (read: messy rooms)*
● *they like to learn independently and often resist help and suggestions*
● *they may be super-sensitive*
● *they may be intolerant, judgmental, critical, perfectionistic, sassy, argumentative, and rude.*

In other words, while you may be the light of your parents' life, you probably haven't been the world's easiest child. It's just a little something to keep in mind when you're tempted to rant and rave about parental injustices.

Second (and we'll keep this short), most parents don't really enjoy the get-tough aspects of parenting. Nagging you to do your homework, reminding you to study for tests, asking you for the thousandth time to please clean your room, and grounding you for breaking curfew are not among the pleasures of parenting. Because you're a bright, interesting, capable, intelligent person, they would rather spend their time with you enjoying your company. (Especially because that time is limited now that you're getting older, a fact of which parents are very aware.) The more responsible you are, the less they have to act like drill sergeants, and the more you can all relax and get to know each other as human beings who have more in common than your DNA. Who knows—you might even *like* each other.

Find Out More

To learn more about understanding and getting along with your parents, read:

Packer, Alex J. *Bringing Up Parents: The Teenager's Handbook.* Minneapolis: Free Spirit Publishing, 1992.

If your parents would like to learn more about understanding and getting along with you, suggest that they read:

Ford, Judy. *Wonderful Ways to Love a Teen . . . Even When It Seems Impossible.* Berkeley, CA: Conari Press, 1996. The title probably won't appeal to you, but your parents can relate— and family counselor Judith Ford's advice, insights, and basic respect for teenagers are terrific.

On Being a Teenager

Thirty-four percent of our survey respondents wanted to know more about the emotional stages of adolescence. Thirty percent were curious about how one develops a philosophy of life. Forty-six percent wanted help dealing with strong emotions such as sadness, depression, and anger.

It's no news to you that being a teenager can sometimes be frustrating, exhausting, maddening, saddening, and anxiety-producing. There are days when it seems as if life is one problem after another—a steady stream of hassles too overwhelming to solve, too important to share with just anyone.

> "GIFTED PEOPLE HAVE THE ABILITY TO CREATIVELY FIND WAYS OF MAKING THEIR LIVES NOT ONLY MANAGEABLE BUT WONDERFUL. I THINK WE SHOULD LEARN NOT JUST HOW TO SURVIVE, BUT ALSO HOW TO MAKE THE MOST OF WHO WE ARE—CELEBRATING GIFTEDNESS, BEING AUTONOMOUS, AND KEEPING OUR OPTIONS OPEN." PAULITA, 18

> "I WONDER WHAT MY FUTURE WILL BE, HOW SUCCESSFUL I'LL BE, AND WHAT DIFFICULTIES I WILL HAVE TO FACE." BOY, 11

DEPRESSION
ANXIETY
emotions
Philosophy
SADNESS
MEANING of LIFE
ANGER
GURU

How many of these complaints of being a teenager sound familiar to you?*

● *School is boring and unsatisfying.*
● *My parents don't understand me. They're always on my case.*
● *My parents aren't around much. I wish I could have more of their time.*
● *I wish I were more popular.*
● *I'm not pretty (good-looking, tall, short, thin, athletic . . .) enough.*
● *I can never do what I want.*
● *I don't know what I want to be when I grow up.*
● *Sometimes I don't think anyone really cares about me.*
● *I never have any money.*
● *My car is a piece of junk.*
● *I hate my clothes.*
● *I'm sick of being alone. I want a girlfriend/boyfriend.*
● *I'm worried about the world—every day it's nothing but bad news about hunger, pollution, wars, AIDS, discrimination, crime, homelessness, and pain.*
● *Many of my friends use drugs.*
● *I need a job.*
● *I'm afraid I might be pregnant/I might have gotten someone pregnant/I might have caught some kind of sexually transmitted disease.*
● *I'm afraid of getting beat up or shot or killed.*
● *I wonder if I'm gay or bisexual.*
● *I'm worried that I might not even have a future.*

And the list can go on and on. Sometimes you may get so fed up that you feel like dropping out or worse.

Not that this will necessarily make you feel any better, but almost all teenagers experience some of these problems and doubts to one degree or another. So at least you're not alone. Plus it appears that gifted teenagers have *more* worries than other young people. Their worries seem more pressing, more intense, more urgent and overwhelming.

Jim shares this story from his teaching experience:

> Nathan was an 11-year-old who got physically ill every Wednesday at 2:45 P.M. He didn't tell me about these vomiting episodes; he merely asked to be excused to use the restroom. Only when a concerned classmate returning from the bathroom and whispered, "Mr. D., I think Nate's dying in there!" did the truth come out.

---

* Naturally not all teenagers have all of these concerns, but many teenagers have told us that they have one or more.

In a way, Nate *was* dying, one small step at a time. On Wednesday afternoons, he went directly from school to Hebrew lessons in preparation for his upcoming bar mitzvah. It wasn't the fact of his after-school classes that bothered Nate. Rather, it was something much more profound and personal. As he explained tearfully to me: "My rabbi doesn't take me seriously. When I disagree with him or question something he says, he tells me I'm too young and stupid to have my own opinions about religion."

Nate was a bright, curious student who learned by asking questions. Unfortunately, his rabbi didn't appreciate his inquisitive nature. So when Nate asked, "How do we know there's a God?" and, "If my God is different from the God people pray to in India, who's the 'real' God?" and, "Shouldn't I be able to choose a religion when I'm older instead of being forced to have one while I'm a kid?" his rabbi grew perplexed and angry. To make Nathan feel even more isolated, none of his Hebrew school classmates shared his doubts and concerns. Eventually, Nate came to believe that there was something wrong with him—that he was incapable of understanding issues that both his rabbi and his classmates accepted without question. He turned inward against himself. His clockwork vomiting was a physical reaction to his psychic pain.

I contacted Nate's mother and told her what Nate had revealed to me. After much discussion, Nate's mom decided that her son needed a new spiritual teacher. She found another rabbi who was more intrigued than aggravated by Nate's questions. The vomiting soon stopped and, 18 months later, so did the weekly Hebrew lessons: Nate celebrated his bar mitzvah.

Judy remembers a student from her years as a classroom teacher:

Janine was 13, soft-spoken, well-mannered, and a straight-A student. One day she came running into my class (the gifted resource room) and burst into tears. I comforted her as best I could and finally got her to tell me why she was so upset: She had gotten a B on a test in her social studies class. Since she normally got all A's, this alone was a shock to her. But what made it unbearable was the teacher, who held up her test in front of the class and proclaimed, "Look what Janine got on her test! And *she's* in the gifted class."

The damage was done, and I couldn't undo it. I told Janine that the teacher's remarks had been abusive and uncalled for. I asked her to describe how she felt about the incident, and others in our group recalled times when they'd been similarly embarrassed. (Even though few teachers are this insensitive, when it happens it's painful and infuriating.) Janine's experience gave our gifted class a perfect opportunity to talk about the fact that you can't control what other people say and do. We revisited Janine's options related to how she felt about herself, considered some reasons (albeit misguided) why the teacher did what he did, explored the possibility of whether Janine would personally tell the teacher how she felt, and offered suggestions as to how Janine might turn her negative experience into a positive one. I also decided that I would talk to the school principal about how Janine's teacher had humiliated her. My goal was to see that the same sort of treatment was never again meted out to any student—gifted or otherwise.

Although our class didn't accomplish our designated activity for that period, we were able to do something much more important: support an individual classmate. Janine left the class feeling better about herself. She also had some ideas for talking with her social studies teacher that might not only benefit her but other students as well.

These stories underscore what you probably already know: That even though the "real world" can hurt, it won't go away. That avoiding unpleasant topics, events, people, and facts can't make them disappear. That whether a problem is minute or massive, personal or international in scope, it can be accompanied by perceptible anxiety, pain, and fear.

How can we learn to deal with these feelings? How can we keep them from getting us down? How can we make it through the rough times and equip ourselves to cope with those to come?

You're Not "Just a Kid"

When a group of gifted teenagers from New York was polled about questions they have about themselves and the world, they came up with these:

- *"Does God really exist?"*
- *"What will it feel like to die?"*
- *"Is there someone (anyone) who thinks and looks at life the way I do?"*
- *"Are scientific experiments in the search for truth always justifiable?"*
- *"Will the universe ever come to an end?"*

Some of these questions have many possible answers, depending on individual philosophies, beliefs, experiences, and so on. Others seem more rhetorical—the kinds of questions that pit you against Aristotle, Gandhi, or your parents when *your* sense of truth differs from *theirs*. The hardest part of answering the above questions (and others like them) often comes in trying to justify *why* you believe what you believe.

Former Beatle John Lennon once explained:*

> "There was something wrong with me, I thought, because I seemed to see things other people didn't see. I thought I was crazy or an egomaniac for claiming to see things other people didn't see. As a child I would say, 'But this is going on!' and everybody would look at me as if I was crazy."

When you see black while everyone else sees white, or when you see shades of gray that no one else seems able to perceive, you may start to feel lonely, afraid, or different. Well-meaning others may try to convince you that your perceptions will change as you mature, or they may try to persuade you to ignore your ideas in deference to theirs. As in:

- *"You'll feel different when you're older. Trust me."*
- *"There's no point in thinking about that now. That's a grown-up issue."*
- *"When you have kids of your own, you'll understand."*
- *"You're not mature enough to make those kinds of decisions. Let me make them for you."*

What can you do when someone puts you off, puts you down, or insists on doing your thinking for you? Here are two suggestions that have worked for gifted teenagers we know. They might work for you, too.

1. Respect Yourself

Have you ever asked an adult a question only to be told, "Don't worry about that, you're just a kid"? Usually, this response comes from someone who thinks you're too young to be thinking about "such things." ("Such things" usually translates into questions about sex, sexuality, religion, politics, money, or other supposedly "adult" topics.)

In fact, you can't *not* think about ideas that enter your mind at an earlier age than they're "supposed to." It's like telling a bumblebee that it's not "supposed to" fly. Interestingly, there's a scientific theory that says just that. According to the Theory of Uneven Weight, the bumblebee is too top-heavy to support itself in flight. Yet the bumblebee flies anyway because it doesn't know how *not* to.

> "The real questions are the ones that obtrude upon your consciousness whether you like it or not, the ones that make your mind start vibrating like a jackhammer, the ones that you 'come to terms with' only to discover that they are still there. The real questions refuse to be placated."
> Ingrid Bengis

---

* From "The Me I See: Self-Images of the Gifted Child" in *Teaching Gifted Children*, July/August 1981, p. 9.

Perhaps the tendency to ask big questions and think big thoughts early in life is part of what being gifted is all about. And although this may make some social interactions more difficult than you'd like them to be, you're going to have to live with it—because that's the way it is, and, more importantly, that's the way you are.

So don't give in to people who tell you to turn off your brain. Your cranium is private property, and what goes on up there is up to you. Respect your abilities, your questioning nature, your curiosity, your desire to seek the truth, your persistence—and *respect yourself*.

It may help to know that when others try to put you on intellectual "hold," this may be an instinctive reaction against an idea they don't understand. And when they won't answer your questions, it may be because they can't.

Where can you go for answers? The library, for starters. Read what other great thinkers past and present have thought, written, and said. (They won't always agree with each other, which will give you even more to think about.) Find out the facts on issues that concern you. Then find out where to go to learn more; research can be a long and fascinating path. Then get involved with people who have concerns similar to yours. You'll find them in groups from the Sierra Club to Greenpeace, the National Wildlife Federation to UNICEF, the National Organization for Women to the NAACP.

Find adults you can talk to; they're out there. Your parents may welcome the opportunity to have serious conversations with you. So may a teacher or two (or more). Take your questions about religion to a minister, priest, or rabbi—or all three. Use a class project or an assignment for the school paper as a chance to interview politicians, scientists, university professors, health professionals, whoever.

Don't give up! If *you* think a question is important enough to pursue, *it is*.

2. Learn to Put Up with Other People's Faults and Foibles

Did you ever go to a movie you knew would be awful, just because your friends wanted to see it? Have you come up with an answer in class and kept it to yourself, waiting for other students to arrive at the same solution? Have you resisted the urge to point out a teacher's mistake or argue with your parents when you're positive you're right?

If you've done any of the above, without thinking too hard about it or passing negative judgments on the other people in-

volved, then you've probably learned how, why, when, and where to suffer in silence. You've discovered that there are times when it's best—even smartest—to choose not to assert your opinions and rights as an individual. This doesn't mean you're a bad person, a phony, a wimp, or two-faced. It shows that you know how to play the game of life.

Why not go to the movie? It may not have won first prize at Cannes or Sundance, but that doesn't mean you can't have fun watching it with your friends. Why not give others in your class the chance to speak up and shine? You might learn something from them. Why not keep silent about a teacher's blunder? If you must talk about it, arrange to meet privately after class. Why not go along with your parents for a change? Maybe they know something you don't, or maybe the point isn't important enough to argue about.

Think of the times when others have put up with your shortcomings. (Just because you're smart doesn't mean that your ideas are always the best or the brightest.) Your parents have doubt-less endured all kinds of nonsense from you over the years. Your teachers have probably been patient on a number of occasions when you've gone off on tangents. And your friends have stuck by you in spite of your quirks and flaws.

> "What I cannot love, I overlook. Is that real friendship?"
> Anaïs Nin

Naturally, it's important to know when *not* to suffer in silence: when your safety is at stake; when "the crowd" puts others in danger, or humiliates or hurts them; when your values, morals, beliefs, or integrity are at risk of being compromised. When in doubt, ask yourself: "If I go along with this, will it make any difference a year from now?" If the answer is no, then swallow hard, smile, and try to enjoy yourself. If the answer is yes or maybe, then swallow hard, say "no thanks," and pat yourself on the back for making a tough and not too popular decision.

Understanding Adolescence (Or Trying To)

One reason why it's tough being a teenager is that you have to be an adolescent at the same time. It would be nice to be able to postpone adolescence until you were ready for it, but unfortunately that's not possible. Actually, adolescence is a 20th-century invention. In the 1800s, a person went directly from childhood to adult responsibilities like work and family. A mere three generations later, a person might spend the years between 13 and 24 going to high school, then college, then graduate school without dipping more than a toe into the real world. There's no social track record for what's supposed to happen during this long and often tumultuous period.

Why do some people sail through adolescence seemingly effortlessly, while others fall apart at the first hint of hormones? Why do some have good looks and energy to spare, while others lurch around like Quasimodo in a semicoma? Why do some later think back on their teenage years as "the best years of my life," while others compare theirs to an extended stay in Motel Hell?

Experts who study adolescents have discovered some similarities among this group of very different individuals. The most obvious are the physical changes that pave the road from childhood to young adulthood. Who doesn't know about growth spurts, cracking voices, pimples, the sudden compelling and confusing interest in sex, and the myriad other burdens of puberty? These combine to create the feeling of being out of control and overwhelmed by strange and powerful forces from within. Add to this the expectations the world lays on you just because you're growing up, and it's no wonder teenagers get cranky.

Then there are the social and emotional issues. On the one hand, you're learning that you're different from everyone else, an individual, unique. On the other, you're finding out fast how important it is to fit into society and the world. Just as you're starting to figure out your family, you're preparing to leave it and go off on your own. One day you're getting your act together, and the next you're taking it on the road.

Thomas M. Buescher, a clinical social worker, adolescent therapist, and founder of the Center for Exceptional Development, has identified six issues of special relevance to gifted adolescents. They are:*

1. Ownership ("Who says I'm gifted?")

In junior and senior high school, being popular usually means being normal or familiar. Popular leaders represent the more dominant values of the group; popular girls look and dress according to group tastes; popular guys use language adopted by the ruling clique. In other words, popularity depends on conformity—something gifted students often aren't very good at.

It may seem better to deny your ability in order to appear normal and fit in. And it may be easy to do this—for a while. The eventual and unavoidable result is internal conflict. Resolving this conflict means going back to owning who you are, what you are, and what you're capable of. The only real answer to "Who says I'm gifted?" is "I do!"

> "To think is
> to differ."
> Clarence Darrow

2. Dissonance ("If I'm so smart, why can't I do everything right?")

Prone to perfectionism from an early age (for more on this topic, see pages 70–79), gifted kids have an especially hard time during adolescence. Already off balance because of the physical, social, and emotional changes going on, they feel a dissonance between how well they *do* and how well they *think* they should do.

Your talents and abilities are growing, but even you have limitations. Becoming aware of them and learning to live with them doesn't mean you're giving up. It means you're growing up.

> "Striving for
> excellence
> motivates you;
> striving for
> perfection is
> demoralizing."
> Harriet Braiker

3. Risk taking ("Should I or shouldn't I?")

One of the characteristics of the young gifted child is the willingness to take risks. Gifted adolescents, on the other hand, seem to become *more* cautious while their "normal" friends become *less* cautious by the minute.

No one seems quite sure why this happens. Maybe it's because gifted teenagers are more aware of the consequences of risky

> "Fear is a
> question. What
> are you afraid of
> and why? Our
> fears are a
> treasure house
> of self-knowledge
> if we explore
> them."
> Marilyn French

---

* Adapted from "A Framework for Understanding the Social and Emotional Development of Gifted and Talented Adolescents" by Thomas M. Buescher. *Roeper Review*, Vol. 8, No. 1 (September 1985), pp. 12–15. Used with permission.

actions and more skilled at checking out the advantages and disadvantages ahead of time. In any case, they seem to need security—and may scale back their activities and aspirations to get it.

Are you avoiding honors courses because you can't be sure of getting A's? Are you choosing not to challenge yourself because you can't predict the outcome? There's such a thing as being too careful. Remember the old saying: "Nothing ventured, nothing gained."

4. Others' expectations ("Who's in charge here?")

You have goals for yourself. Your parents, teachers, friends, and relatives have goals for you, too, and they're probably not shy about making them known. What happens when their push meets your pull? A competition of Olympic proportions that can leave you feeling frustrated, resentful, confused, and usually exhausted.

Multipotential makes this especially difficult (for more on this topic, see pages 96–105). The more you can do, the more you (and others) think you *should* do, and the more people around you try to guide you "for your own good."

What's the solution? Until you're on your own, you'll have to put up with some outside interference. Just remember that in the final analysis, it *is* your life, and you're the only one who can live it. Set your goals where you can be proud to reach them.

5. Impatience ("I want it NOW!")

Gifted teenagers don't hold the patent on impatience, a universal adolescent trait. They can, however, carry it too far. They tend to want clear-cut answers to everything—from complex problems to career choices and personal relationships.

Sometimes those clear-cut answers don't exist. Sometimes they take a long time to emerge and make themselves known. Impatience can lead to hasty resolutions that leave you feeling angry and disappointed.

This doesn't mean that you should spend hours each day agonizing over which socks to wear (if any). But when it comes to the Big Issues—like what to be when you grow up, or how to resolve a difference with a friend—it makes sense to go slow, to be patient, and to ask for help when you need it.

6. Identity ("I know who I am and what I want to be!")

Competing expectations and impatience can propel gifted adolescents toward deciding their futures too soon. The 14-year-old who declares that she's going to be a doctor is closing the door to other opportunities. And the 16-year-old who's determined to be a dancer may never discover his talents in science or math.

> "There are no shortcuts to any place worth going."
> **Beverly Sills**

One man in his late 20s recalls an argument he had with his father at age 13:

> "I had decided that I wanted to be an English teacher. My dad wanted me to take more science courses. I told him that those didn't have anything to do with teaching English. 'Take them anyway,' he suggested. 'Why narrow your options?' 'I know what I want to be,' I shouted, 'and I'LL NEVER CHANGE!' Today I remember that as one of the dumbest things I ever said."

Narrowing your interests too early can sometimes prevent you from reaching your full potential. It can keep you from the satisfying, integrated careers and relationships that make the most of your abilities. Besides, whoever said that you have to decide now what you'll be for the rest of your life?

Conclusion: It's okay to stay a kid for a few more years. One of the bonuses of adolescence is that it buys you time to experiment, explore, and experience a variety of possibilities and choices.

Teen Angst

John Lennon once observed that "one thing you can't hide is when you're crippled inside."* Poet Langston Hughes wondered where dreams go when they die; do they wither like a raisin in the sun, or do they fester like a sore or stink like rotten meat? Turn on your favorite radio station, and you'll hear songs about love gone wrong and the world gone bad. In their own ways, all of these artists are coping with *angst,* a German word meaning "foreboding, anxiety, worry, fear, and dread." To you, angst is much more than a dictionary definition. It's a powerful, invisible magnet drawing you toward questions without firm answers or issues without specific resolve:

- *"What do you mean, we can't do anything about homelessness? We're the richest nation on earth!"*
- *"My parents won't recycle because they say it's a pain, but it's my future they're throwing away!"*
- *"I'm sorry if it's required that I dissect a frog for biology. I won't do it. It's not right to have to kill something to find out how it lived."*
- *"Why must life be the way it is?"*

---

* All right, so we *like* quoting John Lennon. Maybe too much. Send us *your* favorite quotes and we'll start a collection for the next edition of this book.

Angst is a frequent visitor to gifted people of all ages. It usually comes rapping uninvited at your cerebral door, refusing to leave even after you ask it to ("I'm *not* going to worry about this. It has nothing to do with me. I can't do anything about it. Why should I worry?"). Try to ignore it, and it creeps up on you at unexpected times—at a movie, in class, at bedtime—demanding your attention. For gifted students, angst is part of the package, one of the by-products of an overactive brain and a tendency to care too much. It's the reason you challenge what everyone else gladly accepts; the reason you lose sleep over issues that don't even bother your friends. And just like your eye color, birthmarks, and (increasing) foot size, angst is here to stay.

What You Can Do

"Birds sing after a storm, why shouldn't we?"
Rose Fitzgerald Kennedy

Now for the good news: You can use angst to your advantage. The ability to see things other people don't easily see, or to dissect life situations with a sharp mental scalpel, give you insights into this sometimes crazy, frequently wacky world. But you're not the first person to walk through this valley of angst, which allows you to study and learn from those who have gone before you and emerged successful. Examples:

- Twelve-year-old Ohio student Tara Jones read about two newspaper reporters who went undercover and pretended to be homeless for a week. She called the reporters and invited them to her social studies class to talk about her findings. Tara and her classmates were so moved by the reporters' stories that they started a campaign to raise money and donate children's books to family shelters in Cleveland. This became a schoolwide project, raising hundreds of dollars and collecting hundreds of picture books.

- Sixteen-year-old Catherine Murray hated the gang wars and drug deals that were always going on in her Oakland, California, neighborhood. She decided that the best way to end such actions was to get to kids early, replacing their harmful and dangerous behaviors with constructive ones. So she began The Global Teen Club, an organization of ethnically diverse and globally aware teens who tackle problems ranging from AIDS discrimination to school violence, teenage nutrition to eating disorders. Catherine's work, as reported in her monthly newsletter, has been applauded by world leaders and young people alike.

- When 12-year-old Andrew Holleman learned of a developer's plans to build 180 condominiums in a wetlands near his family's home, he read the developer's proposal, researched the wetlands, drafted a petition, collected signatures, helped to organize a neighborhood association, spoke in front of a series of town meetings and debates, and eventually stopped the project. Because of his efforts, his beloved wetlands are safe from large developers.

Each of these students took a giant step forward in his or her growth. Instead of relying on other individuals, groups, or organizations to remedy a wrong, they put themselves in charge of trying. They cared deeply about their world and the people in it, but rather than simply saying "I care," they acted on their convictions and concerns. They refused to believe that since they were "just kids," their scope was limited. They realized that youth was not a barrier to effectively solving a problem.

"Dear Me": How and Why to Write Yourself a Letter

Everyone likes to get mail (except bills, of course), and gifted students are no exception. But did you ever get a letter from the person you know best—yourself? Writing a letter to yourself and opening it six months from now will reveal how your cares and concerns (and angst) can transform over time. On the other hand, it might reveal that no matter how much time passes, your cares and concerns (and angst) stay the same. Either way, a letter written to you, by you, will be an eye-opener.

After an especially meaningful experience at home or at school, write yourself a note expressing your feelings about what just occurred. You might find yourself commenting on little things, like a smile from a stranger or an uplifting comment from a teacher. Or your letter might describe something major, like a decision you've made to take charge of your life, to break a harmful habit, or to end an unhealthy relationship. Whatever your focus might be, you can assume one thing: If you don't write down your thoughts promptly, they will dissolve as surely as those vivid dreams you sometimes have during the night but can't recall in the morning. So write a letter to yourself, put it in a self-addressed stamped envelope, add a stamp, and give it to someone you trust with instructions to mail it six months from the day you wrote it. (TIP: It helps if the person you choose is both organized and responsible.) You'll be surprised to learn how much you've changed—or how much you haven't changed.

"Although the
world is full of
suffering, it is full
also of the over-
coming of it."
Helen Keller

What's the connection between action and angst? Simply this: The reason most people feel overstressed or overwhelmed by life is because they feel powerless to change the status quo. But when you make the effort to do something—anything—positive, you put yourself in charge. Action by action, you start taking back the personal control that was lost when you thought the situation was hopeless and you were helpless. Angst has a way of diminishing when you realize that your actions can make a difference.

So if angst is an issue with you (or even if it isn't), look for ways, large or small, to move beyond your own small world. Has a family in your town lost their home to a fire? Begin a toy drive at school to help the youngest victims of this tragedy. Did a local bank donate money to the family? Write a thank-you note to the president expressing your appreciation. These actions won't guarantee that you'll never again have a moment of inner conflict, but they will give you practice in viewing problems from a perspective that is greater than your own backyard.

GIFTED PEOPLE SPEAK OUT
Jessica Wilber, 14

When you hit about 11 or so, your body starts going haywire. It's your hormones' gentle way of saying "Hello! We're here, too." (Though often it seems like your hormones are jumping up and down and screaming "NOTICE ME! NOTICE ME!") Add being "gifted" to that, and you've got a slight dilemma.

Journaling can help. The following suggestions are some of my favorites, but you can try anything you want.

1. Get a blank piece of paper and a pen or pencil. Close your eyes and make a mental, emotional, and physical inventory of yourself. If you find anything that's blocked or bothered, dialogue with it. For example: If your back hurts, promise that you won't spend so many hours on the computer if it stops hurting. If you're feeling depressed, promise that you'll be nicer to yourself if your depression lightens up. Write down your promise and the response. (Your back might say, "It's not enough to spend less time at the computer. Get some exercise, too!")

Don't laugh! Dialoguing with different parts of yourself doesn't make you certifiably insane—and it really works.

2. Write a poem about anything you choose: your body image, why school is boring, why you're so mad at your parents that you could scream. This is an excellent release, and because you're writing in your journal, you don't have to worry about anyone seeing your poem (unless you want them to—more about that in a second).

3. Make lists of things you enjoy doing, however small or insignificant they might seem. Your list might include bird watching, taking a bubble bath instead of a shower, eating strawberries, going for a long bike ride, calling a long-distance friend on the phone. The next time you're feeling bored, tense, or stressed, look at your list to find healthy, creative ways to feel better.

4. Set goals for yourself and write them down. For example, if you have written a really good short story that you'd like to get published, resolve to send it to three different places this month. If you like a certain boy or girl in your class, resolve to say hello to him or her (and smile when you say it). Every time you accomplish one of your goals, put a check mark by it. You'll feel great.

5. If you're wondering if there are other teens out there like you, there are. So start a 'zine to meet each other and share your thoughts, ideas, and concerns. A 'zine is a do-it-yourself magazine. You can call it whatever you want and include articles, poems, stories, journal entries, artwork, etc. You can include your name, a "pen name," or no name at all. You can request pen pals. You can write and design your 'zine by hand, type it, or desktop publish it on a computer. You can print out or photocopy several copies, staple them, and sell them or pass them out for free (slip them into people's lockers, give them to friends, advertise them online).

Whatever you decide to do, have fun!

Peace,

Jessica

Jessica Wilber is the author of Totally Private and Personal: Journaling Ideas for Girls and Young Women *(Minneapolis: Free Spirit Publishing, 1996). She has won awards in creative writing contests at school and has a monthly column on the Teen Page of her local newspaper. She lives with her family in Wisconsin.*

The Top Ten Teenage Lies

The teen years are often associated (at least by adults) with terms like these:

rebellion . . . showing off . . . arrogance . . . restlessness . . . high energy . . . low energy . . . laziness . . . boredom . . . sarcasm . . . experimentation . . . raging hormones . . . "testing" . . . attitude.

No matter who you are at age 12, by the time you reach 13 your parents expect you to wake up one morning and be somebody you've never been before: an overly critical, cynical, hormone-driven creature whose favorite three words are "me," "me," and "me." While this description might fit some teenagers (and some adults), it's hardly accurate for the majority of 13- to 19-year-olds. In fact, in our experience with teenagers, we've found that the ones who are *most* out-of-control are those whose parents and teachers expect them to act this way. Gifted or otherwise, teenagers are far more complex, compassionate, sensitive, and caring than society gives them credit for.

Still, there are certain ways in which teenagers tend to be similar, especially in the area of misconceptions. Over the years, we've collected quite a few of these, and we've chosen to call the most common ones the "Top Ten Teenage Lies." We don't expect that all of you (or even many of you) will adhere to each one of these mistruths, but we suspect that more than a few will sound familiar to you.

Lie #1: "I don't care!"

"There is no map for life; unfair things happen. The challenge is what you do with these things."
Elizabeth Glaser

The most widespread lie is also the most egregious, because—like it or not, admit it or not, accept it or not—you *do* care. You care whether your teachers like you and your parents love you. You care about the pain-in-the-neck sibling sharing your house. You care about succeeding in things that matter to you. You care about whether our planet stays green. You care about your future; you care about your cat.

When you claim that you don't care, you're attempting to relieve the frustration you feel when things aren't going the way you thought or hoped they would. There's nothing wrong with that, as long as you (and the people within hearing distance) don't really believe what you're saying—and as long as you don't get permanently stuck in "I-don't-care" mode. In a world where people are either part of the problem or part of the solution, those who genuinely don't care belong to the first category.

Lie #2: "School is a waste."

So Algebra II is boring, History of the World seems trivial, and school lunches remind you of the table scraps you feed your pet. Also, where do they find those teachers? Under a collapsed ruin from one of those long-lost civilizations you're supposed to be studying? These all might seem like reasons to dismiss school as a waste of your precious time and energy. Don't you have better things to do than sit in some uncomfortable, graffiti-filled desk listening to lectures, correcting homework, and taking tests?

Frankly . . . no. There may be a lot of things wrong with your school—including teachers who don't care about you (or themselves), irrelevant assignments from outdated textbooks, cliques, gangs, and pervasive apathy—but if you look more closely, you'll usually find something else beneath the thin veneer of the typical high school or junior high:

- *Like Mrs. Johnson, the 6th-period teacher who encouraged you to pursue your latent writing talent. "Keep writing," she once wrote across one of your homework assignments. "I want an autographed copy of your first novel."*
- *Or Mr. Bennett, the guidance counselor you didn't think knew your name—until he walked up to you in the hall and asked how your dad was doing since coming home from the hospital.*
- *Or Toya, the girl in homeroom who began the canned food drive that ended up collecting thousands of items for local shelters.*

Generally speaking, most educators don't enter the field without at least *some* interest in helping kids. Over time, some teachers might lose the sense of purpose that brought them to their profession, becoming discouraged by low pay, weekends filled with grading papers, and students whose attitudes, facial expressions, body language, and mumbled comments communicate their disrespect. If you're caught up in Lie #2, you may want to find some reasons (and people) to make school worthwhile for you. At the very least, think in terms of your own self-interest: You spend about 1,100 hours a year at school, so why not get something out of it? When you adopt an approach that's more upbeat than downtrodden, you might be surprised at what you find in your school—and in yourself.

> "To learn is to change. Education is a process that changes the learner."
> George B. Leonard

Lie #3: "Been there, done that."

How jaded, bored, and blasé we've become! Thanks to cable and MTV, the Internet and Prodigy, Sony and Nintendo, we've got the whole world at our fingertips. We need only go as far as our computers to travel anywhere and try anything—reality or fantasy. We can talk to people in other cities, states, and countries without ever meeting them face-to-face. Wherever you look, the world seems like a smaller, more impersonal place.

So what's left to explore? What adventures remain? In an era when we can journey thousands of miles and access tens of thousands of newsgroups and Web sites at the click of a mouse, many teenagers have begun to wonder, "Is that all there is?"

The answer is no, but only people wise enough to appreciate both the possibilities and the limits of our modern age ever realize this. Appreciating the limits means realizing that an E-mail friend in Paris can't replace the kid down the block who's been your sidekick since the second grade. Or that downloading video clips doesn't compare to watching the original, non-colorized version of *The African Queen* with your family, while your sister squeals with horror at seeing the blood-sucking leeches attack Humphrey Bogart's legs.

Your dog licking you awake in the morning . . . the beauty of winter's first snow, or the tangerine hue of a warm sunset . . . the touch of a friend's hand . . . the fragrance of cookies baking. . . . These are the quiet joys of life, the ones you forget the moment they pass—and then, for some reason, remember first and most distinctly when you're homesick or lonely.

Been there, done that? Do yourself a favor and free yourself to explore, experience, and delight in life's little moments.

Lie #4: "I'm not gifted, I'm normal."

People who are supposed to know something about giftedness—educators, researchers, authors—have done a terrible job of explaining why giftedness should be perceived as an asset. Using jargon that only they understand—"differentiated curriculum," "dysynchronous development"—these otherwise intelligent people are often clueless when it comes to the day-to-day lives of gifted young people. They don't realize that the word "gifted" provokes all kinds of negative reactions. Examples:

> **Girl, 11:** " 'Gifted' sounds too powerful. I think the term 'capable' is better because it doesn't sound as if you have ESP."

> **Girl, 13:** "Sometimes people think 'gifted' means stuck up and they think that you are going to make fun of their grades because they don't make as good grades as you do."

> **Boy, 12:** "I do not like being called 'gifted.' It makes me think something is wrong with me. I don't know of any other word to replace 'gifted,' but I wish someone would think of something."

But just because the word "gifted" is one that very few bright students like or approve of is no reason to deny the talents you do possess. Like it or not, your mind reacts more quickly and intensely than the minds of most young people your age. That's nothing to be ashamed of, nor is it something to hold over other people's heads, but it's absurd to deny it.

When someone asks you if you're gifted, you might try answering, "In some things." That's not a lie, and it allows for another reality: that the person asking knows more about or is better at some things than you are. Find out what those things are, and you'll both win.

Giftedness may be atypical, but it's not abnormal. There's a big difference.

Lie #5: "But, Officer, I was going the speed limit."

This lie is genetic—you inherit it from your parents. And you'll probably pass it on to your children, if you have children. There is no cure, no solution. Just smile, take the ticket, and slow down next time.

Lie #6: "My way or the highway."

The answers you give in school are usually correct, and on tests—even essay tests—your opinions are validated by high grades. So it seems reasonable to think that your opinions in social situations will be just as well regarded and universally accepted.

Don't count on it. There's no correlation between being right at school and being right with friends. Your teachers might applaud the logic behind your theory of why dinosaurs became extinct, but that doesn't mean your friends will automatically go along with your choice for a night on the town. They might have different (and better) ideas. Be ready to give in once in a while—especially important if your social group happens to include a lot of other gifted students, each of whom is equally used to being bright and right. If you're not careful, you could end up with eight leaders and no followers, each person convinced that the others are wrong, stubborn, or selfish.

Listen to your friends' choices and their reasons for them. Go along with the wishes of others once in a while. Don't be concerned with always being right. Sometimes, especially in social situations, there are no good guys or bad guys—just a group of people intent on having a good time.

Lie #7: "I'll never touch the stuff."

"Stuff" in the context of this lie might mean anything that is taboo for you and other people your age, including:

1. illegal drugs (or someone else's prescription drugs)
2. tobacco products, including those you smoke, snort, or chew
3. alcohol, including wine and beer
4. sexual activity (protected or otherwise)
5. violence toward others (or yourself).

Each of these things is harmful and addictive; the more you get, the more you want. "But not for me," you might insist. "I can control my habit." And maybe you can . . . or maybe you can't. Your willpower may be strong, but is it strong enough to withstand pressure from stress or friends?

Still, saying "I'll never touch the stuff" might be an overstatement, at least for some of these teenage behaviors. If you're smart, you'll forever avoid numbers 1, 2, and 5; they're dangerous to you and the people around you. Number 3 may be part of your life at some point; your decision to drink alcohol will probably depend on whether you enjoy its taste and effects. Number 4 is the only teenage taboo we hope you'll enjoy regularly (and safely) as an adult. The physical and emotional feelings of sexual activity are intense, enjoyable, and worth repeating. But please, please keep in mind (we know you've heard this before, blah blah blah) that in the age of AIDS, unprotected sex—even with people you love and know very well—is potentially lethal. When you and your partner have decided that you're mature enough for sex, use a condom.

Lie #8: "Depressed? Me? Never!"

There are many myths about giftedness, including the myth that "smart people don't have problems." Because of your superior mind, you're supposed to be able to handle even the most emotionally draining and/or tumultuous times without help from others. In other words, you're supposed to be immune from depression.

But gifted people get depressed, too. Left unacknowledged, unchecked, and untreated, depression can be as dangerous as some of the taboos listed in Lie #7. The signs of depression are remarkably similar to the warning signs of suicide, which shouldn't be surprising, since suicide is an extreme reaction to extreme depression. Here are some of depression's calling cards:

● *lack (or loss) of appetite*
● *low (or lower) grades in school*
● *the desire to be alone instead of with others*
● *negative views of the future*
● *focusing on mistakes you've made in the past instead of on your successes*
● *an overall lack of initiative; you're almost always tired or bored*
● *lack of concern (or less concern) about physical appearance*
● *frequent arguments with others*
● *long periods of sleep*
● *an overall attitude that everything is hopeless*
● *loneliness and a sense that you've "lost" some part of yourself.*

Of course, you *will* have the occasional bad day, when all you want to do is pull the covers over your head and sleep for a week. That's not depression, it's a natural reaction to stress or boredom. Depression, in contrast, is long-term (lasting more than a couple of weeks) and intense. Each day, the pit you're in gets deeper, the wall you've built around yourself gets taller, shutting people out becomes easier, and although you can't say you *enjoy* your isolation, there is a predictability about it that you find comforting. When this happens, it's time to get help. Which leads to . . .

Lie #9: "I can survive anything."

As noted in Lie #8, the signs of depression are similar to the warning signs of suicide. Logically, this makes sense: If you begin to believe that your future and the planet's are hopeless, then logic tells you that it makes little sense to stick around. Fortunately, logic doesn't (or shouldn't) always prevail. There's also something called *intuition,* which silently tells you to give yourself another chance. And *self-preservation,* an enormously strong instinct that insists that life is always preferable to the alternative. Plus there's your high intelligence which, despite your occasional feeling that it's more of a burden than an asset, enables you to consider an issue or a problem from more than one side.

However, each of these alternatives to logic may require a gentle push from someone else—a friend, a parent, a counselor, a religious leader, or someone else you trust and can turn to when you're hurting. Like it or not (and when you're depressed, you probably won't like it), human beings are social creatures. You are a human being, therefore you are a social creature. Before you can reach inside yourself, you may first have to reach out to someone else. Think of that person as a human life preserver, an emotional buoy in the choppy seas of adolescent angst.

Strange but true, it's only by seeking out others that you can fully understand and appreciate yourself. But that's the way it's always been, and as long as people continue to live as helpmates rather than hermits, that's how it always will be.

We know that when you're hurting, it may be even more painful to reach out to someone else for help. But we promise you this: If you take the first step, each successive step will be easier.

Lie #10: "Don't worry, Mom (or Dad), everything will be okay."

Usually this lie surfaces when you're trying to convince your parent(s) that something they perceive as potentially dangerous or troublesome is really no big deal.

Lies Your Parents and Teachers Tell You

So you don't think we're branding all teenagers liars and implying that all adults tell the truth, here are a few lies you've probably heard:

From parents:
1. "None of my children get special treatment."
2. "This will hurt me as much as (or more than) it hurts you."
3. "I had to walk two miles to school, uphill both ways."
4. "Brussels sprouts are good for you."
5. "I remember when I was your age. . . ."

From teachers:
1. "I don't have favorites."
2. "I don't believe in homework."
3. "The test will be easy."
4. "If you don't learn this now, you'll be behind next year."
5. "I enjoy bus duty."

Example: You and a couple of friends want to drive to a nearby big city to see a concert.

"Be careful," they say. "You're not used to city driving. Don't talk to anyone you don't know. Don't stop for strangers. Don't turn down any dark streets. Don't . . ." etc., etc., etc.

"Don't worry, Mom (or Dad)," you say, giving them your most sincere look. "Everything will be okay."

And there they are: the words all parents hate to hear. This casual reassurance seldom satisfies any but the most gullible or laid-back parents. Remember that no matter how old or how tall you eventually get, to your parents you're still the little kid who couldn't sleep without your special "blankey."

To avoid a verbal ping-pong match of warnings (theirs) and assurances (yours), change the wording of lie #10. Since you don't know that "everything will be okay" (the best intentions and most careful planning can go awry), try this alternative: When your parents finish reading you the safety bulletin (don't interrupt, and wait to make sure that they really have finished speaking), say, "Mom (or Dad), I promise to be responsible." Then follow this statement with specifics that fit your particular situation. Maybe you'll say that you won't go anyplace by yourself, or you won't do anything stupid, like getting into a car with someone who's been drinking.

When you say that you'll be responsible and illustrate your claim with examples of what you will and won't do, you may find that your parents grow more accommodating and less restrictive. They won't stop worrying—if they did, they wouldn't be parents— but as long as you live up to your end of the bargain, they are more likely to grant you increasing amounts of freedom and respect.

And Now a Few Words About Drugs, Sex, and Death

As a teenager, you're statistically part of the age group most prone to accidents, homicides, drug use, and sexually transmitted diseases, including AIDS. You're also in the *only* age group affected by teen pregnancy (duh). Harsh as they are, those are the facts.

Some people assume that gifted students are immune from these woes, arguing that your advanced intelligence leads you to make the right decisions when it comes to smoking, drinking, sex, and other temptations. Others assume the opposite: that your heightened awareness of things around you, coupled with a driving curiosity to explore almost anything new or different, leaves you more susceptible to dangerous experimentation.

The truth lies somewhere in between. In 1995, 3,351 outstanding students took part in a nationwide survey. Some of the survey results may surprise you . . . or not.*

● *86 percent of the students surveyed have never tried marijuana, 98 percent have never tried cocaine, and 52 percent don't drink alcoholic beverages. BUT: 47 percent said that it was easy or not very difficult to obtain drugs at their school, 45 percent think some of their friends have a problem with alcohol, 11 percent admit to driving after drinking, and 27 percent have been passengers in cars whose drivers have had too much to drink.*

● *88 percent of the students surveyed haven't yet engaged in sexual intercourse. Of those who have, 44 percent wish they had remained a virgin. BUT: 44 percent of those who are sexually active don't use a contraceptive device regularly, 37 percent would engage in sexual intercourse if a condom were not available, 85 percent refuse to believe they have even a moderate risk of contracting AIDS, and 61 percent are convinced that their risk of pregnancy is low or nonexistent.*

● *45 percent of the male students surveyed claim to own or have access to some kind of gun.*

There is no way that an entire group of people clumped together under the label "gifted and talented" will all behave in precisely the same way under any circumstances. You are an individual, and your personal choices and decisions will be based on factors including:

● ***How you were raised.*** *Strict adherence to rules and fear of parental retribution may cause you to behave differently from someone who was raised in a family that rewards independence and free thinking.*

● ***Your moral/ethical/religious convictions.*** *Some people choose not to engage in certain behaviors because they consider these behaviors morally wrong. Others weigh each situation independently, choosing a response based on their feelings and needs at the moment (this is called "situational ethics").*

● ***Your self-esteem.*** *People who don't believe they are valuable may do dangerous things because they think that no one cares or they want to fit in with their social group. Others respect themselves enough to say no in the face of peer pressure and possible rejection.*

● ***Your long-term vs. short-term concerns.*** *A popular expression in the 1960s was "If it feels good, do it." This contrasts sharply with the young person who asks, "How might the consequences of this decision affect me next week? Next month? Next year?" People who live only in the present are bound to make more mistakes than those with an eye toward the future.*

---

* As reported in the *Who's Who Among American High School Students' 26th Annual Survey of High Achievers*, published by Educational Communications, Inc., 721 N. McKinley Road, Lake Forest, IL 60045. Of the 3,351 high-achieving 16- to 18-year-olds who participated in the survey, all have an A or B average, and 98 percent plan to attend college after high school graduation.

- *Your common sense.* You already know that using illegal drugs, having sex with someone you barely know, and smoking two packs of cigarettes a day are not intelligent choices. Yet teenagers do these things and more all the time. Common sense (which, according to Mark Twain, "is not all that common") often serves as the dividing line between acquiescence and resistance.

It's not our place to tell you what you should or shouldn't do. You already get plenty of lectures at home, in DARE classes, sex education, family life, social studies, homeroom, etc. We simply want to remind you that a first-rate brain is good for more than solving calculus problems. You might use yours to sift through the best and the worst of what life has to offer, so the decisions you make today are the ones you can live with tomorrow.

Find Out More

To learn more about adolescence, read:

Berman, Phillip L., editor. *The Courage of Conviction.* New York: Ballantine Books, 1986.

Gordon, Sol. *The Teenage Survival Book: The Complete Revised, Updated Edition of You.* New York: Times Books, 1981.

Rubin, Nancy. *Ask Me If I Care.* Berkeley, CA: Ten Speed Press, 1994.

Death with Honors: Suicide Among Gifted Adolescents

There are a few topics that are so taboo and painful to discuss that many people choose to ignore them entirely. Teenage suicide is one of them. Working under the misguided assumption that "If you don't talk about suicide, it will go away" (or "If you do talk about it, more suicides will occur"), many teens and adults dismiss teen suicide as something that happens to *other* families in *other* towns. And a lot of people believe that gifted adolescents are too smart to even consider ending their own lives.

Katy Amundson* was 17 when she killed herself. She was an A student and a regular member of her school's Honor Society for academic achievement. She was also a cheerleader, a model, a

> "Suicide is a permanent solution to a temporary problem."
> **Phil Donahue**

---

* Her name has been changed, but the story is true.

beauty contestant, and a driven perfectionist who battled both anorexia and bulimia. One February afternoon, she drove to a state park, poured two cans of gasoline over herself, and lit a match.

Teenage suicide is a far bigger problem than most people think. Here are some scary facts:*

● *According to the American Psychiatric Association, suicide is the third leading cause of death among teenagers. Among college students, it's the second leading cause of death.*

● *According to the Centers for Disease Control (CDC), suicide rates for teenagers are rising steadily. Between 1980–1993, the suicide rate for 10- to 14-year-olds rose 120 percent; for 15- to 19-year-olds, almost 30 percent.*

● *In a 1993 CDC study of 16,000 high school students, 1 in 12 said that he or she had attempted suicide during the previous year.*

● *Of the 3,351 high-achieving teenagers who took part in the* Who's Who Among American High School Students' *26th Annual Survey (1995), 26 percent have considered suicide, and 4 percent have attempted suicide.*

● *According to Covenant House, which provides crisis care, counseling, outreach, and special programs for homeless and runaway youth, 33 percent of U.S. teenagers say they have considered suicide, 15 percent have thought seriously about it, and 6 percent have actually tried it.*

If you read your local newspaper, you've probably seen stories about teens who have killed themselves. If you went to the library, you could easily find many more. A large number will describe teens who were "bright," "top students," "successful," "attractive," "college-bound," and so on. Perhaps you know someone who attempted suicide or committed suicide. We do.

Who is the typical candidate for teenage suicide? Here's a composite picture: male or female, smart or average, a social isolate or a social mixer, from a broken home or a secure one, wealthy or poor, religious or not, black or white, from a suburb or a small town. In other words, there is *no such thing* as a "typical" suicidal teenager. There do appear to be some patterns or trends among suicide victims, but the majority don't fit any particular mold.

● *Like Katy Amundson.*

● *And Keith, who hanged himself in a public restroom. This handsome, intelligent teen from a New England state was a football team captain who, according to his father, "still kissed me good-night even though he was 16."*

● *And Melissa and Mary, two 15-year-olds who left suicide notes asking their parents for forgiveness. "I love you all, so please don't be sad," wrote Mary. "It's not your fault for having the gun around."*

---

* Sources: The American Psychiatric Association; *Who's Who Among American High School Students' 26th Annual Survey of High Achievers,* Lake Forest IL: Educational Communications, Inc., 1996; the Covenant House Web site (http://www.covenanthouse.org/). CDC figures reported in *Time,* July 22, 1996, p. 41.

- *And Steven, a blonde, blue-eyed 13-year-old who shot himself in the head during reading class. Steven was an A student who had been identified as gifted. He was also a star player on his school basketball team.*

- *And David, who learned one month before graduating from high school that he had missed being valedictorian by .36 of a point. Fearing that he had disappointed his parents, he took a shotgun from his dad's closet and killed himself.*

We could fill this book with stories as tragic as these.

Giftedness and Suicide: Some Possible Explanations

Although there is no firm evidence that gifted teenagers are more likely to attempt or commit suicide than less able adolescents, some aspects of being gifted may in some cases contribute to suicidal behavior. (We have deliberately qualified this statement with "may" and "in some cases" because it is simply *not true* that being gifted makes one more prone to suicide.) Examples:

- *A perception of failure that differs from others' perceptions of failure. (For example, feeling that a B is equivalent to an F if your personal standard of success calls for an A or above.)*

- *External pressures to always be #1 and a life orientation that identifies one as a "future leader" or a "mover and shaker of the next generation."*

- *The frustration that comes when one's intellectual talents outpace his or her social or physical development. ("For being so smart, I'm awfully dumb at making friends," or "Starting school early and skipping second grade was fine, but now I'm the freak of the locker room—I'm so puny!")*

- *The ability to understand adult situations and world events while feeling powerless to effect positive change.*

These problems don't plague all (or even most) gifted teenagers, and you may not identify with any of them. If so, that's fine; you can ignore the next two sections. But if any of these things do concern you, please read on.

Knowing and Accepting Yourself

If you take a moment to consider how people behave differently in similar circumstances, the complexity of the human animal becomes clear. Some people are so sensitive to criticism that an unfriendly glance causes shame and tears. Others would interpret a brick thrown through their windshield simply as an odd way of saying hello.

The Gifted Kids' Survival Guide

It's the same with issues related to growing up. What one teenager may view as a catastrophe, another may perceive as an opportunity. And it's the same with issues as heavy as suicide. The science of understanding human behavior is a "soft science" at best. There are no guarantees that people will always respond in the same way to the same situation. This is what makes human psychology so fascinating (and frustrating).

Psychologists and educators do seem to agree that there are two keys to coping with bad times: *understanding yourself* and *developing and maintaining a positive attitude toward yourself and others.* They have come up with some suggestions, based on research studies and life experiences, for directing people toward a healthy outlook on life.

1. Read about who you are and others like you who have gone before.

Psychologists call this *identification.* What it means is that you should try to find another person—a historical figure or the person next door—who shares some of your goals, attitudes, fears, and beliefs.

Books like *The Courage of Conviction* will show you that many successful people—Billy Graham, Lech Walesa, Jane Alexander, Joan Baez, and Mario Cuomo, to name a few—have developed a philosophy of life that allows for human frailties and fears. For example, here's Steve Allen describing why there is no "right answer" that applies to every life situation:*

> "No philosophy, sadly, has all the answers. No matter how assured we may be about certain aspects of our belief, there are always painful inconsistencies, exceptions and contradictions. This is as true in religion as it is in politics, and is self-evident to all except fanatics and the naive."

2. Try to remember that life isn't always fair, winning isn't always best, and many questions don't have "one right answer."

Our society does a lot to encourage and reward achievement—which is okay to a point, because winning is nothing to be ashamed of. Still, the prevailing attitude seems to be that achievement is the only measure of success. This discredits a lot of very good ideas (and the people behind them) that never achieve #1 status.

---

* From Philip L. Berman, ed., *The Courage of Conviction.* New York: Ballantine Books, 1986.

The Seven Great Myths of Adolescence: Roadblocks to Self-Appreciation

1. Everyone has to like me.
2. I have to like everyone.
3. Happiness is achieved solely through wealth or power.
4. No one will find me physically attractive enough to want to date me.
5. Asking for help from parents, teachers, friends, and others is the same as admitting failure.
6. There's nothing left to learn and no one around who can teach me anything.
7. If I can't do something perfectly, I shouldn't do it at all.

For example, after four years of high school, only one person is chosen to be valedictorian, which leaves many "also rans" wondering, "What's the point?" The point is that life isn't fair. This is a cliché, but it's true anyway. So is the old saw that says, "It's not whether you win or lose but how you play the game." There's comfort to be derived from platitudes like these.

Do your best not to get too upset when your burning questions about God, the meaning of life, and the pursuit of happiness don't get answered immediately or to your full satisfaction. Life is a journey, not a destination, so answers that seem solid now may seem silly in two years. And questions that mean nothing to you today may represent great challenges later.

3. Cultivate and maintain a healthy skepticism.

Henry James, the nineteenth-century author of *A Turn of the Screw,* once wrote: "Steer safely between the opposite dangers of believing too little or believing too much." More recently, a popular bumper sticker has put this more succinctly: "Question Authority."

Sometimes the right path for you may not be the most popular one. Being gifted, you have the ability to detect nuances that aren't obvious to other people. You can draw connections between ideas that seem totally unrelated to those around you. If you choose to act on your convictions, you may find yourself in a minority of one. As a gifted 21-year-old observed, "True genius requires creativity along with (or perhaps in spite of) intelligence. The invention of new ideas . . . can be painful, lonely, and difficult."

Don't put yourself down by minimizing your powerhouse ideas—if, in fact, you believe in them and in yourself. You may not find anyone who agrees with you, but you'll be in impressive historical company. Many of the world's great thinkers have stood alone in their attitudes and philosophies.

What does all of this have to do with teenage suicide? Plenty. Nobody really wants to die; instead, there are people who don't want to live. There's a *big* difference. The circumstances that prompt suicidal gestures are the everyday frustrations that people feel alone in facing or impotent to overcome.

Although it may not seem true at times, we all share a common bond called *humanity*. To feel the way it holds us close, we must take a few moments now and then for deep personal reflection.

> "Life is better than death, I believe, if only because it is less boring, and because it has fresh peaches in it."
> Alice Walker

Intervening with a Friend in Need

According to data from the health professions, the incidences of depression now outnumber those of all other medical symptoms put together. Blame it on world strife, the decline of traditional family values, or the sense of personal isolation that results from living in complex and uncompromising times.

"How can I help friends who are having problems?" Liza, 18

Whatever the reason, the reality is that some young people see more bad than good. They wonder if life is all it's cracked up to be. They fail to see alternatives to living the way they do.

They need help.

Not everyone is a counselor, and not every teenager is equipped to offer the long-term treatment a depressed friend may require to weather emotionally troubling times. But most can listen, and sometimes that's enough.

Depression is an illness. A depressed person can't fight it by himself or herself, any more than you can fight strep throat with cough drops. Often, depression requires medical attention. Most of the time, however, depressed adolescents will go first to age mates, not to adults, to discuss what's bothering them. That's where you come in, ears wide open and shoulder ready for a cry.

There are a number of ways you can help a friend in need. To make them easier to remember, we've organized them around the acronym REALITY.

On Being a
Teenager

Respect

Respect your friend's self-doubts and sadness. Don't dismiss his feelings or beliefs as being silly or trivial. Share some of your own fears and losses. Let him know that you appreciate his willingness to open up to you; this implies trust, and it takes courage to admit "I hurt."

Evaluate

Evaluate your friend's words and ask, "So how can I help?" or "How do you plan to deal with these problems?" If she even hints that suicide is a possibility, keep her talking! The more specific her plans are, the more imminent the danger is.

Act

Act specifically. Too often, teenagers feel that they can't share with others (especially adults) things that were said to them in confidence. While this applies in many cases, it *never* applies to life-threatening situations. Let your friend know that while you'd never do anything to hurt him, you will do whatever you can to keep him alive. Then talk to an adult—a sympathetic teacher, a school counselor, someone in your church or synagogue, anyone who can help you intervene.

273

A suicide claims more than one victim. It leaves behind a host of people who carry the burden of believing that they could and should have done something to stop it. Don't put yourself in this wrenchingly painful position.

Listen

The most difficult of all human relations skills, true listening involves understanding the other person's words *and intentions*. It doesn't mean waiting for your turn to talk, nor does it lead to a verbal battle of "I'm right/you're wrong." As one suicidal teenager wrote, "I didn't expect anyone to give me all the answers. I only wanted someone to hear my questions."

Investigate

Investigate local agencies. Know where to go for more help than you can give. Find out where teenagers in your community can get confidential information and advice about problems they're unwilling to discuss with someone at home or school. Start by checking your local Yellow Pages under "Crisis Intervention Centers." (Additional resources are listed on page 276.)

Take

Take preventive steps. One Texas town where the population grew from 3,000 to 93,000 people in ten years had big problems with teenage suicide, delinquency, and drug abuse. In response, a task force of teenagers, teachers, and community leaders began to meet regularly with newcomers and anyone else who wanted to talk or listen. The result? Drastic reductions in teenage suicide.

Talk to school or church leaders about starting a peer support group to serve as a forum for discussing the problems (and joys) of growing up. These meetings can perform much the same function as an annual medical checkup or car tune-up: detecting potential problems.

Yourself

Just because we don't have degrees in counseling, we assume that we can't help a friend in need, pain, or crisis. Wrong! Each of us can help simply by serving as the initial contact person. We can listen, ask questions, smile, and reach out a comforting hand. Just by being supportive, we can bolster a friend's feelings of self-worth. We can make a difference.

"The way in which my own life touches those of so many others, those I know and thousands of those I don't, has strengthened my belief that each human has his or her unique place in the ocean of existence."
Jane Goodall

Find Out More

To learn more about suicide and suicide prevention, read:

Nelson, Richard E., and Judith C. Galas. *The Power to Prevent Suicide: A Guide for Teens Helping Teens.* Minneapolis: Free Spirit Publishing, 1994. When teenagers were asked, "Who would you tell about wanting to commit suicide?" 90 percent said they would tell a friend first. This book tells you what to do next.

Bergman, David. *Kids on the Brink: Understanding the Teen Suicide Epidemic.* Washington, DC: PIA Press, 1990. Weaves dozens of stories about suicidal young people into solid facts and information about teen suicide and its causes.

Crook, Marion. *Please, Listen to Me! Your Guide to Understanding Teenagers and Suicide.* Bellingham, WA: Self-Counsel Press, 1992. Written for parents to help them understand why their child might think about or attempt suicide and what they can do to help a troubled child, this easy-to-read, easy-to-understand book also provides insights into why teen suicide happens.

Visit these sites on the World Wide Web:

http://www.save.org/
The Suicide Awareness\Voices of Education (SA\VE) home page.

http://www.cmhc.com/guide/suicidal.htm
Links to self-help resources compiled by Mental Health Net.

http://earth.execpc.com/~corbeau/suicide.html
Links to news groups, FAQ files, online support networks, book lists, other Web sites, and more.

http://www.coil.com/~grohol/helpme.htm
The Suicide Helpline compiled by Dr. John Grohol includes links to helpful mailing lists and online resources.

Suicide Prevention Resources

● **Look under "Suicide Prevention" in your local phone book.** Most cities and many towns have suicide prevention hotlines staffed 24 hours a day, 7 days a week, with people ready and willing to listen. Check the "Community Services" section first, if there is one. You can also find hotline listings in the Yellow Pages.

● **Youth Suicide Prevention (YSP)** can provide information and articles. It has established suicide prevention committees in most states and can refer you to the one nearest you. Call (617) 738-0700, or write to: YSP, 11 Parkman Way, Needham, MA 02192-2863.

● **The American Association of Suicidology** can provide information and listings of support groups around the country. Call (202) 237-2280, or write to: American Association of Suicidology, 4201 Connecticut Avenue NW, Suite 310, Washington, DC 20008. On the World Wide Web, go to: http://www.cyberpsych.org/aas.htm

GIFTED PEOPLE SPEAK OUT
Anonymous

During my junior year in high school, I thought a lot about suicide. I felt isolated, alone, and different, and I had no one to talk to (or so I believed). My father was an alcoholic, distant and preoccupied; my mother was often ill and had problems of her own. Because my parents were very strict, I had almost no social life and, as a result, no friends I felt close enough to confide in. On the surface I seemed fine—a well-behaved, well-adjusted student with A's on my report cards and awards for academic achievement. My teachers liked me and encouraged me. Yet I kept one of my father's razor blades hidden in a dresser drawer, and I always knew where to find my mother's pills, including powerful tranquilizers. I was aware that mixing alcohol and pills (both plentiful at our house) could be fatal. I thought that if I swallowed a handful of Valiums and drank half a bottle of Scotch, that would probably do it.

I even drafted suicide notes to my parents—indictments of their shortcomings as parents that usually ended with a melodramatic "please don't forget me." (As if any family ever forgets a suicide.)

So why didn't I go through with it? I had ample opportunities and, I felt, plenty of good reasons to kill myself. But something always stopped me. Although there were many nights when I cried myself to sleep, I never woke up crying in the morning. At some point, I realized that *I always felt better in the morning*—minutely, infinitesimally, microscopically better, but enough to get me through another day. Maybe it was the sun shining through my bedroom window. Maybe it was the knowledge that I was one day closer to leaving home!

I also discovered that reading was a way to distract me from my sadness. I read anything and everything I could get my hands on—Jane Austen novels, Ian Fleming's James Bond series, science fiction, *Gone with the Wind,* poetry (especially poetry). No matter how miserable I was feeling, I could always lose myself in a book.

That was 30 years ago. Today I have a loving husband, a wonderful son, close friends I can talk to about anything, and a career that I find very satisfying. But I've never forgotten the loneliness and desperation I felt as a teenager.

I first started talking to my son about suicide when he was in junior high school. He often experienced emotional extremes—highs of elation and excitement followed by crashing lows of depression and negative feelings about himself and his life—and I wanted him to know that the lows would pass. I told him about the times when I was a teenager and wanted to die. I explained that while I thought I had no one to talk to, there probably had been someone I could have talked to, if I had looked hard enough. He, on the other hand, had many people in his life he could talk to, and he didn't have to look far to find them. (Once we worked together on a list of names and phone numbers that he could keep in his desk.)

But the main point I tried to make (without pounding him over the head with it) was that no matter how awful he felt at night, *he would always feel better in the morning.* I tried to reinforce that during especially difficult times. Over breakfast,

I would ask him, "Do you feel better now than you did last night? Even a little?" When he said yes (if he spoke to me at all), I would say, "Remember that feeling and trust it."

There will probably be times in your life (if you haven't had them already) when you feel hopeless and lonely—maybe even enough to consider suicide. When they happen, always promise yourself at least one more morning.

P.S. I love this quote from Harvey Fierstein: "The great thing about suicide is that it's not one of those things you have to do now or you lose your chance. I mean, you can always do it *later.*"

Anonymous is a writer who lives in the Midwest.

What's Next?

We've almost reached the end of this book, but it's not quite the end of the story.

The Gifted Kids' Survival Guides (including the original 1983 edition and *Guide II,* published in 1987) have always been strongly influenced and in large part shaped by the results of surveys distributed to gifted teenagers across the United States and around the world. This revised edition is no different. As you've seen, it's full of facts and quotes gathered from our most recent survey. We simply couldn't have written this book without the help of countless teenagers who took the time and made the effort to share their insights, experiences, and wisdom.

The survey that follows on the next four pages is the one we used when compiling information for this book. And we'd like to use it when we start thinking about the next edition.

We need *your* help. Please photocopy the survey, fill it in, and send it to:

Free Spirit Publishing
ATTN: GKSG Survey
400 First Avenue North, Suite 616
Minneapolis, MN 55401-1730
U.S.A.

We hope that you now have some of the knowledge you'll need to understand, accept, and celebrate your giftedness. We hope that you'll be able to carve a bigger, more delectable and challenging slice of life for yourself. And we wish you the very best as you continue on your journey . . . wherever it leads you.

"**C**hesire Puss," [said Alice], "Would you tell me, please, which way I ought to go from here?"

"That depends a good deal on where you want to get to," said the Cat.

"I don't much care where—" said Alice.

"Then it doesn't matter which way you go," said the Cat.

"—so long as I get somewhere," Alice added as an explanation.

"Oh, you're sure to do that," said the Cat, "if you only walk long enough."

Lewis Carroll, *Alice's Adventures in Wonderland*

The Gifted Kids' Survival Guide Survey

A.   DEMOGRAPHICS

your age _____ your gender   M:_____   F:_____

number of years in an enrichment/gifted program or class
(please circle one):

0   1   2   3   4   5   6 or more

B.   GIFTS AND TALENTS
(check as many as apply; circle the one that interests you the most)

I want to know more about . . .

B1: ❑ new definitions of intelligence
B2: ❑ the latest findings about intelligence (Where does it come from?
        Can we improve on our own intelligence? Can intelligence be "lost"?)
B3: ❑ new definitions of giftedness
B4: ❑ IQ and achievement tests (what they mean, what they don't mean, etc.)
B5: ❑ the difference between being "gifted" and being "talented" (if there
        is a difference)
B6: ❑ how to explain giftedness to my friends
B7: ❑ how to explain giftedness to adults (parents and teachers)

C.   EXPECTATIONS
(check as many as apply; circle the one that interests you the most)

I want to know more about . . .

C1: ❑ the difference between "perfectionism" and "striving for excellence"
C2: ❑ how to set realistic goals
C3: ❑ how to manage my time more effectively
C4: ❑ how to give myself "permission" to fail sometimes . . . to be more
        gentle with myself
C5: ❑ how to deal with people who think, "If you're so gifted, why don't
        you get straight A's?"
C6: ❑ how to cope with comparisons between siblings

D.   EDUCATION
(check as many as apply; circle the one that interests you the most)

I want to know more about . . .

D1: ❑ the pluses and minuses of "tracked" or "ability grouped" classes
D2: ❑ how to earn college credit while I'm still in high school
D3: ❑ how to have successful conferences with guidance counselors
D4: ❑ why some gifted students do poorly in school
D5: ❑ how to survive in the regular classroom
D6: ❑ how to be more productive in school
D7: ❑ non-traditional learning (e.g. community service work, mentorships)
D8: ❑ the pluses and minuses of cooperative learning
D9: ❑ getting teachers to be more flexible (e.g. letting you skip some assignments because you already know the material and can "test out" to prove it)
D10: ❑ how to integrate the fine arts into your education
D11: ❑ options for after high school

E.   FRIENDS AND RELATIONSHIPS
(check as many as apply; circle the one that interests you the most)

I want to know more about . . .

E1: ❑ the emotional stages of adolescent development
E2: ❑ the importance of age in friendships
E3: ❑ the differences between intellectual maturity and physical maturity
E4: ❑ coping with peer pressure
E5: ❑ how to make friends

F.   BEYOND ADOLESCENCE
(check as many as apply; circle the one that interests you the most)

I want to know more about . . .

F1: ❑ selecting a career or field of study
F2: ❑ alternative lifestyles
F3: ❑ what to expect the first year of college
F4: ❑ how to develop a philosophy of life
F5: ❑ how to deal with strong feelings like sadness, depression, and anger
F6: ❑ how to define success
F7: ❑ how to cope with loss (of a parent, a friend, ideals, etc.)
F8: ❑ how to get along better with parents

The Gifted Kids' Survival Guide Survey. © 1996 by Judy Galbraith, M.A., and Jim Delisle, Ph.D. Free Spirit Publishing Inc.
This page may be photocopied.

• •

Please answer the following questions (add extra paper if necessary):

1. The *Roeper Review* reported that gifted kids have a tendency to deny their intelligence and downplay their talents. Do you think this is true? Why or why not?

2. Do you think gifted girls and young women have to deal with any special problems or dilemmas? If yes, what are they?

3. Do you think gifted boys and young men have to deal with any special problems or dilemmas? If yes, what are they?

4. Do you think a gifted student's ethnic background can cause any special problems or dilemmas? If yes, in what ways?

5. How can teachers help gifted students?

6. How can parents help gifted students?

7. Are there any topics you are interested in that aren't mentioned on this survey? Please list them here:

• •

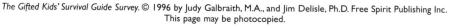

Please tell us what you liked best about *The Gifted Kids' Survival Guide.*
(Check all that apply.)

_____ quotes from gifted teenagers
_____ first-person essays by gifted teenagers and adults
_____ quotes from gifted adults
_____ suggestions for additional reading that address the topics
_____ names/addresses of groups/organizations that offer
information and/or assistance
_____ use of humor/cartoons in discussing the topics
_____ educational and psychological research
_____ questions that guide independent thinking
_____ lists (e.g. "12 Tips for Making and Keeping Friends")

Is there anything not mentioned here that you especially liked about
this book?

Are there aspects of this book that could be improved? Please explain:

OPTIONAL:

Your name:_____

Your school:_____

Your city/state:_____

Thank you for your comments!

Judy Galbraith and Jim Delisle

Please return your completed survey to:

Free Spirit Publishing
ATTN: GKSG Survey
400 First Avenue North, Suite 616
Minneapolis, MN 55401-1730
U.S.A.

Additional Resources

Books and Publications

Creative Kids Magazine

Prufrock Press
P.O. Box 8813
Waco, TX 76714-8813
1-800-998-2208
http://www.prufrock.com/

Activities, games, essays, opinion, brain teasers, and more written by and for creative kids ages 8–14. Free trial issue. Write, phone, or query through the Web site for subscription information.

The Gifted Child in Contemporary Fiction

Available as ISD #728 from:
Elk River Public Schools
Elk River, MN 55330
(612) 441-1003, ext. 189

An annotated bibliography of books with main characters who are gifted, compiled by Stephen Schroeder-Davis, Coordinator of Gifted Services for Elk River Area Public Schools.

Imagine: Opportunities & Resources for Academically Talented Youth

Center for Talented Youth
The Johns Hopkins University Press
P.O. Box 19966
Baltimore, MD 21211
(410) 516-6989 or 1-800-548-1784
http://jhunix.hcf.jhu.edu/~setmentr/imagine.html

Published by the Study of Exceptional Talent (SET), a project of the Johns Hopkins University Center for Talented Youth (CTY), *Imagine* is a newsletter for talented students in grades 7–12. Published five times a year, it helps students identify options at home, in school, and in the community that will satisfy their intellectual curiosity and need for greater academic challenge. Topics include preparing for and entering academic competitions, writing for publication, choosing stimulating extracurricular activities, and finding appropriate college programs. *Imagine* also provides a forum for student creative writing, book reviews, and evaluations of colleges. Write, phone, or query through the Web site for subscription information.

Associations and Programs

The Council for Exceptional Children (CEC)

1920 Association Drive
Reston, VA 22091
(703) 620-3660

Information and support for parents and teachers of individuals with exceptionalities, including gifted children and those who are both gifted and LD.

Institute for the Academic Advancement of Youth (IAAY)

Center for Talented Youth (CTY)
Johns Hopkins University
3400 N. Charles Street
Baltimore, MD 21218
(410) 516-0337

See page 286 for description and Web site information.

The International Dyslexia Association

Chester Building, Suite 382
8600 LaSalle Road
Baltimore, MD 21204
(410) 296-0232

Information and support for parents and families of gifted children with LD.

National Association for Gifted Children (NAGC)

1707 L Street NW, Suite 550
Washington, DC 20036
(202) 785-4268

Information about and support for appropriate educational experiences for gifted students.

National Resource Center on the Gifted and Talented (NRC/GT)

University of Connecticut
362 Fairfield Road, U–7
Storrs, CT 06269-2007
(203) 486-4826

See page 286 for description and Web site information.

Parents of Gifted and Talented Learning-Disabled Children

2420 Eccleston Street
Silver Spring, MD 20902
(301) 986-1422

Information and support for parents and families of gifted children with LD.

Supporting the Emotional Needs of the Gifted (SENG)

Dr. James Delisle
SENG—College of Education
405 White Hall
Kent State University
Kent, OH 44242
(216) 672-2294

An international organization that helps parents, educators, children, and teens better understand the high points and hassles of growing up gifted. Each annual SENG conference includes a program for children ages 8–14 staffed by local teachers of the gifted, graduate students, and certified counselors.

UConn Mentor Connection

Dr. Jeanne H. Purcell
University of Connecticut
362 Fairfield Road, U-7
Storrs, CT 06269-2007
(860) 486-0283
http://www.ucc.uconn.edu:80/~wwwgt/mentor.html
purcell@uconnvm.uconn.edu

An annual three-week summer program at the University of Connecticut for academically talented secondary students, UConn Mentor Connection provides students with opportunities to participate in creative projects and investigations under the supervision of university mentors. Topics for one summer's programs included "Biostatistics: Where Do the Numbers Come From?," "AIDS Prevention: How Can Outreach Efforts Be Made More Effective?," "Environmental Science and Geography," "Metabolic Calculations, Fitness Testing, and Energy Metabolism," and "We Met on the Internet: Personal Relationships in Cyberspace." Admission is by application and selection. To apply or request a brochure, contact Dr. Jeanne H. Purcell at the address above.

Web Sites*

The Gifted and Talented (TAG) Resources Home Page

http://www.eskimo.com/~user/kids.html

The best place to start surfing the Net in search of information about giftedness and gifted education, this amazing page (updated often) contains links to all known online gifted resources, enrichment programs, talent searches, summer programs, gifted mailing lists, and early acceptance programs. It also contains contact information for many local gifted associations and government (mostly U.S. state) programs.

EPGY—Education Program for Gifted Youth

http://kanpai.stanford.edu/epgy/

Run by Stanford University, EPGY offers mathematics, physics, and writing courses for gifted youth. EPGY is sometimes referred to as a DLP (distance learning program).

ERIC Clearinghouse for Exceptional Children

http://www.aspensys.com/eric/index.html

ERIC is a large and useful online resource. You can read or download ERIC Digests about giftedness, gifted education, and gifted children at this site.

---

* The Internet is dynamic and fluid; Web sites go up and come down, URLs change, and what might be current information today is old news tomorrow. We can't promise that everything on this list will still be accurate when you read it, but it should give you a start in the right direction. When in doubt, use a search engine.

The Gifted Child Society

http://www.gifted.org/

The Gifted Child Society is a non-profit organization that was founded in 1957 to further the cause of gifted children. Its goals include educational enrichment and support services specifically designed for gifted children, assistance to parents in raising gifted children to full and productive adulthood, professional training to encourage educators to meet the special needs of these youngsters, and a greater effort to win public recognition and acceptance of these special needs. Since 1957, the Society has served over 40,000 children and their families. In 1975, the U.S. Department of Education named it a national demonstration model.

Institute for the Academic Advancement of Youth (IAAY) Center for Talented Youth (CTY)

http://www.jhu.edu:80/~gifted/

Formally established at Johns Hopkins University in 1979, IAAY is dedicated to identifying young people with exceptional intellectual abilities and offering them accelerated academic programs specially suited to their own individual rates of learning. IAAY's original mission has grown to reach a broader student base, giving youth the opportunity to fully explore their individual academic abilities. CTY Academic Programs support and nurture academic talent by providing motivated, academically talented students with a chance to study at a pace and/or depth appropriate for their abilities. Qualified students, generally between ages 7 and 16, choose from a wide range of courses in the humanities, mathematics, and sciences held at six sites in the United States. CTY Academic Program staff specifically design these courses to be challenging and exciting.

National Resource Center on the Gifted and Talented (NRC/GT)

http://www.ucc.uconn.edu:80/~wwwgt/

Based at the University of Connecticut, directed by Dr. Joseph Renzulli, the NRC/GT is a collaborative effort of the University of Connecticut, City University of New York/City College, Stanford University, University of Virginia, Yale University, 52 state and territorial departments of education, over 339 public and private schools, over 167 content area consultants, and stakeholders representing professional organizations, parent groups, and businesses. Its mission is to plan and conduct research about giftedness.

The TAG Family Network

http://www.teleport.com/~rkaltwas/tag/

An organization dedicated to appropriate education for talented and gifted youth and advocacy. Run by and for parents, it disseminates information, supports parents, monitors and influences legal issues. TAG's home page contains current information on gifted education with links to many other Web sites of interest to parents, educators and children.

TAGFAM—Families of the Gifted and Talented

http://www.access.digex.net/~king/tagfam.html

TAGFAM is an online support community that seeks to provide mutual help and support for gifted and talented individuals and their families. Its home page contains many links to other web sites, definitions of terms related to gifted education, mailing list instructions, and much more.

YAHOO Resources for/about Gifted Youth K-12

http://www.yahoo.com/text/education/k_12/Gifted_Youth

A gifted youth information/search page, with links to many online resources and sites.

Additional Permissions and Credits

Some of the information on giftedness, intelligence, and IQ in "On Being Gifted," "Intelligence," and "IQ, Tests, and Testing" is from *The Survival Guide for Parents of Gifted Kids* by Sally Yahnke Walker (Free Spirit Publishing, 1991) and *It's All In Your Head* by Susan L. Barrett (Free Spirit Publishing, 1992).

Some of the information about "twice exceptional" students on pages 22–23 is from *Teaching Kids with Learning Difficulties in the Regular Classroom* by Susan Winebrenner (Free Spirit Publishing, 1996), p. 27.

"What if you're not sure of your answer?" on page 57 is from *School Power* by Jeanne Shay Schumm and Marguerite Radencich (Free Spirit Publishing, 1992), p. 79.

"12 Test-Taking Tips" on pages 61–64 is adapted from *Get Off My Brain* by Randall McCutcheon (Free Spirit Publishing, 1985), pp. 93–104 and *The Best of Free Spirit* (Free Spirit Publishing, 1995), pp. 136–137.

"Problems of Perfectionists" on page 75 and "Ten Tips for Combating Perfectionism" on page 78 are adapted from *Talk with Teens about Self and Stress* by Jean Sunde Peterson (Free Spirit Publishing, 1993), pp. 41–43.

"Seven Cardinal Mistakes of Self-Esteem" by Sol Gordon on pages 81–83 is from *The Best of Free Spirit*, pp. 29–30.

The "Think About It, Talk About It" questions on page 107 are adapted from *Talk with Teens about Feelings, Family, Relationships, and the Future* by Jean Sunde Peterson (Free Spirit Publishing, 1995), pp. 168–170.

"Two Tried-and-True Ways to Really Relax" on pages 132–36 is adapted from *Fighting Invisible Tigers: A Stress Management Guide for Teens* by Earl Hipp (Free Spirit Publishing, 1985; revised and updated edition, 1995), pp. 73–81.

"Ten Tips for Talking to Teachers" on pages 155–56 is adapted from *Free Spirit: News & Views on Growing Up Gifted*, Vol. 2., No. 1 (1988).

"Gifted People Speak Out: Jerry Simmons" on pages 167–69 is adapted from *The Best of Free Spirit*, pp. 69–70.

"Gifted People Speak Out: Bryan A. Mantz" on pages 210–11 is adapted from *The Best of Free Spirit*, pp. 5–6.

"How to Talk to Parents: Strategies for Successful Conversations" and "Ten Tips for Talking to Parents" on pages 233–36 are adapted from *The Best of Free Spirit*, pp. 169–170.

Some of the "Think About It, Talk About It" questions on page 239 are adapted from *Talk with Teens about Feelings, Family, Relationships, and the Future*, pp. 100–101.

Some of the information in "Enough About You—What About Them?" on pages 239–41 is from *The Survival Guide for Parents of Gifted Kids* by Sally Yahnke Walker and *Bringing Out the Best* by Jacqulyn Saunders with Pamela Espeland (Free Spirit Publishing, 1991).

The story of Andrew Holleman on page 254 is adapted from *Kids with Courage* by Barbara A. Lewis (Free Spirit Publishing, 1992), pp. 143–150.

All are used with permission of the publisher.

Index

About the Authors

Judy Galbraith, M.A., is the author of *The Gifted Kids' Survival Guide (For Ages 10 & Under)*. She is also coauthor with Connie Schmitz of *Managing the Social and Emotional Needs of the Gifted* and coauthor with Peter L. Benson and Pamela Espeland of *What Kids Need to Succeed*. She has a master's degree in guidance and counseling of the gifted and has worked with and taught gifted youth, their parents, and their teachers for over ten years. In 1983, she started Free Spirit Publishing, which specializes in SELF-HELP FOR KIDS® and SELF-HELP FOR TEENS.®

Judy lives in Minneapolis, Minnesota, with Chloé, her comic Airedale "terror." She recently achieved a major life goal: building a house on Madeline Island in Lake Superior. Her future goals include getting her captain's license (for sailing) and renovating a historic office building.

Jim Delisle, Ph.D., is the author of seven books including *Guiding the Social and Emotional Needs of Gifted Youth* (Longman Publishers), *Kidstories* (Free Spirit), and *Growing Good Kids* with Deb Delisle (Free Spirit). He is a professor of education at Kent State University, a part-time middle school teacher, and the parent of a gifted teenager. He also serves as Co-Director of SENG (Supporting the Emotional Needs of the Gifted), an international organization of

parents, educators, and students. His work has been excerpted in the *New York Times, Washington Post, LIFE* Magazine, and on *Oprah Winfrey*.

Jim and his family share their time at their homes in Kent, Ohio, and North Myrtle Beach, South Carolina. In his spare time, Jim enjoys hiking, reading, and tough crossword puzzles. One day he will walk New Zealand's Milford Track and explore Antarctica.

Other Great Books from Free Spirit

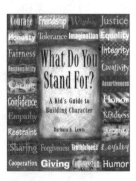